## THE PAGES THAT MADE HISTORY

The "Echoes of Liverpool" book is published by :

# Trinity Mirror NW²

Trinity Mirror North West & North Wales
PO Box 48
Old Hall Street,
Liverpool L69 3EB

Trinity Mirror S.M. Executive Editor:
Ken Rogers

Design / production:
Daisy Dutton, Jonathan Low, Emma Smart

Echo library:
Colin Hunt, Brian Johnston, Leslie Rawlinson

Contributors:
Gary Bainbridge, Ian Hargraves, Tony Martin,
Sharon Pell, Natasha Young, Peter Grant

ISBN 978 1 905266 34 0

# From the Editor

**For the last 128 years the Echo has faithfully recorded the history of Liverpool.**

**The good times, the bad times.**

**The triumphs, the tragedies.**

But Liverpool's story goes back long before Merseyside's best-selling newspaper hit the streets in 1879.

This year our city celebrates 800 years of history. 800 years since King John granted 'letters patent' to the Steward of West Derby – the charter which founded the Borough of Liverpool.
Back then, and for years to come, it was word of mouth, church records and town criers that gave the people the news and information they needed.

But how WOULD the Echo have dealt with the massive news events that shaped our city long before the presses started rolling?
We turned our modern-day Echo journalists loose on the big stories from days of yore.
Then we asked them: What will life be like in years to come?
And how will the Echo handle the news stories that are yet to break?

Wish Liverpool the happiest of birthdays and join Britain's best newspaper for a mind-boggling journey through the past, present and future of Britain's best city.

## Love history? Love the Echo!

**Alastair Machray**
Editor, Liverpool Echo

# Contents

## ECHOES OF THE PAST

## ECHOES OF THE PRESENT

## ECHOES OF THE FUTURE

# 1207–1878
## ECHOES OF THE PAST

The Liverpool Echo grabbed the hearts and minds of the people of
Merseyside from the moment its first edition was published
on October 27, 1879.

Originally launched as powerful ally to the well-established
Liverpool Daily Post (1855), the Echo was to become one of the most
influential publications in the history of British newspapers.
Its arrival on the Merseyside scene saw the company move from a small
printing shop in Lord Street to a vibrant new headquarters in Victoria Street
from where new presses would ultimately deliver millions of copies
onto the streets of Liverpool.

Today the Echo and Post operate from a high-tech media centre
in Old Hall Street, the headquarters of parent company
Trinity Mirror North West. From this base a string of highly successful
weeklies, special editions, glossy magazines and books are published
alongside the Liverpool Echo and Daily Post.

In Victorian times, the Echo mushroomed into the populist voice of Liverpool,
becoming part of the very fabric of Merseyside. It would power on into a new
century to report on every major story that engulfed the city.

This book – helping the city celebrate its 800th birthday – is the people's
history, with a new chapter added every time the Echo hits the streets.

In this first section, we take a trip in a time machine back to 1207 before
moving forward into the medieval city. No Liverpool Echo in those days,
of course, but how might the paper have treated events like the historic
granting of a town charter by King John and the pounding
of the city with cannon balls from the heights of Everton
by Prince Rupert and his Royalist army?

Read on and enjoy a glimpse of days gone by before we bring you
right up to date with the story of Liverpool through the Echo headlines
that are now part of history.

# King John grants Royal Charter to Liverpool

LIVERPOOL was a tiny little hamlet, too small to be mentioned by name in the Domesday Book in 1086.

King John became direct lord of the area between the Mersey and Ribble rivers and needed a handy port so he could send men and goods to Ireland. Liverpool was the perfect spot, but it needed to be built up.

Days after taking possession of Liverpool from Henry Fitzwarin, John issued the charter at Winchester.

It invited settlers to come to Liverpool, offering them 'burgages' – small plots of land – for a small rental charge every year.

Liverpool was declared a freeport, which meant it was exempt from some taxes, making the little town a good place to trade.

*Right: In 1907, Liverpool people re-enacted the sealing of the Royal Charter for an ECHO supplement*

## What the Charter says

'JOHN, by the grace of God, King of England, Lord of Ireland, Duke of Normandy and Aquitaine, Count of Anjou, to all his faithful people who have desired to have Burgages in the township of Liverpool, greeting. Know ye that we have granted to all our faithful people who have taken Burgages in Liverpool that they may have all the liberties and free customs in the township of Liverpool which any Free Borough on the sea has in our land. And there we command you that securely and in our peace you come there to receive inhabit our Burgages. And in witness hereof we transmit to you these our Letters Patent. Witness Simon de Pateshill at Winchester on the twenty-eighth day of August in the ninth year of our reign.'

## Another Charter

THERE were various other Charters for Liverpool over the years, including one in 1329 given by King Edward II. But the most important after King John's was granted by Charles I in 1626.

This charter made Liverpool a 'body corporate and politic', settled the town's legal system, set up a commercial court for the recovery of debts and gave the borough its own mayor and council.

# WHO NEEDS A LIONHEART?
## We love King John more than his brother

AT LAST, Liverpool has been given the status it deserves.

King John has been given a bad press in some quarters. Certainly his brother, Richard the Lionheart, has been a tough PR act to follow.

And he has been unfairly maligned thanks to the tall tales of a socialist hoodie who hangs

### Voice of the ECHO

around the woods near Nottingham with a band of so-called Merry Men.

**But today, the people of Liverpool can hail our monarch** as a true visionary.

He has moved quickly since taking over the region and spotted the potential of our hamlet.

While his brother has been gallivanting over in the Holy Land, King John has been efficiently running the country. By granting this historic charter, King John has ensured a bright future for the port of Liverpool.

**That's more than his brother ever did.**

*How today's ECHO might have reported the historic granting of the Royal Charter to Liverpool by King John in 1207*

# LIVERPOOL ECHO

**Toxteth fashion**

How to cut a dash in the King's favourite hunting ground - See Page 23

00,001 MAIN TUESDAY, AUGUST 28, 1207 1 GROAT

## KING MAKES US OFFICIAL AT LAST

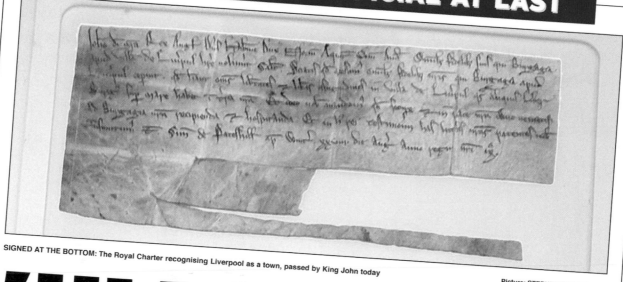

SIGNED AT THE BOTTOM: The Royal Charter recognising Liverpool as a town, passed by King John today

Picture: STEPHEN SHAKESHAFT

# 'ULLO JOHN, GOT A NEW CHARTER!

BURGAGE KING: John wants traders to come to Liverpool

## BIGGEST DAY IN OUR HISTORY - PAGES 2,3,4,5,6,7,8,9&10

# Monks lose right to run Mersey ferry

LIVERPOOL is famous for its iconic ferry service, celebrated in the song Ferry Cross The Mersey by Gerry And The Pacemakers. But the ferry had humble origins. The first regular ferry service was started by monks at the Benedictine monastery at Birkenhead.

## LIVERPOOL ECHO

00,002    MAIN    MONDAY, FEBRUARY 18, 1536    1 FARTHING

### Tight fit for a king

Can men really get away with wearing hose? We ask style experts **Look**

### END OF THE PIER

**Henry puts a stop to monk quay business**

By ISLA MANN

MONKS today lost their right to charge fees for the Mersey ferry.

For over 200 years the Benedictine monks – based at Birkenhead Priory – have been rowing travellers to Liverpool and back.

But King Henry's review of monastery finances has recommended that the ferry rights of the Papist brothers should be handed over to the Lord of the Manor.

It is believed the new ferries will be quicker,

● Turn to Page 2

You know you can still count on ...ABACUSWORLD

It received the Royal seal of approval from Edward III, who allowed the monks to charge a toll forever.

But his successor 200 years later, Henry VIII, snatched back this right as part of his looting of the monasteries, handing it to the Lord of Birkenhead Manor, who later sold it on to private operators.

## Henry VIII and the monasteries

FOLLOWING the Pope's refusal to annul Henry VIII's marriage to Catherine of Aragon so he could marry Anne Boleyn, the King broke the Church of England's ties with Roman Catholicism.

After this split, Henry made his chief minister, Thomas Cromwell (right) tour England's monasteries to assess their wealth.

In 1536, Parliament allowed Henry to seize the wealth of the smaller monasteries, including Birkenhead Priory.

In 1638, Henry authorised the destruction of Roman Catholic shrines, and one year later he dissolved all monasteries in England with their property transferred to the Crown.

A view of Liverpool between 1160 and 1189.
On the left is the Chapel of Our Lady, on the spot where St Nicholas' Church is now situated.
On the right is Liverpool Tower, on the site of the current Tower Buildings

## The original monks' ferry

IT is believed that a group of Benedictine monks, who established Birkenhead Priory in around 1150, were the first to start a regular ferry service across the Mersey. The monks were obliged to offer food and shelter to travellers who wanted to make their way across the river.

They asked King Edward III for permission to run a toll-paying ferry service from Birkenhead to Liverpool. The King assented in 1330, granting a charter to the priory and its successors forever:

"the right of ferry there... over the arm of the sea, for men, horses and goods, with leave to charge reasonable tolls."

Birkenhead Priory, which in recent years has been reopened for tourists and visitors

## After the monks

THE new owners of the ferries switched to fully rigged sailing ships, which could carry more people.

But the infamous thick fog of the Mersey, and the unpredictabilty of the wind on the river meant the service was even more at the mercy of the weather.

There were terminals operating at Eastham, New Ferry, Rock Ferry, Birkenhead, Seacombe, Tranmere, Woodside, Egremont and New Brighton, with Liverpool terminals at the Pier Head, Otterspool and Garston.

All routes were privately owned until the mid 1800s when the Birkenhead and Wallasey corporations bought them and introduced the first steam ferry.

In the 20th century, several terminals closed, partly owing to competition by the Mersey tunnels.

The ferries are now owned by Mersey Ferries and three vessels are in operation – Royal Iris of the Mersey, Royal Daffodil and Snowdrop.

## It's all over for priory

● From Page One

being powered by the most up-to-the-minute sail technology rather than the monks' old-fashioned oars.

But the pressure group Wirral Commuters (WC) have expressed concern about reliability.

Spokesman Tim Gruel: "The Mersey is notoriously foggy, and there is little wind in winter. Can a wind-powered

Left: How today's Echo might have reported the end of the monks' ferry

# Horrocks observes the transit of Venus

ON November 24, 1639, Jeremiah Horrocks, an astronomer from Otterspool, was the first man to observe a transit of Venus.

A transit of Venus is similar to a solar eclipse, where the moon blocks out the sun's light.

But because Venus is so far away, and so much smaller than the sun, during a transit of Venus it appears as a small black dot on the sun's surface. Transits of Venus are only seen twice a century, and occur eight years apart. Astronomers believed there would only be a near-transit in 1639, but Horrocks, who had been studying Venus, was convinced it would occur that year.

Horrocks' observations of the transit enabled him to estimate the size of Venus and the distance between the earth and the sun, making calculations which changed the world.

## How did it change the world?

HORROCKS estimated that the sun was 59 million miles from the earth, thanks to his observation of the transit of Venus. This was inaccurate - today we know it to be 93 million miles away - but it was much closer to the truth than was believed in the 17th century. Suddenly people became aware that if the distance between planets was so immense, the distance between stars must be so much greater. The universe immediately became a bigger place. His calculation affected the definition of the Astronomical Unit -

the distance between the sun and earth. And his confirmation of the date of the transit prompted expeditions in 1761 and 1769 to different vantage points around the world to get more accurate measurements.

These expeditions included the voyage of Captain James Cook, who discovered Australia and New Zealand. Cook's superiors at the Admiralty were convinced Australia must exist, and used his mission to measure the transit of Venus at Tahiti as cover for his search for the continent.

## When is the next transit?

THERE was a transit of Venus on June 8, 2004, which means the next will be on June 6, 2012.
The bad news is, if you want to see it, you will have to

visit North America or the southern hemisphere. Otherwise you will have to wait until 2125, which is when the next transit is visible from Europe.

## HO X IN sport TONIGHT

1 FARTHING

The weekend's bear baiting action. PLUS: Witch ducking

AYS SCOUSE STARGAZER

# SKY'S

E: Venus makes its transit in front of the sun on Saturday

### By URSA MAJOR

A TOXTETH PARK astronomer today overturned everything we know about the universe.

Jeremiah Horrocks, of Lower Lodge, Otterspool, used a rare astronomical event this weekend to measure the distance of the sun from the earth.

And he says the sun is...

# still count on

# ACUSWORLD

Left: How today's Echo might have reported Horrocks' discovery

## A brief and brilliant life

Above: Horrocks safely observes the transit

JEREMIAH HORROCKS (or Horrox) was born in Lower Lodge, Otterspool in Toxteth Park in 1618. His father was a farmer and Horrocks was relatively poor. He went to Cambridge University in 1632, but left in 1635 without graduating and went to live in Much Hoole, near Preston.

At Cambridge, he studied the astronomer Johannes Kepler, who believed there would be a near-miss transit of Venus in 1639. Horrocks believed he was mistaken.

On November 24, 1639, he focused the image of the sun through a telescope onto a piece of card. The tiny shadow of Venus appeared at 3.15pm and he watched it for half an hour until sunset.

Horrocks went on to surmise correctly that the moon's orbit was an ellipse rather than a circle, and suggested that the sun also affected the moon's orbit - anticipating Sir Isaac Newton's theory. Horrocks returned to Liverpool in summer 1640 and died suddenly on January 3, 1641. He was just 22 years old. His paper on the transit was only revealed to the Royal Society 18 years later.

# Jeremiah's just sun-believable

● From Page One

away from the earth, around 100 times further than scientists and scholars currently believe.

Farmer's son Horrocks observed this weekend's transit of Venus – a rarely witnessed event in which our neighbouring planet passes between the earth and the sun, casting a small shadow.

His calculations have given astronomers a better idea of where we are in space.

They will now be used to measure more accurately the distance between stars.

Horrocks' mum told the

# Prince Rupert takes Liverpool Castle

*Right: Prince Rupert took Liverpool Castle back from the Roundheads*

AT THE outbreak of the English Civil War, Liverpool's noblemen – the West Derby Hundred – were firmly on the Royalist side, unlike the Parliamentarians in Manchester. By 1643, Liverpool was one of the two Royalist strongholds in Lancashire (the other was Lathom). In early 1643, Manchester's Parliamentarians attacked and overran Liverpool.

Prince Rupert, leader of the Royalist cavalry, made the recapture of Liverpool his top priority.

He surveyed the defences from his headquarters in Everton, and said Liverpool Castle was indefensible – "a mere crow's nest which a parcel of boys might take."

He sent his forces, from his headquarters in Everton Village, to besiege Liverpool Castle. For 18 days, Rupert's men pounded the castle with cannon fire. In the battle he lost 1,500 men.

Eventually, he decided to attack at night. Aided by the local knowledge of Caryll, the brother of Lord Molyneux, he led his men into the fight down through the northern fields to the Old Hall, at 3am.

The ramparts were deserted but 400 men remained. Fierce fighting broke out in the streets of Liverpool, but, after several hours, the Parliamentarian forces surrendered and Prince Rupert took his place at Liverpool Castle.

## Roundhead forces put to sword

● From Page One

castle and was making plans to move on to Lathom, which has remained loyal to King Charles.

Official figures are yet to be released for the number of dead in today's battle, which was concentrated around the Old Hall.

But one onlooker told the Liverpool ECHO: "Prince Rupert's men did slay almost all they met with, to the number of 360, and among others ... some that had never borne arms, ... yea, one poor blind man."

Caryll, brother of Lord Molyneux, is thought to have helped the Prince with his strategy, thanks to his local knowledge.

Insiders today credited the nobleman with the plan to take the town centre from the north, springing a deadly surprise on the Manchester invaders.

A source close to Colonel Moore, former governor of Liverpool, said: "Caryll Molyneux killed seven or eight poor men with his own hands."

**Today's battle brings to an end 18 days of conflict around Liverpool Castle – a conflict which has left thousands dead and injured.**

From his base in Everton, Prince Rupert concentrated hi-tech fire power – the latest in cannon technology – at the castle, on Lord Street.

Today, Prince Rupert said: "This is a beautiful day for the people of Liverpool. Yea, we have smited the enemy.

"God Save The King."

*Right: How today's Echo might have reported the Battle of Liverpool Castle*

LIVERPOO
ECO
00,004    MAIN    SATURDAY, JU
BRAVE RUPE
HUN
DIE
BATT
OLD H

Right: A copy of Liverpool Castle created in 1907 for the city's 700th birthday celebrations

## The castle

ACCOUNTS of Liverpool Castle are sketchy. No accurate plans or drawings of the castle exist. All we know is it was built before 1235 at the top of Lord Street, facing down Castle Street. It was demolished in 1720.

## The English Civil War

THE English Civil War began because King Charles I (above right) had been riding roughshod over the will of Parliament. After a rebellion in Parliament, Charles assembled an army of noble horsemen, who were nicknamed the Cavaliers.

Their Parliamentarian enemies, led by Oliver Cromwell (above left), were nicknamed Roundheads. Religion played an important role in which side people were on. Anglicans and Catholics usually supported the King, while Puritans were Parliamentarians.

The war raged from 1642 to 1648, when Charles was taken prisoner and executed. It is believed around 100,000 soldiers died during the war. Cromwell ruled cruelly as Lord Protector from 1653 until his death in 1658. In 1660, Charles' son, Charles II was restored to the throne.

---

# HO

**1644**        **1 FARTHING**

## Thanks, but no Mancs!

Victory for Everton against Manchester United – Back

## KING OF THE CASTLE

## DREDS
## N
## LE OF
## ALL ST L3

### By MAURICE CAVALIER

PRINCE RUPERT'S forces today liberated Liverpool Castle.

The Royalist men stormed through the town centre early this morning, taking the Manchester Parliamentarians by surprise.

By noon today, the Prince had occupied the

● Turn to Page 2

## Who was Prince Rupert?

PRINCE Rupert was born in Prague in 1619, and was the grandson of James I. He settled in England in 1635 and was put in charge of the cavalry. He used tactics that he had learnt fighting in Sweden which involved charging at the enemy, with horses kept close together and the men firing their pistols at the last moment. Early in the Civil War, the Roundheads were cowed by this tactic and ran away. But Oliver Cromwell realised that men armed with 16-foot-long pikes, who stood their ground, could defeat Rupert's cavalry. In 1646, Rupert surrendered and was expelled from England. He took command of the Royalist fleet in 1648 and attacked English shipping, but was defeated by Admiral Robert Blake and escaped to the West Indies. Prince Rupert returned to England in 1660 with Charles II and died in 1682.

# End of the slave trade

LIVERPOOL grew rich through trade - in cotton, silk, sugar, tobacco... and slaves.

The evidence of the city's trade in slavery is all over Liverpool. From carvings on Water Street's Martin's Bank building to the names of streets like Penny Lane, Rodney Street and Exchange Flags - where slaves were traded - the wealth created through exploitation and human misery is proof of the city's shameful past.

But if we are ashamed of the merchants who took part in the slave trade, we can be proud of the Liverpudlians who helped to end it. We can be proud of people like William Roscoe MP, who fought alongside William Wilberforce to make Parliament ban the trade, which it did on March 25, 1807.

An exhibition at Merseyside Maritime Museum, depicting a master with his slaves in the West Indies

Manacled figures of child slaves at the entrance of the Martin's Bank building

## Atrocity at sea

ONE of the most evil acts in slave history centred around a Liverpool vessel.

Luke Collingwood was master of the ship the Zong, travelling from Africa to the West Indies. During the Zong's voyage, due to the appalling conditions on board, many slaves became ill. As the insurance companies would not pay out if a slave met a natural death, Collingwood ordered his crew to throw 133 victims overboard to drown. He successfully claimed for 150 lost slaves at £30 a slave.

## Roscoe and the abolitionists

WILLIAM ROSCOE, along with other city worthies including William Rathbone and Dr Jonathan Binns, worked hard to bring an end to the slave trade.

A prominent banker and lawyer, and friend to several slave ship captains, he nevertheless published poems attacking slavery. In The Wrongs of Africa, he wrote: 'Blush ye not, to boast your equal laws, your just restraints, your rights defended, your liberties secured, whilst with an iron hand ye crushed to earth the helpless African; and bid him drink that cup of sorrow, which yourselves have dashed, indignant, from Oppression's fainting grasp?'

In 1807, he was briefly elected to Parliament, where he joined with William Wilberforce finally to help abolish slavery, just three months after taking his seat.

## The evidence

PROOF of Liverpool's involvement in the slave trade is all over the city. Many streets are named after traders and supporters of the slave trade, including Admiral William Rodney, the Duke of Clarence, the Tarleton family and John Manesty. Even Penny Lane, made famous by the Beatles song, was named after James Penny, a slave trader who spoke in favour of the slave trade to Parliament.

City of Liverpool
PENNY LANE L18

## A good first step, now finish the job

IT has taken a long time, but finally the despicable trade in humanity has been banned.

The ECHO, like most Liverpudlians, was initially sceptical about the case for the removal of this trade.

It has to be said that

**Voice of the ECHO**

most people were concerned more about the effect on Merseyside's economy than on the morality of making Africans slaves.

But William Roscoe MP deserves credit for turning around opinion. Thanks to his recognition that compensation needs to be paid and his assertion that slavers are decent if misguided, he has won over hearts and minds.

Liverpool's economy will recover from this setback and grow.

But the priority now is really to break the chains. The trade in slavery may have been abolished.

**Now it is time for all slaves to be freed.**

*Right: How today's Echo might have reported the abolition of slavery*

## Market leaders

BETWEEN 1783 and 1804 Liverpool ships carried around 650,000 African slaves, making the town the principal European centre of the slave trade.
When it appeared slavery was to be abolished, the city council at the time pleaded with Parliament for the trade to continue, as it feared the loss of money brought in by the practice would damage Liverpool's prosperity.

*A 1766 advertisement for slaves in Liverpool paper the Williamson Advertiser*

*One of Liverpool's slave ships*

# LIVERPOOL ECHO

**JOBS**

Can't make a living on the slave ships anymore? We've got 20 pages of jobs

00,006 MAIN MONDAY, MARCH 26, 1807 1 PENNY

## END OF AN ERA AS ROSCOE'S MEN WIN

# SLAVE TRADE ABOLISHED

**VICTORIOUS: William Roscoe**

**BREAK THE CHAIN** AN *ECHO* CAMPAIGN

By WILL FREEMAN

THE battle to ban the trade in slaves is over.

The King last night gave Royal Assent to the bill brought to the House by Foreign Secretary Charles Fox.

The bill was supported by newly-elected city Whig MP William Roscoe, a long-standing opponent of the slave trade, and Tory William Wilberforce, who failed in his bid to end the trade two years ago.

Mr Roscoe spoke passionately in favour of the bill, which prohibits the sale of slaves, but does not make slavery illegal.

● Turn to Page 2

# William Huskisson dies in first railway accident

WILLIAM Huskisson was MP for Liverpool, a cabinet minister and statesman who served his country with distinction.
Sadly, his achievements have been overshadowed by the manner of his death.
Huskisson was the first person to be killed by a train.
During the unveiling of the Liverpool to Manchester railway line, Huskisson was one of the first passengers, riding down the line with the Duke of Wellington.
At Newton-le-Willows, the train stopped so the passengers could watch a cavalcade. Huskisson and company left the train to see the fun, just as the locomotive the Dart was approaching down the parallel track. Huskisson was unable to avoid the train and his left leg was crushed by it.
The wounded man was taken by train to Eccles, but he died later that day.

## The Liverpool to Manchester line

THE Liverpool & Manchester Railway was the first recognisable intercity passenger line in the world.
It was the first to have a fully timetabled service and operated mostly by steam locomotives.
The line was built mainly to transfer goods and raw materials between the port of Liverpool and the industrial powerhouse of Manchester, and to bypass the canal system which was making excessive profits.

The construction of the 35-mile line was overseen by George Stephenson, whose men cut through rock and placed foundations in bogland to complete a remarkable engineering feat.

George Stephenson's own locomotives, including his famous Rocket, were chosen by the owners of the railway to run on the new line.
The Liverpool to Manchester line

*Left: Stephenson's Rocket on the Liverpool-Manchester railway line*

*Below: George Stephenson*

opened on September 15, 1830, a momentous day – for more than one reason.

## Mercy dash too late for MP

THE creator of the Rocket, Mr George Stephenson, took stricken MP William Huskisson for medical attention.
He placed Mr Huskisson in a locomotive and sped along the new railway towards Eccles at high speeds approaching a breakneck 10 miles an hour.
But the effort was for nothing as Mr Huskisson died hours later at 9pm last night.
Mourners told today how the MP's last thoughts were of his fellow passenger and great political rival the Duke of Wellington.
The duke had reluctantly continued to Manchester after the accident.
As he heard the guns announcing the duke's arrival in Manchester, Mr Huskisson said: "I hope to God the Duke may get safe through the day."
It has emerged that Mr Huskisson was accident-prone. On honeymoon he was nearly crushed by a falling horse and he had broken his arm three times.
His funeral will take place on September 24.

*Right: How today's Echo might have reported the first rail accident*

TERROR ON THE LINE: The sce

## The Rainhill trials

IN October 1829, the directors of the Liverpool & Manchester Railway held a competition to decide whether stationary steam engines or locomotives would be used to pull the trains.

A £500 prize was on offer to the winner of the trials, which were held near Rainhill, St Helens.

Only five locomotives began the tests and only one of those completed the trials – George and Robert Stephenson's 'Rocket'. The Stephensons were given the prize and a contract to produce locomotives for the line.

*A 1980 reconstruction of the Rainhill competition*

## Lunardi flies over Liverpool

LIVERPOOL saw its first train in 1830, but transport pioneers would have looked to the skies 45 years before.

On July 20, 1785, the first balloon flight over Merseyside took place. Standing in the ornate gondo hanging under the gas balloon was Vincent Lunardi, secretary to the Neapolitan Ambassador to England. The September before, Lunardi had become the first person ever to fly over England.

At 6pm on July 20, Lunardi took off from the old Liverpool Fort – the current site of Princes Dock – watched by crowds. At 6.20, he passed through a cloud and snow fell on the balloon. But eight minutes later, he had a "most beautiful view of Liverpool".

At 6.57, he started to descend, landing in a cornfield near Symmond's Wood, about 12 miles from Liverpool, at 7.06pm.

## ECHO — SHOCK AT RAILWAY OPENING

SEPTEMBER 16, 1830 — 1 PENNY

# KILLED Y TRAIN

day just before William Huskisson MP (inset) was struck by George Stephenson's Rocket

Picture: STEPHEN SHAKESHAFT

TURNS TO DESPAIR - PAGES 2,3,4&5

ECHO Flying tonight

## LUNAR-TIC

At 6pm today, this madman plans to strap himself to a balloon and fly through the skies of Liverpool. We say: Don't stand underneath him!

FULL STORY – PAGES 4&5

You know you can count on ... ...ABACUSWORLD

19

# 1879–2003
## ECHOES OF THE PRESENT

Having taken you back to those days before the Echo's launch in 1879,
it is now time to look at the pages that made history in Victorian England
before we bring you hurtling forward into the 21st century and the city's
emergence as a world heritage site and European Capital of Culture 2008.

The first of these events is pre-Echo, but crucially important to the
city – the laying of the St George's Hall foundation stone – covered by the
Liverpool Mercury. Then it's Echo pages all the way.

As the 20th century dawned, Liverpool's status as a world famous port
and second city of the Empire gave its citizens every reason to believe
Scouse Power would last forever.

Little did the avid readers of the Echo know that they would soon
be reading headlines declaring the start of two devastating world wars.
Of course, the incredible spirit of the people always shone through, even
when German planes destroyed the heart of the city during the Blitz.

Those frightening days of the Forties became the functional Fifties that in
turn became the swinging Sixties. The Beatles were at the heart of a musical
revolution and the city once again seemed to be the centre of the universe
with the our football clubs also top of the game.

The Echo has remained at the heart of all things Liverpool,
always reflecting the drive and imagination of its citizens.
The voice of the Echo – and therefore the voice of the people – has never
been silenced. The modern Echo headlines highlight the remarkable
regeneration of the city in this 800th birthday year.

In this section of "Echoes of Liverpool" we look back at many contrasting
stories – local, national and international – that were not just newsworthy,
but worthy of a place in history.

These include the building of historic gems like St George's Hall;
the laying of the foundation stones for Liverpool's cathedrals and the
emergence of entertainment institutions like the famous Empire Theatre.

We headline disasters along the way like the loss of the Thetis and the
Lusitania that are at the heart of the city's maritime history.

We highlight more modern international headline grabbers like the
first moon landing, the shooting of John Lennon and 9/11 in New York.

Now the Echo reports daily on the changing face of modern Liverpool,
European Capital of Culture 2008 as the "Echoes of Liverpool"
continue to make history.

# St George's Hall foundation laid

WHEN it opened in 1854, St George's Hall was hailed as a symbol of Liverpool's greatness and pride as much as for its splendour as one of Europe's finest neo-classical civic buildings.

The first stone was laid on the coronation day of Queen Victoria on June 28, 1838, on a sandstone hilltop on the edge of an area known as The Great Heath.

A design competition was won by Harvey Lonsdale Elmes and his £300,000 building won fame for its fabulous Minton-tiled floor, beautiful Small Concert Room and fascinating decorations.

The concert room has been graced by no less than Charles Dickens who gave regular readings there, and the building's assize court was the setting for many notorious trials, none more so than when Florence Maybrick was convicted of the murder of her husband James by poisoning him with arsenic.

*Above: A rare commemorative medallion given to dignitaries who attended the opening of St George's Hall*

*Right: An illustration of St George's Hall in 1854*

*Below: Architect Harvey Lonsdale Elmes's finished competition perspective of the assize courts*

*Harvey Lonsdale Elmes, the architect who won the contest to build St George's Hall*

The Mercury, a predecessor to both the Daily Post and Echo, reported the laying of the foundation stone. The Mercury, which went to press on Cowper's Patent Printing Machine, left, merged with the Daily Post in 1904

## Queen Victoria

*Right Reports of Queen Victoria's coronation; and the young queen in her ceremonial gown*

THE Victoria monument in Liverpool is one of the city's icons; it survived the Blitz unscathed and now looks on benignly as the Grosvenor shopping centre takes shape.

It is a tribute to a woman who reigned as Queen for more than 60 years. Forever in our imaginations as the mourning-clad old lady, many forget that on her Coronation, Victoria was just a girl of 18.

# The year the city of Liverpool was born

FOR many years now, Liverpool has boasted two cathedrals, but for more than 200 years, the city relied on the famous St Peter's Church in the street named after it, for its religious reputation.

Completed in 1704 on the south side of the street, with a steeple 108 feet high that was fitted with a peal of eight bells, it cost £3,500 and was said to be the first church consecrated in Lancashire since the Reformation.

The church contained many interesting features, including four portals, each in a different style of architecture, a handsome altar and a stained glass representation of St Peter.

In 1880 it was declared a pro-cathedral foundation, enabling Liverpool to become an official city.

The church finally closed its doors in August 1918 after the consecration of 84,000 marriages, the baptism of 360,000 babies and the burial in its cemetery of 43,000 people, but all that remains today is a small cross in the pavement near Woolworth's.

*Top Right: Gardens on St Peter's Church site, 1919*

*Right: Echo article reporting Liverpool's new city status*

*Below: St Peter's Church*

## LIVERPOOL A CITY.

### LETTERS PATENT SEALED.

Liverpool is no longer a "town;" it is to-day a "city." This morning the Town-clerk received a letter from the Home Office, stating that the letters patent constituting Liverpool a City had been sealed and dated yesterday. The documents are expected to-day, but they take effect from yesterday, according to their date.

A FURTHER REDUCTION

**BOURNVILLE COCOA**

NOW 7½ᴰ ¼ lb tin

See the name 'CADBURY' on *every piece* of Chocolate

*Above: Liverpool had its 19th Century chocoholics as this advert for Bournville Cocoa shows*

*Right: How the Echo reported Liverpool becoming a city*

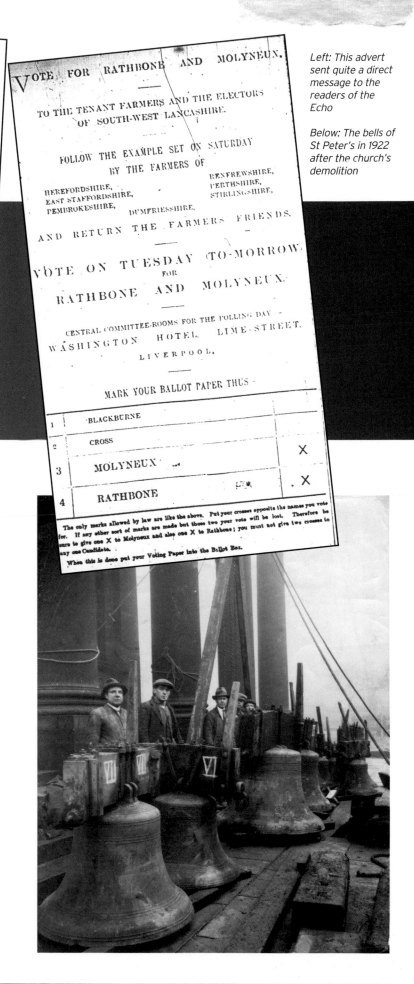

# THE CITY CHARTER FOR LIVERPOOL.

In our first edition we announced the receipt by the Mayor of the charter conferring on Liverpool the title of city. Through the courtesy and kindness of the Mayor we are enabled to publish the full text of the charter, which is as follows:—

Victoria, by the grace of God of the United Kingdom of Great Britain and Ireland Queen, Defender of the Faith,

To all to whom these presents shall come, greeting.

Whereas the Mayor, Aldermen, and Burgesses of the borough of Liverpool, in our county of Lancaster, have by their memorial humbly represented unto us that our Royal predecessor, King John, by his charter, dated on or about the 28th day of August, in the ninth year of his reign, was graciously pleased to incorporate the inhabitants of that town and borough and their successors. That under and by virtue of an Act of Parliament passed on the 10th day of August, in the forty-second year of our reign, and intituled "an Act to provide for the foundation of four new bishoprics in England," the Ecclesiastical Commissioners have certified to us, under their common seal, that the endowment fund required by the said Act for the foundation of the bishopric of Liverpool has been provided. That the memorialists prayed if it should please us, by Order in Council, to found the said bishopric, that our Royal Letters Patent, authorising the change in the name and denomination of the said body corporate, and conferring upon Liverpool the title of "City," and declaring that the memorialists shall be hereafter called and known as "The Mayor, Aldermen, and Citizens of the City of Liverpool," might be issued. The memorialists, therefore, most humbly prayed that we should be graciously pleased to authorise and direct the issue of a Royal charter conferring upon Liverpool the title of city, and upon the memorialists the name and description of "The Mayor, Aldermen, and Citizens of the City of Liverpool." And whereas the said bishopric has been duly founded, and we are minded to accede to the prayer of the said memorial. Now, therefore, know ye that we, of our especial grace and favour, and mere motion, do, by this our Royal Charter, will, ordain, constitute, declare, and appoint that our said Borough of Liverpool shall henceforth for the future and for ever hereafter be a city, and shall be called and styled "The City of Liverpool, in the County of Lancaster," instead of the Borough of Liverpool, and shall have all such rank, liberties, privileges, and immunities as are incident to a city; and we further declare and direct that the said Mayor, Aldermen, and Burgesses of our said Borough of Liverpool shall henceforth, and by virtue of this our Royal Charter, be one body politic and corporate, by the name and style of "The Mayor, Aldermen, and Citizens of the City of Liverpool," with such and the same powers and privileges as they have hitherto had as the Mayor, Aldermen, and Burgesses of the Borough of Liverpool, and as

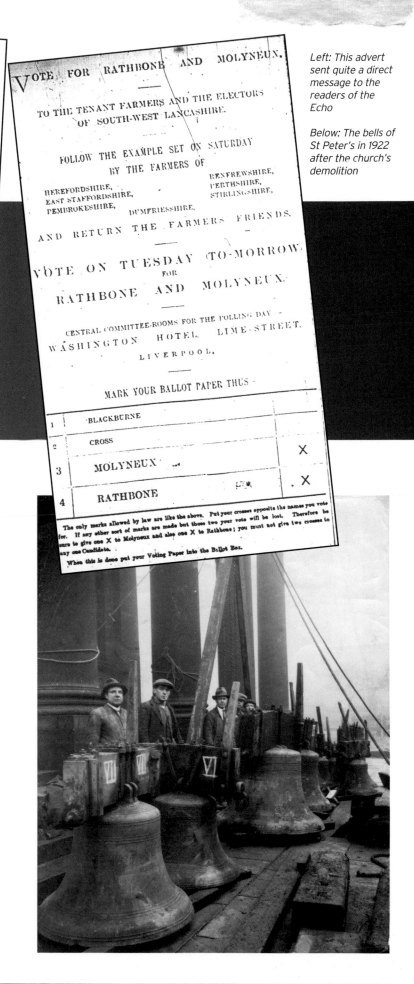

*Left: This advert sent quite a direct message to the readers of the Echo*

*Below: The bells of St Peter's in 1922 after the church's demolition*

# Some things never change

HOW different life was back then... or was it? There are some striking similarities between the stories appearing in the Echo in 1884 and those in our modern papers.

Technology has rapidly progressed and life has changed beyond recognition but some things never alter. After all, people are still people!

**45, GREAT CHARLOTTE-STREET.**

**ARTIFICIAL TEETH.**—A complete Set, One Guinea. Single Tooth, 2s 6d. Precisely the same as advertised by other firms. Guaranteed for five years.—E. F. L'ESTRANGE, Surgeon Dentist, 24, Mount Pleasant (near Adelphi Hotel).

*Here's an offer to get your teeth into...*

## ALARMING SCENE IN BOLD-STREET.

Yesterday an alarming scene was witnessed in Bold-street, but fortunately no disastrous result followed. It appears that Mr. Alfred Castellain, corn merchant, of St. Anne's-road, Wavertree, had occasion to alight in Bold-street from a one-horse brougham. His coachman, James Pickles, got off the box to hold the horse's head, when the animal darted off at a furious pace into Church-street and along Lord-street to the corner of North John-street. At this point, but for the prompt interference of Police-constable 466, it would have collided with a passing omnibus. The constable, at great risk and with much difficulty, seized the animal, and succeeded in arresting its progress. If it had not been that the streets were tolerably clear of vehicles, some damage might have resulted.

SUNDAY TRADING

*What was more amazing – the policeman's quick thinking, or the fact that Bold Street was clear of vehicles?*

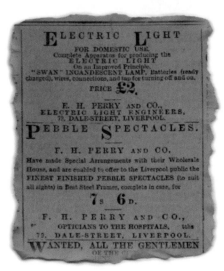

*Be a sight for sore eyes in pebble spectacles. Were they just for the stoney-faced?*

*Great value? You butter believe it!*

## A THIEF IN FOUR PAIRS OF TROUSERS.

At the City Police Court, this morning, before Mr. T. S. Raffles, stipendiary magistrate, a sailor named John Smith was charged with having broken and entered the captain's cabin on board the Cunard steamer Bothnia, which was lying in the Alexandra Dock yesterday, and stolen four uniform coats, five vests, four pairs of trousers, one silk handkerchief, one marine glass, and a revolver, valued at £30, the property of Horatio M'Kay, the master. Mr. Marks prosecuted. The cabin was secured on the afternoon of the 21st inst., but on the following morning it was found to have been broken open and the articles mentioned taken away. The same evening the prisoner was arrested in Great Howard-street, with the glass in his possession, and on arrival at the Detective Office he was found to be wearing the four pairs of trousers, which belonged to the captain of the steamer. A search was afterwards made in an empty house in Fulford-street when the stolen coats and vests were discovered.—Prisoner now pleaded guilty to the offence, and was committed to gaol for six months with hard labour.

THE GRAND DUKE OF HESSE

*OK sunshine, drop 'em. And them. AND them. Them too!*

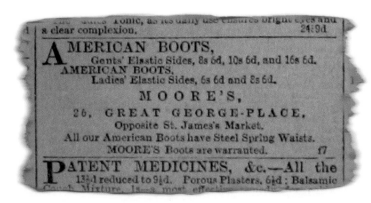

*American boots: one previous owner, used for kicks on Route 66*

## THE POCKET-PICKING NUISANCE.

At the Liverpool Police Court, this morning, before Mr. Raffles, three boys, aged from ten to twelve years, named David Miller, John Miller, and Edward Pearson, were charged with frequenting the Landing-stage with intent to commit a felony. Detective Robbins stated that he saw the prisoners attempt to pick the pockets of several people on the George's Landing-stage yesterday, and took them into custody. The lads, who it is believed are connected with the gang of juvenile pickpockets who have been brought before the court during the last week, were remanded for seven days.

## THE MANCHESTER UNITY

*No ASBOs, just named, shamed and jailed*

## STONETHROWING BY BOYS.

To-day, at the City Police Court, Dale-street, before Mr. P. H. Rathbone, upwards of a dozen lads (some of them of thoroughly respectable appearance) attended to answer summonses taken out against them by the police for stonethrowing in different parts of the city. The offences were proved, and the young defendants were fined 1s and costs each, the chairman observing to each of them that he was empowered to inflict a penalty of 40s and costs in respect of every such offence. The fines were paid by the parents of the boys, who attended. The Rev. Gustavus Carson, incumbent of St. Augustine's Church, Shaw-street, who occupied a seat at the solicitor's table, addressed their worships at the conclusion of the hearing of the charges, and stated that for a long time past there has been a very large number of complaints by respectable inhabitants of Shaw-street and the neighbourhood respecting this stonethrowing nuisance, and he himself had on several occasions reason to complain on account of the windows of the church of St. Augustine being broken. Over and over again he had forgiven the lads, on account of their otherwise respectable position, some of them being attendants at his school, but he found it of no use. He was glad that official action had at last been taken, and he trusted that good consequences would arise.

## MANSLAUGHTER IN LIVE

*Its not just the scruffs that throw stones*

---

N.B.—Shippers, Dealers, and the Trade contracted with.

## CRANE AND SONS, 217, SCOTLAND-ROAD.

## EASY PAYMENTS FOR PIANO-FORTES, AMERICAN ORGANS AND HARMONIUMS,

AT
CRANE AND SONS,
217 TO 225, SCOTLAND-ROAD,
PIANO-FORTES
By Collard and Collard, Broadwood and Sons.

PIANOS ..................... FROM £5

ORGANS..................... FROM £4

HARMONIUMS............. FROM £3

FOR HIRE OR FOR SALE,
OR
SOLD UPON THE HIRE-PURCHASE SYSTEM,
FROM 5s PER MONTH.

£3 10s.—Square Piano-forte, very cheap.—Crane and Sons, 217, Scotland-road.

*When I were a lass, you could buy two pianos, an organ AND a harmonium and still have change of a twenty*

---

## CHARGE OF SELLING DRINK TO A POLICE-CONSTABLE.

At the City Police Court, Dale-street, to-day, before Mr. Thomas Cope, Dr. Gill, and Mr. H. L. Gregory, John Charles Lowe was summoned for supplying drink to a constable on his licensed premises, 132, North Hill-street, while he was on duty. Inspector Clingan, who laid the information, said that on the night of Thursday, the 1st inst., at half-past ten o'clock, he, in company with Police-constable 980, entered the premises of the defendant, and found there Police-constable 1,022, who was on duty at the time, with a pint of beer, and having his armlet on. The constable at once acknowledged the fact, adding that a friend had paid for it for him. This statement was corroborated by the barman, John Paine. The inspector told Mrs. Lowe that she would be summoned for supplying the constable with drink.—Mr. Lewis, solicitor, who defended, called Police-constable 1,022, who denied that he had his armlet on in the house.—The defence was that the defendant supplied the drink to the constable unknowingly.—After further evidence was given the charge was dismissed.

## BREACH OF THE LICENSING

*Was this constable let off because the charges were based on just 5% proof?*

## BRUARY 1, 1884.

## A SKILFUL POLICE-OFFICER.

At a quarter to six o'clock last evening, an old man named James Ryan, living in a court off Birkett - street, was knocked down and run over by a horse and spring cart owned and driven by Peter Norris, greengrocer, 198, Westminster-road, Police-constable 401 (Fitzsimons) being on duty close by, was promptly upon the scene, and having been instructed in surgery as one of the members of the St. John's Ambulance Corps, he found that one of the old man's legs had been badly fractured. Thereupon he sent for splints and bandages, which he applied until the arrival of the horse ambulance and Dr. Horrocks from the Northern Hospital, where the patient was removed. Dr. Horrocks complimented the officer upon his skilfulness, and said that if it had not been for the ready treatment death might have ensued.

## THE DARING POST OFFICE ROBBERY.

*St John's Ambulance saves the day*

---

## HALF-YEARLY CLEARANCE SALE AT THE BON MARCHE, IN BASNETT-STREET.

## BOYS' AND YOUTHS' CLOTHING. GREAT REDUCTIONS.

|  | Sale Price. | Former Price. |
|---|---|---|
| 90 Suits, suitable for the Nursery and School Wear; various Tweeds and a few Serges, in the military and Norfolk shapes, will be cleared at . . . . All sizes one price. | 4/6 | 10/6 to 15/0 |
| 80 Suits, including finer Summer Tweeds in drab and grey, will be offered at . . | 7/6 | 15/0 to 21/0 |
| 50 Serge and Tweed Sailor and Sefton Suits, trimmed various, will be offered at . . | 7/6 10/6 | 22/0 to 25/0 |
| 40 Boys' and Youths' School Suits (three garments), made from durable Scotch Tweeds and Homespuns, will be cleared at . . | 15/0 | 25/0 to 30/0 |
| 60 Youths' Long Trousers Suits, for ages from 12 to 15 years old, made from strong Scotch Tweeds, well finished, will be sold for . . | 15/0 21/0 | 25/0 to 42/0 |
| 40 Little Boys' Kilt Suits, made from wool Cheviots and checks, will be sold for . . | 10/0 | 15/0 to 25/0 |
| OVERCOATS. 200 Various Overcoats have been turned out for absolute sale, to fit Boys from 5 to 9 years old, with and without capes, including some of the most expensive kinds. These will be sold for . . | 7/6 10/0 | 10/6 to 30/0 |

ODD KNICKERS.
200 Pairs to be cleared, all sizes.
One price, 2s 11½d ; value, 4s 6d, 5s 6d.

SALE THIS MORNING,
AT THE
BON MARCHE,
IN BASNETT-STREET.

*Unusual underwear, anyone?*

---

## THE CHARGE OF BIGAMY AGAINST A BASKET MAKER.

At the Birkenhead Police Court, to-day, before Mr. Preston, Benjamin Walker, a basket maker, employed in Birkenhead Market, was charged on remand with having committed bigamy by marrying Sarah Baldock at St. James's Church, Toxteth, on the 21st inst., his wife Eliza, whom he had married at Old Basford, Nottingham, on the 16th July, 1877, being still alive. Sarah Baldock, a young woman, now residing in Grange-lane, Birkenhead, proved having been married by licence to the prisoner when the case was before the court on Monday last. She now further stated that she was a cook before her marriage, and had known the prisoner about eleven months. About three months ago she asked him if his first wife was still alive, as he had heard so, and he gave her no answer.—Lucy Walker, sister of the prisoner, who lives at 90, Manning-street, Nottingham, deposed that she was present when her brother was married to Eliza Slaney, on the 16th July, 1877, and she signed her name as a witness. She saw Eliza on Tuesday evening last. Her brother had been separated from her for about four years.—Detective Hughes, who arrested the prisoner, produced certified copies of the two marriage certificates. When charged by the officer with bigamy, on his arrest on Monday last, he said, "I had information some time ago that my wife was dead, and that was the reason I got married. I did not make any inquiries at Nottingham to see if that was true. She was a bad wife to me, and I never could live with her."—He was committed for trial.

## INVALID LIVERPOOL

*Talk about putting all your eggs in one basket*

## THE "SOUTHPORT POET" AGAIN IN TROUBLE.

At the Southport Borough Police Court, to-day, Henry Berry, well known in that town by the sobriquet of the "Southport Poet," was charged with sleeping in a farmyard in Trap-lane, this morning. Evidence in support of the charge having been given by Police-constable Wild, Berry, in reply to the bench, stated that on the previous night he stayed out watching the soldiers until it was too late to go to his lodgings, and he therefore wended his way to the farmyard in question, got amongst some straw, and made himself as comfortable as he could. He was not in a fit condition to be out, and he ought to have been in gaol a week ago. He would sooner go to gaol than to the workhouse (laughter). After a pause he said he had done more for Southport than anyone in it (renewed laughter).—Alderman Robinson, after consulting his colleagues, was proceeding to say that the bench saw no reason why they should not grant his request and send him to prison, when Berry interrupted him, and said he was not yet done talking to them. He could talk to them for half an hour (laughter).—Alderman Robinson remarked that the magistrates had heard quite sufficient, and he (Berry) would have to go to gaol for seven days.—Berry : Thank you, gentlemen ; and I hope when I come out I shall be a wiser and better man (loud laughter).—He was then removed to the cells. This made the prisoner's twenty-third appearance before the court.

*Poet strings together a week-long sentence*

## STEALING INFECTIOUS CLOTHES AT BOOTLE.

At the Bootle Police Court, this morning, before Messrs. W. Barrell and C. Taylor, Michael Ryan, 17, Aber-street, was charged with stealing a quilt and a pair of trousers, valued at 8s 6d, the property of John Sullivan, with whom he lodged. From the evidence it appeared that a man who lodged in Sullivan's house, and who had been suffering from typhus fever, had been removed to the hospital. The prisoner entered the room where the sick man had been staying and carried away the quilt and a pair of trousers. He tried to pawn them, but did not succeed, and the pawnbrokers gave information to the police. The prisoner now stated that Sullivan had given him the trousers, but admitted that he had no right to the quilt. This had not been disinfected, and was likely to spread disease. The magistrates fined the prisoner 21s, or a month in default.

*This tenant got more than he bargained for*

# Lifeboat disaster claims 27 lives

THE worst British lifeboat disaster of all time took place off Southport on December 9, 1886, when two vessels, the Eliza Fernley from Southport and the Laura Janet from St Annes, sank with the loss of 27 lives while attempting to rescue the crew of an iron barque, the Mexico, from Hamburg.

A mayoral ball in Southport was actually in progress at the time the two boats were launched, but all attention was soon turned on the dreadful disaster, which saw both of them overturned by huge waves before either could reach the Mexico.

Ironically, a third lifeboat, the Charles Biggs from Lytham, managed to reach the stranded Mexico and rescue its crew of twelve.

Public grief was so enormous that an appeal for money to help the victims' families reached £30,000 within a fortnight.

The Mexico was subsequently repaired for a mere £45 and became a tourist attraction at Lytham before making a journey to the Falklands and later sinking in Scottish waters.

*Right: An artist's impression of the Eliza Fernley capsizing within sight of the Mexico*

*Right: How the Echo reported the Lifeboat disaster*

*Left: Survivor Henry Robinson*

*Below: Survivor John 'The Shark' Jackson*

## THE WRECK OF THE MEXICO.

### HER CREW SAVED.

### GALLANT LIFEBOAT RESCUE.

### THRILLING SCENES.

[SPECIAL TELEGRAM.]

Early this morning the new Lytham lifeboat the Charles Biggs, which was only launched a fortnight ago, rendered one of those brilliant services for which the noble Institution it represents is famous. Before ten last night signals of distress were observed from the Lytham beach. The boat was speedily launched, amid cheers. Along she sped under oar and sail before a head wind and strong sea in a westerly direction. Signals continued from the locality of the wreck, and were answered from the shore. About one o'clock this morning the ship was sighted lying between Southport and Formby. The lights were then out, but the shouts of the crew for help were to be heard by the lifeboat men three hundred yards against the gale. At this point the sea ran mountains high, and the water was very broken, and occasionally filled the lifeboat. The gallant crew, under the orders of Coxswain Clarkson, persevered against these great odds, and all the unfortunate sailors—twelve in number—were lowered into the lifeboat, the captain being the last to leave the ship, which had by this time listed considerably. When the lifeboat returned at 3.30 this morning, having been out over five hours, ringing cheers from the assembled crowd greeted her on the one side and expressions of thanks from the exhausted crew of the vessel on the other. Hot stimulants were speedily served to the shipwrecked crew as well as to the gallant rescuers. The vessel is the iron ship Mexico of Hamburg, from Liverpool to Guayaquil with a valuable mixed cargo. Captain Burmester states that she left Liverpool on Sunday, and had since Tuesday been drifting about, and had experienced frightful weather.

## Homage to sea heroes

THE worst disaster in lifeboat history, which killed 12 Southport crewmen, will be commemorated on Sunday next week at a memorial service in Lytham St Annes.

A total of 27 lifeboat men were killed in the tragedy 100 years ago when they rescued 12 men from a foundering German ship, the Mexico, which ran aground in a storm at Ainsdale.

*Above: A memorial for the disaster held in 1986*

*Right: Stories of the survivors as reported in the Echo*

# THE LIFEBOAT DISASTERS.

## NARRATIVES OF SURVIVORS.

Late on Thursday night (as reported in our columns yesterday) the ship Mexico, which left Liverpool for Guayaquil a few days ago with a valuable mixed cargo, was driven back before a terrible north-westerly gale and finally went ashore on the banks near Fernby, between Liverpool and Southport. The signals of distress sent up were noticed at Southport and also at Lytham and St. Anne's, on the other shore of the Ribble estuary. A lifeboat put off at once from each place to the rescue, but only the boat from Lytham managed to reach the ship. Two of the masts had been cut away, and the crew, twelve in number, were lashed in the mizzen rigging. They were taken off, and safely landed at Lytham early yesterday morning.

The other boats unfortunately met with disaster. That from Southport, the Eliza Fernley, had got within a few yards of the wreck when she capsized. Instead of righting immediately, as was expected, the boat remained bottom upwards, with several of the crew underneath. In this position the boat drifted on to the sands at Southport, where three men, the only survivors of the crew of sixteen, got ashore. Three dead bodies were found in the boat, and ten others were discovered on the beach afterwards.

The fate of the St. Anne's lifeboat men was even more tragic. They left on their errand of mercy late on Thursday night, and were not heard of again until yesterday afternoon, when the boat was washed ashore near Southport, with three of her crew dead inside. Thirteen men went out with the boat, and they have all perished. The bodies of nine have already been recovered. Telegrams were sent to Blackpool, and the lifeboat was launched in a heavy sea. After searching vainly the whole day along the coast, however, the crew put into St. Anne's at dusk only to hear of the casualty to the sister boat.

A message has been received from the Queen expressing her sorrow at the calamity and her sympathy with the bereaved. The Secretary of the National Lifeboat Institution has also telegraphed a similar message.

## NARRATIVES OF JOHN JACKSON AND HENRY ROBINSON.

An account of the occurrence was furnished by two of the survivors which cannot fail to be interesting. I found John Jackson in the midst of his family at his house in West-street. He is a middle-aged, strong-built man, with very dark hair and eyes, a broad, intelligent forehead, and copious black whiskers. He looked much exhausted, and a child of about four summers, with golden curly head, clung fondly to his knee.

"Yes, I've had a very narrow escape, sir," he replied to my greeting; "but the other poor chaps are gone." Asked to give a succinct account of the whole affair, he went on:—" We saw the vessel at three o'clock in the afternoon, but she was riding at anchor, and nobody thought she was in any danger, but about half-past nine o'clock she gave signals of distress. We got the boat out and started about ten minutes to ten, going along the sands until we got right opposite the vessel. Then we launched her, the vessel not being above half a mile out. When we got up to her we saw that she had a light on her mizenmast; her foremast and mainmast had been carried away. There was a terrible gale blowing, and the sea was awfully rough. We could hear no shouting; we could hear nothing but the sea roaring. The vessel seemed to be drifting ashore, and we ourselves kept drifting towards Southport. When about twenty yards off the vessel we had gone to help, the sea caught us, and the lifeboat went over to the port side, with our heads pointing to Southport. The coxswain (Hodge) and Fisher were at the helm, and I was just about to throw out the anchor when she capsized. Some of us scrambled out as well as we could, but others could not. There were several of us in the sea clinging to the ropes alongside the boat. Richard Robinson was beside me doing the same. He got very exhausted, and I held him up until a sea came and carried him away, and I never saw him again.

*Above: The Eliza Fernley on her horse drawn carriage and the Mexico stranded on Southport beach after the fatal rescue attempt*

## Also this year...

- The Hockey Association was formed in England
- German Karl Benz patented the first successful gas-driven automobile
- American pharmacist Dr John Stith Pemberton invented Coca-Cola
- US President Grover Cleveland dedicated the Statue of Liberty in New York Harbour
- Parisian music hall The Folies Bergère staged its first revue

# Maybrick: The great poisoning mystery

WAS Florence Maybrick an innocent wife or a cunning murderess? Controversy still rages more than a century after young Florence was sentenced to death for poisoning her husband with doses of arsenic.

Florence and her husband James first met on a trans-Atlantic liner and after a comparatively short relationship got married even though as a girl of 18 she was 24 years his younger.

After a short spell in the United States, they moved to live in Battlecrease House in Aigburth but, with little to occupy her, Florence never really settled and in fact had quite a lively relationship with one of her husband's friends.

Shortly after that relationship was broken up,

James suddenly fell ill and after a relatively short time died from what was said to be a dose of arsenic. His wife was found to have purchased arsenic and despite her desperate denials the finger of blame was pointed.

Despite arguments by the defence lawyer to the effect that James had been taking arsenic as a tonic, she was convicted of murder and sentenced to death, though that was reduced to imprisonment shortly before the execution was due.

Florence always denied murder, and she was released from prison after 15 years, living for a further 37 years before dying in poverty in her native United States.

*Left to right: How the action unfolded in the Echo*

*Above: James Maybrick died of poisoning*

*Right: Florence Maybrick, convicted of her husband's murder*

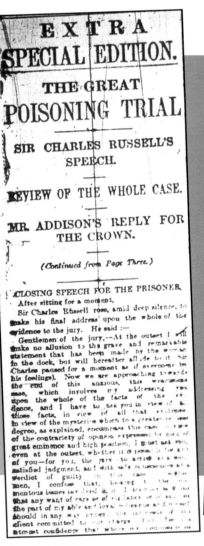

EXTRA
SPECIAL EDITION.

THE GREAT
POISONING TRIAL

SIR CHARLES RUSSELL'S
SPEECH.

REVIEW OF THE WHOLE CASE.

MR. ADDISON'S REPLY FOR
THE CROWN.

*(Continued from Page Three.)*

CLOSING SPEECH FOR THE PRISONER.

*August 5, 1889*

THE
MAYBRICK TRIAL

SEVENTH DAY.

VERDICT AND SENTENCE

THE JUDGE'S SUMMING-UP.

SEVERE CONDEMNATION

THE SCENE AT THE END.

THE PRISONER'S DEMEANOUR

THE JUDGE AND JURY HOOTED.

PETITIONS FOR A RESPITE

CONDUCT OF SIR C. RUSSELL.

There was electricity in the atmosphere yesterday, when Mrs. Maybrick made her appearance in the dock for the last time, and when it was known that that day would decide the question of her fate. The multitude who surrounded St. George's Hall was larger and more eager than ever, and hundreds of privileged persons swarmed round the corridors and were contented with the glimpses of the court they caught through the occasionally opened doors, while only the most fortunate of these were permitted to enter the court as room was made.

*August 9, 1889*

## NINTH EDITION.

## THE MAYBRICK CASE.

## DECISION OF THE HOME SECRETARY.

The Decision of the Home Secretary is to the effect that Mrs. MAYBRICK shall

### BE RESPITED.

## THE HOME SECRETARY AND MRS. MAYBRICK.

### GREAT EXCITEMENT.

### QUESTION IN THE HOUSE.

In the House of Commons, to-day, Mr. W⸺ Macdonald asked the Home Secretary when he expected to be in a position to announce to the public (cries of "No, no") and the house (renewed cries of "No, no") the sentence ("No, no") the decision to which he had arrived in the case of Mrs. Maybrick (cries of "Don't answer").

Mr. Matthews, who arose amid dead silence answered: The advice which I may feel it to be my duty to offer to her Majesty on the subject is not a matter for a question in this house (loud cheers).

Sir John Puleston had twice previously put similar question to the Home Secretary, but Mr. Matthews, upon attempting to rise, was restrained by the general cry of "No" which came from all parts of the house. When at length, however, he rose in his place intense anxi⸺

*August 22, 1889*

## THE MAYBRICK REPRIEVE.

### THE FEELING IN THE COUNTRY.

### CONDITION OF THE PRISONER.

### BRIERLEY LEAVES FOR AMERICA.

### HOW MRS. MAYBRICK'S MOTHER RECEIVED THE NEWS.

There was a general rush to the telegraph offices last night by people who desired to telegraph other people instantly. Among these was a friend of the Baroness Von Roque. He followed his telegram to Blundellsands, and had the pleasure of overtaking the telegraph boy on the road. Taking the despatch from him, he entered the house, and found the poor mother, wan and weary, diligently engaged on a message of entreaty. She jumped up, heard only the words "She is sav⸺" and then sank back strengthless on a couch. It was some minutes before she recovered herself, but then she rose, grasped the messenger by both hands, shook them warmly, and then seized the despatch and tried to read it, and the newspaper extra confirming it through her tears. It was a long time before she was quite herself, and then she was overjoyed. She seized her bonnet and macintosh, and would have immediately started for Walton Gaol to clasp her daughter in her arms, but was restrained by the remembrance that even under such circumstances prison rules would not relax. Then she calmed down, and talked the matter over rationally. The poor lady has great y aged during the past weeks. She has grown thinner and paler, but the news seemed to bring all the freshness and brightness back again.

She said, "Oh! the suspense has been something terrible. I thought I had strength to endure anything, but the fearful agony of the last few days has been more than I thought could be. If Florrie had not broken down I should. Only her misery and weakness kept me up. I have not slept a moment since the verdict. I could not sleep, thinking that every moment brought her one step nearer to her grave, and that I must use that minute in the way that would do most good to her. I felt I knew that the Queen could never depart on her trip to Wales without doing this gracious act. She is a mother herself, and she knows what a mother feels."

*August 23, 1889*

*Left: The Maybrick home, Battlecrease House*

## MRS. MAYBRICK'S RELEASE.

### A NEW AGITATION.

A New York correspondent telegraphs that Mrs. Maybrick is expected to arrive there early in August. Her friends are prepared to welcome her something in the light of a martyr. The fact that she has been released only on ticket of leave has determined her friends to agitate for a full pardon to be granted her, but it is not believed that the British authorities will take this step. Mrs. Maybrick's release yesterday is supposed to have been

MRS. MAYBRICK.

agreed upon because it marked the end of the fifteenth year since her trial began on July 21, 1889. The "Publishers' Press" states that in the early part of 1901 Mrs. Maybrick was transferred from among the ordinary prisoners at Aylesbury to the infirmary, where she acted as servant and nurse, being given not the ordinary prison fare, but practically anything she wanted. This largely brought back to her the health she had lost during her imprisonment.

*July 21, 1904*

# The Overhead Railway opens for business

ONE of the most innovative and successful engineering projects anywhere in the world was introduced to Liverpool in 1893 with the completion of an electric Overhead Railway to serve the then enormous dockland system, which stretched for many miles.

Electrification was still very much in its infancy, but the scheme took off from the start.

The railway was officially opened by Lord Salisbury and that was followed by a public opening of the section between the Alexandra and Herculaneum docks. Soon after, the system was extended to Seaforth sands and in 1896 the Dingle tunnel and terminus were completed.

Plenty of people were upset when a decision was taken to pull the railway down in the mid-1950s.

Although the docks have been greatly reduced since the demolition of the railway, there are still many who wish it remained, as it took plenty of traffic away from roads that are getting more and more overcrowded.

*Above: The overhead station for Gladstone Dock, opened in 1930*

*Excerpts from an Overhead Railway programme*

THE LIVERPOOL FOOTBALL ECHO, SATURDAY, FEBRU

**OPENING OF THE OVERHEAD RAILWAY.**

PRESENTATION TO LORD SALISBURY.

CEREMONY AT THE BRAMLEY-MOORE DOCK.

**LIVERPOOL OVERHEAD RAILWAY. CENTRAL STATION.**

LORD SALISBURY'S VISIT TO LIVERPOOL.

ADDRESS FROM THE CHAMBER OF COMMERCE.

IMPORTANT SPEECH BY THE EX-PREMIER.

FREE TRADE AND TARIFF WARS.

THE PROPOSAL TO TAX FOREIGN WHEAT.

A STOCKPORT FOOTBALLER MISSING.

IF YOU WANT ELECTRIC LIGHT

ELECTRIC BELLS,
ELECTRIC INDICATORS,
ELECTRIC BURGLAR AND FIRE ALARMS
ELECTRIC TELEPHONES,
ELECTRIC BATTERIES, COILS, MOTORS

Send at once for Prices and Samples to

LANCASHIRE ELECTRICAL ENGINEERING COMPANY.

OFFICES AND SHOWROOMS—

26, NORTH JOHN-STREET

Estimates Free.

ESTABLISHED 1804.

TYRER'S CELEBRATED "INVALID" STOUT.

INVALID STOUT. Strongly recommended by the Faculty, being a wholesome, nourishing and STRENGTHENING BEVERAGE, less heavy and more digestible than ordinary Stout.

INVALID STOUT. It will be found in many cases equal to preferable to wine in restoring health.

Sold in Bottles of all sizes. None genuine without bearing our Capsule and Label.

JOHN TYRER AND SON,

WINE MERCHANTS.

46 AND 48 HANOVER-STREET, LIVERPOOL.

BRANCH OFFICES:

21E EXCHANGE STATION, TITHEBARN-STREET

## Also in the news

- The Independent Labour Party in the UK had its first meeting
- Rudolf Diesel received a patent for the diesel engine
- New York stock exchange crash led to a depression
- Gold was found in Kalgoorlie, Australia
- The first car number plates were issued in Paris, France
- New Zealand was the first country in the world to give women the vote

*Left: Passengers on board the Overhead Railway*

# Liverpool Cathedral foundation stone laid

IN 1901 a decision was taken to build a great Anglican Cathedral for the recently formed Diocese of Liverpool and the top of St James Mount was cleared for the purpose.

The construction began in 1904 to a design by 22-year-old Giles Gilbert Scott.

The Foundation was the largest single stone used and was laid by King Edward VII and Queen Alexandra on July 19, 1904.

Their Majesties travelled to Lime Street arriving at 1.40pm and were then taken to the Town Hall for a 2pm lunch.

Meanwhile ticket holders for the event at 4pm, settled in their seats one hour before the ceremony.

Soon after 4pm the grand service began culminating in the laying of the majestic stone by the King with a trowel and mallet of gold and ivory. After a fanfare of trumpets, everyone sang 'O God Our Help In Ages Past'. The Archbishop of York pronounced the final blessing.

In a souvenir programme for the day, The Lord Bishop of Liverpool, The Rt Rev Francis Jas Chavasse, praised the building which he said "was built by all and for all - rich and poor".

## THURSDAY, JULY 21, 19

### THE ROYAL VISIT TO LIVERPOOL

### LETTER FROM THE KING.

### HIS MAJESTY'S APPRECIATION AND GRATIFICATION.

The Lord Mayor has received the following letter from Lord Stanley, Minister in attendance on the King, with reference to the visit of his Majesty the King and Queen Alexandra:—

H.M. Yacht Victoria and Albert,
July 20, 1904.

My Lord Mayor,—I am commanded by his Majesty the King to convey to you his appreciation of the loyal welcome given to him and her Majesty the Queen by the citizens of Liverpool. Their Majesties were much gratified by the enthusiastic reception accorded to them, and were impressed alike by the orderly behaviour of the crowds, the tasteful decoration of the streets, and the admirable arrangements made by your lordship.—I have the honour to be, my lord, your obedient servant, STANLEY.

*July 21, 1904*

*July 18, 1904*

## ROYAL VISIT TRAFFICS.

### OVERHEAD RAILWAY.

The number of passengers travelling on the Overhead Railway and tramways was 53,022.

### THE UNDERGROUND RAILWAY.

It was ascertained at the offices of the Mersey Underground Railway that on the occasion of the King's visit yesterday the system generally did twice as well as on an ordinary day. As regards local traffic between their own stations, the returns show the travelling to have been considerably better than the heaviest Bank Holiday the company has had. There was, likewise, a very heavy traffic to New Brighton, to which rendezvous twelve special trains were run by the Wirral Railway in conjunction with underground trains.

The Birkenhead Corporation ferry traffics during Monday and Tuesday were as follow:—

Woodside Ferry—Monday, 49,379; Tuesday, 74,976.

Rock Ferry.—Monday, 21,924; Tuesday, 16,820.

New Ferry.—Monday, 5,443; Tuesday, 5,932.

*July 20, 1904*

**Cailler's**
SWISS
MILK CHOCOLATE

*(As supplied to Her Majesty the Queen.)*

...delicious and absolutely pure food sweetmeat. ...ightful refreshment on any occasion, and ...larly acceptable on bicycle trips, boating ...ns, holiday tours, at garden parties, and ...ll similar circumstances. If you want the ...lease see that the word "CAILLER" is on ...age, as many inferior imitations are put ...emble the original.

...6d. & 1s. Tablets, and in 6d. & 1s. Boxes of Croquettes.

**HENOCHSBERG & ELLIS,**
H&E POPULAR TAILORS ISLINGTON L'POOL
The Gold Medal Tailors,
10, 12, 14, 14a & 16, ISLINGTON, LIVERPOOL.

Scotch and Fancy Tweed Suits, to order, 30/-
**Wonderful Value in Cycling Suits, 12/6**

Suit,
Sweater,
Cap,
Shoes,
Belt,
Tie.

COMPLETE
**21/-**

...OYS' AND YOUTHS' CLOTHING.

HENOCHSBERG & ELLIS, ISLINGTON, LIVERPOOL.

*Right: Some pages from the Daily Post and Echo souvenir, which featured an illustration of Gilbert G Scott's original design for the cathedral*

# THE KING'S VISIT.

## A Guide For To-morrow.

### CUT THIS OUT FOR REFERENCE.

#### TIME-TABLE.

.30 p.m.—Arrival of their Majesties the King and Queen at Lime-street Station.
.36 p.m.—Children's Demonstration in front of St. George's Hall.
.50 p.m.—Arrival at the Town Hall.
0 p.m.—Luncheon.
0 p.m.—Presentation of Address by the Corporation.
Presentation of Address by the Liverpool University.
50 p.m.—King and Queen on Town Hall Balcony.
30 p.m.—Leave the Town Hall.
p.m.—Ceremony of Laying the Foundation-stone of the Liverpool Cathedral. St. James's Mount.
0 p.m.—Arrival at the Landing-stage (No. 6. Bridge).
MARINE DISPLAY.
5 p.m.—Embarkation on the Royal Yacht.

#### EVENING CELEBRATIONS.

0 p.m.—Treat to 1,100 Aged Poor, St. George's Hall.
0 p.m.—Treat to Crimean and Indian veterans, St. George's Hall (Concert-room).
to 9 p.m.—Bands of Music in the Parks.
Dusk.—Illumination of the Town Hall and Grand Display of Fireworks in Stanley, Newsham, Wavertree, and Sefton Parks, and in the Wavertree Playground.

#### CUPANTS OF CARRIAGES FROM IME-STREET TO TOWN HALL.

te: Lime-street, William Brown-street, nd Dale-street.

FIRST ROYAL CARRIAGE
r Majesties the King and Queen and

SECOND ROYAL CARRIAGE.
Stanley, Lord Kintore, the Countess of lford, and the Hon. Charlotte Knollys.

THIRD ROYAL CARRIAGE.
Knollys, Admiral Sir John Fullerton, and the Hon Sidney Greville.

FOURTH CARRIAGE.
(Lord Derby's.)
arl of Derby, the High Sheriff, and Captain Fleet, R.N.

FIFTH CARRIAGE.
(Lord Derby's.)
ord Bishop of Liverpool, Sir William ood, and Consul-General for Belgium.
r-General Sir Francis Howard (in com- of the troops) will ride at the side of ajesties' carriage.
Equerries-in-Waiting will ride in the on.
aff of the North-Western District will tendance on horseback.

SSION FROM TOWN HALL TO CATHEDRAL SITE.

Castle-street, Lord-street, Church-, Bold-street, Berry-street, Great -street, Upper Parliament-street. James-road.

---

## ROYAL LIVERPOOL

### 20 years later...

THE first portion of the Anglican Cathedral was consecrated by King George and Queen Mary on Saturday, July 19, 1924.
Liverpool's new 'house of prayer', begun 20 years earlier, was the largest church in the country and only two cathedrals in Europe, St Peter's and Seville, were thought grander.
Leaders of the Anglican Church, English Diocesan bishops and English deans were joined by representatives from Scotland, Ireland the United States and the Dominions. That sunny Saturday morning saw the city centre thronged with people. King George and Queen Mary had spent the night at Knowsley as the guest of Lord Derby and they attended a ceremony at St George's Hall before lunching at the town hall.
The congregation for the consecration were all in their seats by 1.50pm. As with all such ceremonies it was conducted with military precision. The Archbishop of York blessed the building - a cathedral then only one third of its eventual finished size. The King praised the 'noble cathedral' in his address.

*How the auspicious day was recorded in the Echo*

#### TO-DAY'S HISTORIC EVENTS.

##### His Majesty's Fine Tribute; The Archbishop's Sermon.

#### SUNSHINE GRACES THE CEREMONIES

*" Liverpool has risen to the full. This noble Cathedral is a tribute to its piety, generosity, and local patriotism. . . . Neither in site nor architecture need it fear comparison with the masterpieces of past generations. . . . This is the fine spirit of the mediæval builders. . . . It will be an inspiration in every sphere of life."*
— The King to-day.

THE majesty of God, the majesty of the Realm, the majesty of inspired architecture, and the uplifting thoughts of a great people combined to make to-day's Cathedral consecration an event on which centred the reverent interest of the world's Christian peoples.

Liverpool was at its brightest, and amid beflagged and festooned streets, their Majesties the King and Queen—twenty years after King Edward was received tumultuously on coming to lay the Foundation Stone—received a triumphant welcome from hundreds of thousands of people at the ceremonies

The major beauty of the Cathedral, which has been pictured in every civilised country, has captured all hearts, and to-day's events will be historic.

On Page 4 appears a special Cathedral appreciation, a descriptive report of the Pateau across the King's speech, and a list of both-bench guests
On Page 5, a full souvenir of Cathedral pictures
On Page 6 there are some striking "Echo" snapshots to-day.

---

### BOY DESIGNER OF CATHEDRAL.

#### Liverpool's Great New House of Prayer.

#### BEGUN 20 YEARS AGO.

The first portion of Liverpool Cathedral, the foundation stone of which was laid by King Edward 20 years ago, is now completed, and will be consecrated in the presence of the King and Queen on July 19.
This is the first Anglican cathedral to be constructed in the northern province, and the third in England, since the Reformation.
Liverpool's great new house of prayer will be the largest church in the country, inferior in point of size only to St. Peter's and Seville among the cathedrals of the world.
Few people living in Southern England have any vision of the splendour of the great building which, designed in 1904 by a boy of 20, has slowly been growing ever since, high above the banks of the Mersey.

##### PUPIL WINS THE PRIZE.

Mr. Giles Gilbert Scott was a pupil in a Liverpool architect's office when he heard that he had won the open prize for designs for the new cathedral. Then a young dreamer, now a middle-aged man, but still with the same passion for perfection, he sees to-day the completion of the first half of his cathedral.
When the King and Queen go to Liverpool they will see the Lady Chapel, the copper-roofed chapter house, two of the four transepts and the choir.
In the official handbook to the cathedral, published to-day, is given an account of the Lady Chapel windows, which serve as a chronicle of the deeds of good women.
One of these windows is dedicated to "Catherine Gladstone and all loyal-

---

### Our Cathedral Majesty.

To-day, Liverpool was the scene of a deeply moving and historic ceremony which is being followed with devout interest by Christian people in every part of the world.
In the presence of the King and Queen, and an impressive gathering of ecclesiastical dignitaries, among whom there were seven archbishops and forty bishops, the first portion of the city's majestic Cathedral was reverently dedicated to the service of God.
The ceremony marked the first stage in the fulfilment of a great ideal, and nothing that pen can write or tongue can utter can add to the splendour of that has been achieved.
Liverpool's Cathedral, when it is finished, will be the largest house of God in the kingdom; and inferior in size only to St. ter's at Rome and the Cathedral of Seville, throughout the rld.
Its beauty will match its magnitude, for, in the opinion of the most ent architects of the age, it will rank with the noblest buildings of the and possibly be accounted the finest example of modern Gothic. Thus Liverpool will be crowned with a double glory, for already George's Hall, it possesses the greatest modern civic build-the classic style. Both these superb treasures it holds as from youth.
dale Elmes was only twenty-four when he planned St. George's Hall. lbert Scott was even younger than that when he prepared the designs Cathedral. He was only twenty-one.
Liverpool, being young itself, has never been afraid of putting its trust and in both these imposing enterprises its faith has been abundantly

# Dr Crippen shipped back to face trial for murder

DOCTOR Hawley Harvey Crippen was the first person to be arrested with the help of the wireless. Crippen embarked on a relationship with Ethel Le Neve after she started working as a secretary in his patent-medicine firm.

The doctor claimed his wife, Cora, had left for America with another man, but he had secretly poisoned her.

With growing speculation over Mrs Crippen's whereabouts, Dr Crippen and Miss Le Neve fled to Canada, posing as Mr Robinson and his son on the liner Montrose.

A crewmember discovered their true identity when they were caught them squeezing hands 'immoderately', and Scotland Yard was alerted. The prisoners landed in 'boisterous' weather in Liverpool and were then taken on to London. An extensive trial followed where Crippen declared that Ethel Le Neve knew nothing about the murder. The jury decided Ethel was innocent of all charges but Crippen was found guilty and sentenced to death. He was hanged at Pentonville Prison and buried with a photograph of Miss le Neve.

*July 29, 1910*

*August 1, 1910*

*August 22, 1910*

*Below: Crippen's house in Camden Town, where the murder was committed*

*Right: The cuttings from the Echo that followed Crippen's case from arrest to execution*

## CRIPPEN DRAMA.

### THE DENOUEMENT NEARLY REACHED.

### AN EXCITING MOMENT.

### MORE MESSAGES FROM THE MONTROSE.

## CRIPPEN

### Arrested on the Montrose.

### A DRAMATIC MOMENT.

### Detectives in Pilot Garb.

### LE NEVE'S COLLAPSE.

### PRISONERS TAKEN TO QUEBEC.

### DATE OF RETURN.

### Excitement in Two Hemispheres.

Our special correspondent at Father Point, Quebec, cables that Inspector Dew, on boarding the Montrose yesterday morning, identified both Crippen and Le Neve, who were at once arrested. The news is confirmed by Scotland Yard, who received a cablegram to the same effect from Mr. Dew yesterday afternoon. Crippen showed unmistakable nervousness before the arrival of the pilot boat conveying the police authorities, but he submitted to arrest without remark. Le Neve, dressed in boy's clothing, screamed when Inspector Dew approached her in her cabin, but, so far, she has stedfastly refused to answer any questions whatever. In fact, the dramatic nature of the arrest, following the many days of severe tension which she had undergone, completely overcame her, and it was necessary to feed her with brandy and eggs to prevent a total physical collapse.

## CRIPPEN'S HOME-COMING.

### ARRANGEMENTS FOR LEAVING LIVERPOOL.

(Continued from Page 4.)

### CANADIAN TROOPS ON THE MEGANTIC.

The White Star-Dominion liner Megantic left Quebec for Liverpool direct about seven o'clock on Saturday evening. Dr. Crippen and Miss Le Neve, with Inspector Dew and Sergeant Mitchell, and Miss Stone and Miss Foster, wardresses from Holloway Gaol, were transferred by a tug to the liner in the stream at Lawrence.

The liner is bringing first and second cabin passengers, the third-class accommodation having been specially reserved for 650 members of the Queen's Own Regiment of Canada, under Colonel Sir Henry Pellatt, who are coming over to go into camp and undergo training with the Regulars in the South of England.

The Megantic is expected to arrive at the Prince's Stage about noon on Saturday, and it is not known yet whether Dr. Crippen and Miss Le Neve will be landed from the liner in a special tender or whether they will disembark with the saloon and second-class passengers and the troops at the Stage. It is believed that Inspector Dew will leave for London either in the White Star special from Riverside Station or the first train available from Lime-street.

It does not seem likely that Crippen and his companion will be placed in the dock at Bow-street until Monday morning, although, should the Megantic make an exceptionally fast passage, it is possible they will reach London in time to be formally charged and remanded before the court rises at four o'clock on Saturday.

No news has been received at the London office of the company confirming the report that Inspector Dew and his captives are travelling upon the Megantic at the present time.

*November 23, 1910*

## THE CRIPPEN CRIME.

### CONDEMNED MAN EXECUTED.

### SCENES OUTSIDE THE PRISON

### CONFESSION STORY OFFICIALLY DENIED.

[BY "ECHO" PRIVATE WIRE.]

Dr. Hawley Harvey Crippen was executed at Pentonville Prison this morning for the murder of his wife, Cora Crippen, known to the theatrical world as Belle Elmore.

Crippen was called at an early hour and dressed in his own clothes. He spent the last few moments of his life in the company of his spiritual father, and received the last blessing and rites of the Church.

The convict this morning presented a haggard and worn appearance, and he seemed to lose all fortitude as his end approached. Breakfast, consisting of bread and butter and a pot of tea, was brought to the condemned cell shortly before seven o'clock, but the meal remained practically untouched. Just on the stroke of the hour Ellis, of Rochdale, the executioner, with an assistant, entered the condemned cell, which was the only warning that the convict had that his time had come. Crippen rose from his seat and submitted quietly to the process of pinioning. A procession, headed by a Roman Catholic priest, was then formed to the scaffold, which was only a few paces away from the condemned cell. Bareheaded and colourless, Crippen was escorted to the gallows by the warders and quickly placed in position on the drop. At this stage the unhappy man appeared to be on the point of collapse. The noose and cap were quickly adjusted, and the final preparations having been expeditiously performed, the bolt was drawn. Crippen, who weighed just over 10st., was given a drop of 7ft. Death is stated to have been instantaneous, and the execution to have been carried out in all

*Dr Crippen*

*August 27, 1910*

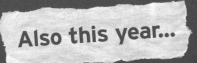

## FIRST PINK EDITION

## THE MYSTERY SOLVED.

### CRIPPEN & LE NEVE LANDED.

### PRISONERS LEAVE RIVERSIDE STATION.

### HOW THE COUPLE LEFT THE MEGANTIC.

### CROWDS AT THE LANDING-STAGE.

### THE JOURNEY TO LONDON.

Ethel on Crippen...
"I never had any reason to believe he would do anything to harm his wife. He was the most kind and gentle man you could meet."

Crippen's last words before he was hanged...
"I send all my love to Ethel."

### KAISER'S TRIBUTE.

During the Kaiser's last visit to England his Majesty caused the following letter to be sent to Miss Nightingale:—

Dear Miss Nightingale.—His Majesty the Emperor, having just brought to a close a most enjoyable stay in the beautiful neighbourhood of your old home near Romsey, has commanded me to present you with some flowers as a token of his esteem for the lady, who, after receiving her education in nursing by the Sisters of Mercy at Kaiserworth on the Rhine, rendered such invaluable services to the cause of humanity during the Crimean War, and subsequently founded a house for the training of nurses in England which is justly considered to be a model institution of European fame.

His Majesty sends you his best wishes.
I have the honour to remain.—Yours sincerely,

P. METTERNICH, German Ambassador.

The reply sent was in the following

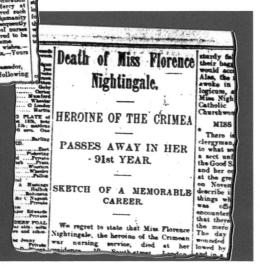

## Death of Miss Florence Nightingale.

### HEROINE OF THE CRIMEA

### PASSES AWAY IN HER 91st YEAR

### SKETCH OF A MEMORABLE CAREER.

We regret to state that Miss Florence Nightingale, the heroine of the Crimean war nursing service, died at her residence...

## Also this year...

FLORENCE Nightingale died on August 13, 1910, aged 90 after tireless work to improve army medical services with notes on hospitals and nursing.

This led to her becoming the heroine of the Crimean war and on her return, Nightingale created a nursing school that changed the future of nursing.

Liverpool pioneered the use of trained nurses in workhouses, with 12 nurses from Nightingale's school.

## Three years earlier...

# A Liver landmark is born

LORD Stanley of Alderley laid the foundation stone of what was to become the Royal Liver buildings on May 11, 1908.

They were being built to provide the Royal Liver Friendly Society with new offices.

Lord Stanley of Alderley was a senior trustee of the society and when laying the stone he performed a ceremony stating that the trustees would own the building and collect rent from other tenants and the committee of management.

Taking three years to complete, it was one of the first buildings to have a reinforced concrete structure, and before the clock was delivered to its resting place at the top of the building, the 25-foot dial was used as a dinner table.

### NEW ROYAL LIVER OFFICES.

Lord Stanley of Alderley this afternoon laid the foundation stone of the new offices which are to be erected for the Royal Liver Friendly Society at the Pierhead. The Lord Mayor presided, and among those present were Mr. J. S. Harmood Banner, M.P. The band of the Indefatigable played during the assembly and the ceremony.

Lord Stanley of Alderley, in performing the ceremony, and speaking as a trustee of the society, said the trustees would own the building and collect a rental from the Committee of Management as well as from the other tenants (applause).

Mr. J. S. Harmood Banner, M.P., and Mr. J. P. Nanetti, M.P. (ex-Lord Mayor of Dublin), were among the speakers, and the proceedings were characterised by great enthusiasm.

*The notice that heralded the beginnings of one of the city's most iconic buildings*

*As these adverts show, we've always been fond of a cuppa and a biscuit while reading the Echo!*

# 1911

# Liver Buildings declared open

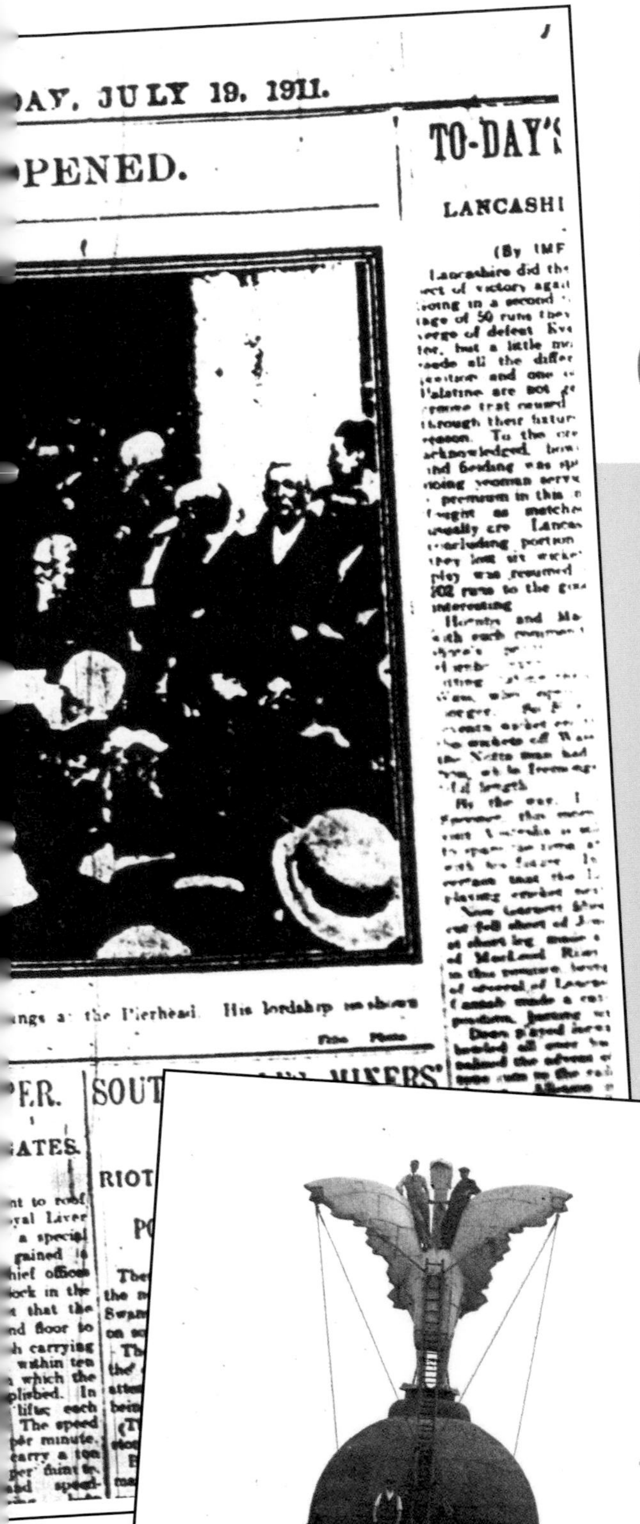

DAY, JULY 19, 1911.

PENED.

TO-DAY'S

LANCASHI

ngs at the Pierhead. His lordship

ER. SOUT

ATES.

RIOT

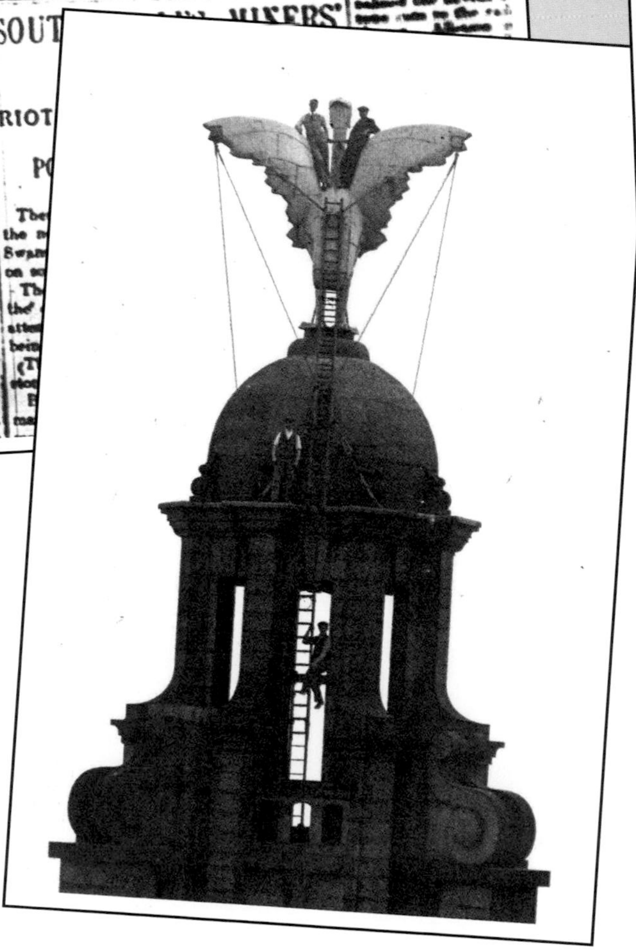

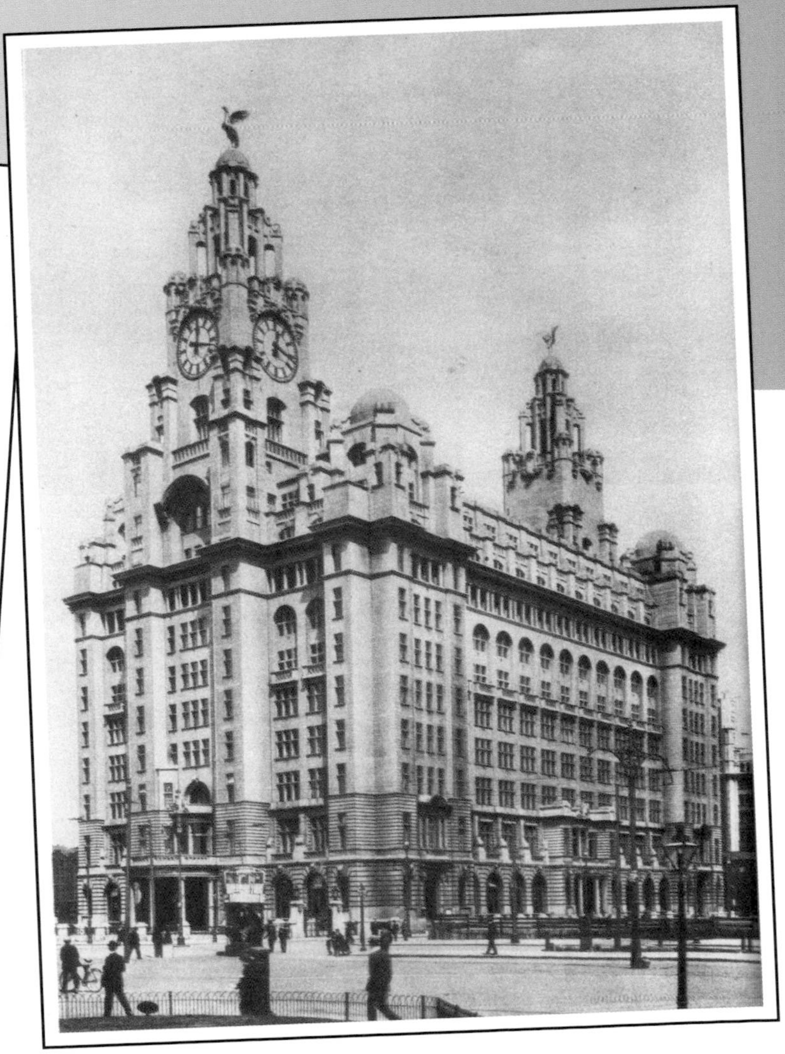

THE opening of the Royal Liver Building, designed by W Aubrey Thomas and built by Nuttall & Company of Manchester, took place on July 19, 1911. Lord Sheffield, a senior trustee of the Royal Liver Friendly Society, was there to do the honours of opening it.

Since then, the building that became the UK's first 'skyscraper' has been home to the headquarters of Royal Liver Assurance, an organisation that started out as a traditional insurance provider and has now stretched to a multi-billion pound financial operation.

The two mythical Liver birds that stand at the very top of the building have become icons for the city.

*From left: Reports from the opening ceremony; Workers climb aboard one of the giant Liver Birds; and the pier head as it was nearly 100 years ago*

LIVERPOOL, LIVER BUILDING AND

OCK BOARD OFFICES.

Left: Steamers outside the Liver Building and, inset, Alfred Gittins, clerk of works during construction, enjoys lunch with collegues around one of the clock faces; and workers hold one of the hands of Liver Building clock Great George before installation

# Archduke assassinated

THE assassination of Archduke Ferdinand, the heir to the Austro-Hungarian throne, and his wife Sophie was one of the factors that led to the outbreak of World War I.

The Royal couple were heading towards a hospital in Sarajevo, Bosnia, on June 28, 1914, to see a wounded officer, having already survived a bomb. In a plot organised by The Black Hand, Gavrilo Princip, a young Serbian assassin, fired two shots from a revolver when the Royal car turned a corner. Ferdinand was shot in the cheek and his wife in a main artery in her body. Angry mobs made demonstrations in Sarajevo until martial law was declared. Austria-Hungary made extreme demands for punishment be given to those responsible, only for the Serbians, who were relying on Russia's allegiance, to decline. War was declared by Austria-Hungary on July 28.

*How the Echo reported the incident that led to worldwide unrest*

# 1914

# The outbreak of World War I

GREAT Britain entered World War I on August 5, 1914 by declaring war on Germany when German soldiers failed to respect Belgium's neutrality and invaded. When the news was received from Brussels, Prime Minister Herbert Henry Asquith made a plea for half-a-million British men to join the army. A motion was also passed in the commons for £100,000,000 war credits and an increased coastguard service.

*From left: Stories flooded in from all over the globe to fill the Echo's pages; A soldier and his horse trudge through knee-deep mud; A map showing progress; A lone soldier in the trenches*

"YOUR COUNTRY NEEDS YOU"

*The iconic image of Lord Kitchener*

# Half-Million More British Soldiers Wanted.

*Above: Men rushed to enlist and cheered when they were accepted*

*Right: The appeal in the Echo*

*Below: The 55th West Lancashire Division held the front line at Blairville. The Liverpool Irish sent a raiding party into the German trenches, killing 55 Germans and gaining much valuable information*

# Your King and Country Need You.

Will you answer your Country's Call? Each day is fraught with the gravest possibilities, and at this very moment the Empire is on the brink of the greatest war in the history of the world.

In this crisis your Country calls on all her young unmarried men to rally round the Flag and enlist in the ranks of her Army.

If every patriotic young man answers her call, England and her Empire will emerge stronger and more united than ever.

If you are unmarried and between 18 and 30 years old will you answer your Country's Call? and go to the nearest Recruiter... whose address you can get at any Post Office, and

# Join the Army To-day!

# Lusitania is torpedoed by German U-boat

*Lusitania and Mauretania featured on this Cunard Line poster*

KNOWN as the Greyhound of the Seas, the Lusitania was the fastest liner of its time, as well as secretly being built to Admiralty specifications so that she could be consigned to government service in the event of a war outbreak.

In 1913, when war was looming, the liner went on to be fitted with ammunition at Liverpool dock. Then on May 7, 1915, tragedy struck. On a voyage from New York to Liverpool, the Lusitania was rumoured to have been torpedoed by a German submarine off the coast of Ireland, causing her to sink.

On May 8 it was confirmed. The disaster had killed 1,119 of the 1,924 passengers that were aboard the ship. Long lists of those who lost their lives appeared in the Echo.

With 114 of the deceased turning out to be American, the incident went on to cause friction between America and Germany.

**CUNARD LINE**

**MONARCHS** OF THE **SEA**

"LUSITANIA"
the LARGEST, FINEST & FASTEST SHIPS in the WORLD.

"MAURETANIA"
QUADRUPLE SCREW TURBINE STEAMERS.
790 FT. LONG.
32,500 TONS.
68,000 HORSE POWER

**LIVERPOOL · NEW YORK · BOSTON**
VIA QUEENSTOWN.

## LUSITANIA RUMOURS.

### STARTLING REPORTS THIS AFTERNOON.

A startling rumour was current in Liverpool this afternoon that the Lusitania had been torpedoed.

Lloyd's Register of Shipping contains two Lusitanias—one the famous Cunarder and the other a London trader of 1,800 tons.

At the time of going to press we have no information as to which of these vessels the report refers to.

The Press Bureau has permitted the publication of a report that a Lusitania has been torpedoed.

Asked if the report passed for publication referred to the Cunarder or to the trader the reply we have just received is:

"No information."

*May 7, 1915*

## ADMIRALTY MESSAGES.

### Only 703 Out of 2,160 Persons on Board Saved.

## NEW RESCUE REPORT

### Forty-Five More People Landed at Queenstown.

## THE CAPTAIN'S ESCAPE.

### A Thrilling Story By Our Special Correspondent.

*May 8, 1915*

May 8, 1915

# .·"Internal Explosion Tore Open Her Side."

## Terrible Stories of the Last Lurch of the Luckless Ship.

### LIVERPOOL CONSUL'S STORY

### Hundreds of Men, Women and Children Struggling in the Water

### AN INTERNAL EXPLOSION.

THE LAST SEEN OF THE GIANT SHIP.

(From Our Own Correspondent.)

QUEENSTOWN, Saturday. Senor Julian Ayala, Consul-General for Cuba at ... was being unwell at the ...

### VANDERBILT DROWNED.

FAMOUS AMERICAN GOES DOWN WITH SHIP.

It is reported to-day that Mr. Alfred G. Vanderbilt, the famous American millionaire, has gone down with the Lusitania. One message says "both Vanderbilts have ...

### "HER BOWS WENT UP."

WHAT A FARMER SAW OF THE TRAGEDY.

A Cork correspondent of the "Daily Mail" sends the following message:—

A farmer who lives on land nearest the Old Head of Kinsale reported that about 1.15 o'clock in the afternoon he heard two shots, and on looking seawards he noticed a large steamer.

Her bows went up in the air, and as far as he could judge about ten minutes later she heeled over on her side and sank.

Very soon after the steam trawler Daniel O'Connell, that had been fishing right down south-west of the Old Head, came on the scene, and picked up two of the ship's boats which were about the spot.

These contained sixty passengers, mostly women and children, of whom were in a desperate condition. The trawler was taking those survivors to Kinsale but was after copied by a Government tug, which took them to Queenstown.

### HARRISON LINERS.

SINKING OF CANDIDATE AND CENTURION.

Further particulars are to hand about the Candidate (5,858 tons) and the Centurion ...

### THE 'COAL KING' SAVED.

MR. D. A. THOMAS RELATES HIS EXPERIENCES.

### LADY MACKWORTH

SAVED AFTER OVER THREE HOURS IN WATER.

Mr. D. A. Thomas, the Welsh "coal king," is amongst the survivors.

The "Western Mail's" (Cardiff) correspondent in Queenstown has obtained an interview with him.

He said he was glad to say Lady Mackworth and his private secretary, Mr. Rhys Davies, were amongst those saved.

They passed through terrible experiences and had very remarkable escapes.

"Lady Mackworth," he added, "went down with the Lusitania, and was picked up unconscious after being in the water three and a half hours."

"The Lusitania was torpedoed without notice about fifteen miles off the Irish coast and sank in twelve or fifteen minutes."

"It was some time before any steamer reached the scene of the disaster ... had arrived ...

### VERY LITTLE WAR NEWS.

WHAT THE OFFICIAL MESSAGES SAY.

There is very little war news to report to-day. The latest official messages are ...

PARIS

(war news text, partially illegible)

BERLIN

(war news text, partially illegible)

---

# 703 Survivors: Little Hope for the Others---Official To-Night

May 8, 1915

The Lusitania at the Canada Dock in 1907

---

## "TITANIC" DISASTER.

### ICEBERG STRUCK IN MID-ATLANTIC.

### MAMMOTH LINER STILL AFLOAT.

### NO LOSS OF LIFE FEARED.

### PASSENGERS ALL TAKEN OFF.

### "VIRGINIAN'S" TIMELY RESCUE.

---

## Three years earlier...

These headlines, the first from April 15, 1912 and the second from April 16, 1912, give very different accounts of the disaster

LUXURIOUS liner, the Titanic, came to a disastrous end on April 14, 1912, as it struck an iceberg while sailing to New York.

The ship was badly holed from the collision in the Atlantic, and sank four hours later.

While many lives were saved, 1,522 people were lost at sea.

The ship that was thought to be the "unsinkable" did not have enough lifeboats for all passengers and crew.

---

## TITANIC SUNK.

### Terrible Disaster in the Atlantic.

### FOUNDERS IN FOUR HOURS.

### APPALLING LOSS OF LIFE.

### LISTS OF THE SAVED.

# City in chaos as looters hit during Police Strike

WORLD War I may have ended, but people in Liverpool must have felt it was still going on when a large proportion of the city's police officers went on strike in the August of 1919 following a new Police Act that banned trade unions.

Greatly misled by trade union propaganda and inaccurate Press reports, people took part in a spectacular orgy of rioting and looting which led a very nervous government to introduce some extremely tough measures.

In all, some 954 officers, about half the total force, went on strike as part of a national protest for improved pay and conditions and, in less than 24 hours, all but a small handful had been sacked, leading a large number to take part in attacks on those who had stayed at work.

The government response was almost unbelievably severe, with the battleship HMS Valiant and a couple of destroyers arriving at Liverpool with some 2,500 soldiers and marines who came in with rifles loaded and bayonets fixed.

Ironically, the government promised to improve pay and conditions for those who returned to work but only about 50 did so and the remainder lost their jobs. Just to rub in their humiliation, the strikers were given their back pay on Christmas Eve before being dismissed.

The biggest irony of all was that one of the strikers who did return to work, PC Joseph Wright, went on to become chief constable of Liverpool in 1960.

*Above: The Echo captured one of the scenes from the 1919 strike*

*Right: How the Echo reported the police strike*

---

**LAST EDITION.**    8——THE LI

## LIVERPOOL BREATHES AGAIN.

### Municipal Strike "Off," Tram Strike "Unauthorised."

### SURPRISE FOR CORPORATION HOTHEADS.

Mr. Milligan Says Dockers, Also, Have No Idea Of Striking At Present.

In the Commons to-night the Home Secretary said there had been no material change in Liverpool to-day.

The Government had full confidence that the authorities would take every step, however severe, to preserve order, and in this the Government would give every assistance.

This afternoon, at 3 p.m., an important conference began of Labour leaders in Liverpool, Mr. Tom Mann being in consultation with representatives of various industries, but the fear of an immediate general strike has faded away.

We were informed to-day that Mr. P. J. Tevenan, general secretary of the Municipal Employees' Association, sent the following telegram from London to the Liverpool branch of the organisation late last night:—

"Other departments must on no account come out. Tramways strike entirely unauthorised."

The term "other departments" in the telegram means the various classes of workmen in the municipal service, other than tramwaymen.

Interviewed this morning, Mr. G. Dorgan, chairman of the Liverpool District Council of the Municipal Employees' Association, and Mr. W. J. Daniels, secretary, made the following statement:—

"The Liverpool District Council of the M.E.A. have decided under no consideration to call out other employees until after consultation with the national executive. The public may rest assured that no hasty step will be taken by the Council. The District Council wishes this statement to be taken by Liverpool members of the Association as an official notice to remain at work."

Mr. Dorgan said that this resolution had been adopted in order to prevent the public being further inconvenienced.

Referring to last night's meeting of municipal employees, at which a resolution threatening 24 hours' notice of the cessation of work on the part of the other sections of municipal workers unless the present strikers' demands were conceded, Mr. Dorgan said that none of these notices had, as a matter of fact, been handed in to-day, and the men should remain at work.

Mr. George Milligan, assistant secretary of the Dockers' Union, stated this afternoon that there was at present no question of the dockers coming out for the reinstatement of the police.

Mr. McCurdy, M.P., Parliamentary Secretary to the Food Ministry, who in Liverpool, made an extremely important statement regarding the possibility of a general strike being declared in Liverpool.

One-third of the country's total available supplies of foodstuffs are now concentrated in the port. As a general strike would result in the paralysis of the port's activities it would be impossible without special organisation to distribute the food supplies for the nation.

Liverpool already is breadless. There were no loaves for sale yesterday, and there will be none to-day.

The Government express their determination to resist with all the for

---

# TROOPS PATROL CITY STREETS TO-DAY.

Men Brought In By Motor Lorry And Billed In St. George's Hall.

## NIGHT LOOTING FOLLOWS THE POLICE STRIKE.

Serious Outbreaks Lead To Ransacking Of Number Of Shops.

## BIRKENHEAD MEN JOIN THE STRIKERS.

As a result of the looting which broke out in Liverpool, following the police strike, certain streets in the city — Scotland-road and Byrom-street — are to-day being patrolled by troops which were brought into the city for the emergency.

Six lorry-loads of troops first arrived. They were in full marching order, and were billeted in St. George's Hall. Other troops have arrived since.

The looting was of a serious character, and in the Scotland-road area a large amount of damage was done and a considerable quantity material stolen by the looters.

The Lord Mayor has issued an appeal to all citizens to assist in the preservation of order, and the Chief Constable is asking for recruits at once.

Volunteers for duty are asked to enrol at the Town Hall from ten o'clock this morning and daily until further notice. Existing "specials" are asked to parade for reserve duty in plain clothes, with armlets, &c., at their divisional stations at six o'clock this evening.

To-day has seen an addition to the number of strikers. A large portion of the Birkenhead men have come out. At Birmingham men came out this morning, and in Liverpool the number, according to the official figure, has increased to 700 (out of a total of ...). In Bootle there are 60 out, but in Wallasey only one man struck.

Sir Nevil Macready to-day stated that there was no difficulty filling the vacancies, and that he could get 5,000 recruits immediately. Nearly 1,000 men are out in London now.

The Liverpool police strikers are actively pursuing their campaign. They ... the official statement that the total of men on strike is 632 and claim is at least double that number.

### UGLY SCENES TO-DAY.

SCOTLAND AREA 'OCCUPIED' BY SOLDIERS.

Scotland-road and Byrom-street, the scene of last night's looting, is territory to-day.

... ruins ... remnants of Peace Day ... still hang in some of the side ...

### BIRKENHEAD NOW.

ONLY FEW OF POLICE ON DUTY TO-DAY.

The police strike has now spread to Birkenhead, and there are only a few men on duty, the streets being unpatrolled.

The men were brought out during the early hours of this morning by the Liverpool strikers, who, after the demonstration last ...

Left: A cutting from the Echo describing the night of looting following the police strike

Above: Shopkeepers assess the damage after looters hit stores in Scotland Road

Below left: Business as usual at Beaty Bros. Ltd

Below: The Lord Mayor appealed for help to police the city

# IMPORTANT AND URGENT NOTICE.

## To ALL LAW-ABIDING CITIZENS

### The LORD MAYOR

Appeals to the Citizens of Liverpool to assist him in the maintenance of Law and Order in the City.

Volunteers for Duty are asked to enrol at the Town Hall from 10 o'clock this (SATURDAY) MORNING and Daily until further notice.

Existing Special Constables are asked to Parade for Reserve Duty in Plain Clothes with Armlets, &c., at their Divisional Stations at 6 o'clock this (SATURDAY) EVENING.

Town Hall, Liverpool.
1st August, 1919.

JOHN RITCHIE,
Lord Mayor.

# 1925

# Empire Theatre's grand opening

LIVERPOOL'S Empire Theatre has been a building of many identities. It started life as the Prince of Wales Theatre and Opera House, which in turn twice changed its name to the Royal Alexandra Theatre and Opera House and then the Empire.

Opening in its current form on March 9, 1925 the Empire claimed to have the largest stage in Great Britain, 160 feet wide and 40 feet deep, something that has obviously enabled it to put on some spectacular shows with which most other theatres could not possibly cope.

The first performance at the new Empire was a production of 'Better Days' starring Stanley Lupino, Maisie Gay and Luke French, but things became even more spectacular in the Sixties.

Merseyside talent took part in the Royal Command Performance in front of the Queen and Prince Charles and, on December 5, the Beatles gave their final Liverpool performance there. Other famous stars to follow have included both Bing Crosby and Frank Sinatra and another show nobody will forget was Blood Brothers which was of course written by Liverpool playwright Willy Russell.

In 1977 Moss Empires looked into the possibility of closure after losing money five years in succession, but two years later Merseyside County Council stepped in to save it, spending £330,000 on a new back stage and a further £350,00 on a new lighting system and extended orchestra pit.

## Empire Timeline

**1866:** The Prince of Wales Theatre and Opera House opened on Lime Street

**1867:** It became the Royal Alexandra Theatre and Opera House

**1894:** The Alexandra closed

**1895:** The Alexandra reopened under the ownership of Empire Theatre Ltd

**1896:** The theatre was sold to Moss & Thornton and re-opened under the Empire Theatre name

**1924:** The Empire Theatre closed and a new theatre was built on the same site

**1925:** The Empire as we know it today opened

*Above: A view of Lime Street showing the old Royal Alexandra Theatre*

*Right: Adverts from the Echo on March 9, 1925*

## LIVERPOOL'S LEAD.

### TO-NIGHT'S BIRTH OF A NEW EMPIRE.

### THE FINEST THEATRE?

### MERSEYSIDE LATEST AS BEST IN KINGDOM.

#### "ECHO" ARTICLE.

Liverpool's new Empire has certainly captured the imagination of people interested in theatrical entertainment. Not only are Press critics and professional experts of wide experience unanimous in their view that the theatre is the finest in existence, but the public, too, are anxious to make their acquaintance with the new palace of entertainment.

As already stated in the "Echo," the application for seats for the first night has been unprecedented, and many thousands of letters containing cheques and postal orders for seats have had to be returned. When the curtain goes up to-night on the big Wylie-Tate production, "Better Days," the house will be filled to its utmost capacity.

#### EXTRA FACILITIES.

So great has been the demand that a new form of booking seats had to be instituted. Previously seats have been booked, but for this week standing room in the theatre has been bookable, and since the announcement of this new departure was

---

**VARIETIES.**

LIVERPOOL
EMPIRE —— EMPIRE,
LIME-STREET.
Proprietors ....... MOSS EMPIRES, LTD.
**GRAND RE-OPENING,**
TO-NIGHT, AT 7 O'CLOCK,
FOR WHICH PERFORMANCE ALL SEATS
ARE SOLD.
But a limited Number of Standing-room Tickets
are available and can be booked in advance.
REMAINING NIGHTS AT 7.30.
MATINEES WEDNESDAY & SATURDAY, at 2.30.
Presenting JULIAN WYLIE'S
New Super Revue,
"BETTER DAYS."
MAISIE GAY. STANLEY LUPINO.
MADGE ELLIOT.
BERTRAM DENCH. BERNARD DUDLEY.
GEORGE BAKER. CONNIE EMERALD.
RUTH FRENCH.
"FROLICKING GODS" BALLET by Michael Fokine.
THE HIPPODROME EIGHT.
Prices of Admission : 7/- to 1/2, including Tax.
All Bookable in Advance without Fee.
BOX OFFICE Open 10 a.m. to 10 p.m.
Telephones 2671 and 2672 Royal.

EMPIRE CELEBRATION BALL,
MAR. 10th. ADELPHI HOTEL.
TICKETS £1 1/-, including Supper.
Apply Empire Theatre, and Adelphi and Exchange
Hotels and Usual Libraries.

Above: The bill for the grand re-opening of the Liverpool Empire Theatre

---

## FAST FACTS

- Upon opening in 1925, the theatre claimed to have the largest stage in Britain at 160ft wide and 40ft deep

- A licensed bar was omitted in the original plans – the theatre was modelled on the New York Theatre which was built at the time of prohibition in America

- International stars Bing Crosby and Frank Sinatra both performed at the Empire

- The Royal Command Performance was held at the Empire in 1963, attended by the Queen and Prince Charles

- The Beatles gave their last concert in Liverpool at the Empire on December 5, 1965

---

Above: A 1925 artist's impression of the Empire Theatre

Right: How the Echo reported the build up to the theatre's opening night

# Strike disrupts services in city

LIKE every other city in the United Kingdom, Liverpool suffered from a nine-day General Strike in 1926, but so far as can be seen, it encountered fewer problems than many other parts of the country, partly because it was not heavily involved with coal mining which was at the centre of the problem.

The Trades Union Congress (TUC) conference met on May 1, declaring the strike would begin two days later, but both their leaders and key figures in the Labour Party were worried that if it was allowed to get out of hand revolutionary actions might start to develop.

Work in the Liverpool docks was disrupted, but at least some ships continued to sail, and car drivers invariably stopped to give lifts to people deprived of their usual bus services.

On May 8 there was a dramatic movement in London's docks, with the Army being used to break pickets and ensure food supplies were distributed, but Liverpool seems to have avoided similar problems.

The TUC agreed to call off the strike on May 12 and most people returned to work soon after, though the miners continued to be involved for some time.

*Left: 1926 Prime Minister Stanley Baldwin*

*Below: The strike made front page news on May 8, 1926*

*Above: Bulletins replaced the Echo's normal news service during the strike*

*Left: The front page reporting the end of the strike*

*Below: Emergency notices were posted outside Liverpool Town Hall*

# Record 60 goals for Blues legend Dixie

*May 5, 1928*

EVERTON hero William Ralph 'Dixie' Dean celebrated a 60-goal league record in 1928 in the last game of the season against Arsenal.

A hat trick secured Dixie Dean's 60th goal in front of an ecstatic Goodison Park crowd, whose celebrations were not deterred by the fact the game finished with a 3-3 draw.

Two men pushed through the police barrier in jubilation while players, including those from Arsenal, queued up to shake Dean's hand. The referee allowed him to leave the field before the final whistle to prevent the rest of the crowd spilling over onto the pitch.

With Dean's goal scoring record it was only fitting that Everton finished the season top of the table, beating Huddersfield by two points.

## THE CHAMPIONS AT PLAY

### Everton And The Arsenal Wind Up An Historic Season.

### CHARLIE BUCHAN BIDS FAREWELL.

#### The Game And The Hectic Scenes At Goodison Park.

#### By "BEE."

EVERTON
Davies.
Cresswell. O'Donnell.
Kelly. Hart. Virr.
Critchley. Martin. Dean. Welden. Troup.
.
Peel Brain Shaw Buchan Hulme
Blyth Butler Baker
John Parker
Paterson

ARSENAL.

Magnificent weather graced the final act of the 1927-28 season at Goodison Park to-day, when Arsenal visited Everton in a match that promised to be historic, because it meant Everton stood No. 1 in the League after starting No. 1 in the League on August 26 last year.

It was Charlie Buchan's final match in football history.

It was Everton's third League championship. It was Dean's best season ever, and opened the possibility of Dean breaking all English League records by getting three goals to-day.

were crazy after this inspiring turn round in the score sheet.

It was all very simple in the making. The first point was from a corner taken by Critchley. Martin turned the ball on to Dean, who headed it to the extreme left-hand corner. This was the second chapter at the second minute.

The third excelled all others. Dean was running through when the long-legged Butler crossed him. It was an accidental collision—to the referee it was a trip, and the consequence was that Dean was able to rise from the ground and take the penalty kick successfully and well.

Three goals in the first five minutes of this championship act was all to the joy of the crowd. It was a fitting start to a fatal game—fatal in the sense that Dean

Everton's team v. Tranmere Rovers, in the final of the Liverpool Senior Cup, on Monday, at Anfield, 6.30, will be:—Hardy, Common, Kennedy; Bain, Griffiths, Reeney; Neston, Easton, French, Jones, and Stem.

was now wanting but one goal to put him top of England in the League section in the course of forty odd years of League football.

#### BEANFEAST OF FIGURES.

Moreover, the goals to Everton meant that Everton were nearing the magic figure of 104 made by West Brom. Albion soon after the war, the total now being 101. Thus the well-primed football fan was having a beanfeast of figures, fun, facts,

## LEAGUE—DIV. I.

| | | |
|---|---|---|
| EVERTON.........3 | The Arsenal.......3 |
| Manchester Utd..6 | LIVERPOOL.....1 |
| Birmingham......2 | Derby County....1 |
| Blackburn Rov... 0 | Bury...............1 |
| Bolton Wan.......1 | Sheffield United...1 |
| Cardiff City.........3 | Burnley............2 |
| Huddersfield Tn. 4 | Portsmouth........1 |
| Middlesbrough... 0 | Sunderland.........3 |
| Newcastle Utd....3 | West Ham Utd...1 |
| Sheffield Wed.....2 | Aston Villa.....1. 0. |

| | P. | W. | L. | D. | F. | A. | Pts. |
|---|---|---|---|---|---|---|---|
| Everton | 42 | 20 | 9 | 13 | 102 | 66 | 53 |
| Huddersfield | 42 | 22 | 13 | 7 | 91 | 68 | 51 |
| Leicester City | 42 | 18 | 12 | 12 | 96 | 71 | 48 |
| Derby Cnty | 42 | 17 | 15 | 10 | 96 | 83 | 44 |
| Bury | 42 | 20 | 18 | 4 | 80 | 80 | 44 |
| Cardiff City | 42 | 17 | 15 | 10 | 72 | 80 | 44 |
| Bolton Wan. | 42 | 16 | 15 | 11 | 81 | 66 | 43 |
| Aston Villa | 42 | 17 | 16 | 9 | 78 | 73 | 43 |
| Newcastle U. | 42 | 15 | 14 | 13 | 79 | 81 | 43 |
| Birmingham | 42 | 13 | 14 | 15 | 70 | 75 | 41 |
| Arsenal | 42 | 13 | 14 | 15 | 82 | 86 | 41 |
| Blackburn R. | 42 | 16 | 17 | 9 | 66 | 78 | 41 |
| Sheffield Utd | 42 | 15 | 17 | 10 | 79 | 86 | 40 |
| Sheffield W. | 42 | 13 | 16 | 13 | 81 | 78 | 39 |
| Sunderland | 42 | 15 | 18 | 9 | 74 | 75 | 39 |
| Liverpool | 42 | 13 | 16 | 13 | 84 | 87 | 39 |
| West Ham U | 42 | 14 | 17 | 11 | 81 | 88 | 39 |
| Manchester U | 42 | 16 | 19 | 7 | 72 | 80 | 39 |
| Burnley | 42 | 16 | 19 | 7 | 82 | 98 | 39 |
| Portsmouth | 42 | 16 | 19 | 7 | 66 | 90 | 39 |
| Tottenham H | 42 | 15 | 19 | 8 | 74 | 86 | 38 |
| Middlesbro' | 42 | 11 | 16 | 15 | 81 | 88 | 37 |

Above includes to-day's matches.

*Above and left: Everton stood number one in the league after beating Arsenal at Goodison Park*

*Far left: William Ralph 'Dixie' Dean*

May 5, 1928

LIVERPOOL FOOTBALL ECHO, Saturday, May 5, 1928.

## PALAIS de LUXE

MON. NEXT | 6d. MATINEES

MARION DAVIES and MATT MOORE in

# TILLIE THE TOILER

OF THE WAYS OF MEN SHE KNEW A LIBRARY FULL.

Thursday: LIL DAGOVER in

## MATRIMONEY

---

# EVERTON DRAW LAST GAME

## Tremendous Scenes At Presentation Of The Cup.

### DEAN MAKES RECORD WITH SIXTY GOALS.

There was an electric start.

They scored for Arsenal in one minute.

After five minutes' play, Dean had scored twice, equalling the Camsell record of 59 goals.

O'Donnell headed a ball back into his own goal at the 38th minute.

Dean created the record of sixty individual goals in a season at the eighty-second minute.

(Continued from Page 8.)

In the second half the tension was naturally increased, especially as the Arsenal continued to play charming football and Blyth had a fine understanding with Peel.

The home captain covered up the extra Yorkshire player in a way that had been foreign to him (Peel) in previous meetings this season.

Dean strove upward and onward, and although angled awkwardly he got full power into the spinning ball, so that Paterson's save at the foot of the post was a brilliant one.

The wind did not prevent the air being sultry, and naturally the pace began to slacken a bit.

However, the home centre forward was not greedy about goals, and at this point

Everton F.C. players will be off to Switzerland on Wednesday, leaving Lime-street at 9.45 a.m.

On Monday night they will be present at the Empire Theatre show ("The Girl Friend"), and the cup will be on view to the audience.

he offered Critchley a pass, and the little man knocked a hot shot against the angle of the goalpost. Davies, at the other end, made a good, confident punch-away, and Baker lifted the ball into the number board.

### ON TENTER-HOOKS.

Everton were facing the sun, facing odds, and were playing a trifle too hard, so that the game travelled anybody's way, and the crowd of probably 60,000 was kept on tenter-hooks, and for the moment had to be content to watch the excellence of Weldon, Virr, and company.

For long spells Dean was crowded out or received unwise passes, and at the hour he broke through and seemed an assured scorer, when the ball swung a yard outside.

Moreover, Martin had a magnificent drive put down by the Arsenal goalkeeper, was Paterson who ended another sprightly affair, this time by Critchley.

Time was flying, and the crowd now really hearty over the main issue of the day—namely, Dean's need for one goal.

A lovely ankle pass from Dean to the centre was headed no more than six inches over the crossbar.

One had to be present to feel the

away from the wee Troup, who stood immediately underneath him.

Weldon came near taking the lead with a ball that cannoned off a defender. With nine minutes to go, the crowd yearned for a goal to Dean or anyone, and nearly got their voices working when Martin shot and Paterson punched away over the bar for a corner kick.

### DEAN'S RECORD 60TH.

This was the beginning of Dean's historic record goal in English football. Troup took the corner kick and out of a ruck of probably fourteen players, Dean, with unerring accuracy, nodded the ball to the extreme right hand side of the goal.

There has never been such a joyful shout at Everton. It was prolonged for minutes and went on to the end of the game. The crowd never stopped cheering for eight solid minutes, and indeed there was a threat of the crowd breaking on to the field of play.

In fact, two men rushed across through the barrier of police, and the referee had to bundle one man off, and out of the way of trouble.

It was a memorable scene, and was followed by another sample of nervous strain, such as one, has become accustomed to in Cup finals. A very simple position was created by Peel, and Davies having got his hands and his chest to the ball, should have made an easy save.

### DAVIES BEWILDERED.

The home goalkeeper was off his game, however, and when the ball struck the near upright and cannoned out to Shaw there was no one to stop the Arsenal score.

---

Above: A cartoon by George Green shows Dixie's record

Below: Dixie Dean in action

# Crowds attend cathedral foundation ceremony

WHEN the Brownlow Hill site was bought in 1930, the vision of a Catholic cathedral had taken on many different shapes and forms.

The foundation stone for a cathedral, designed by Sir Edwin Lutyens, was laid on June 5, 1933. The gates to the site were opened at 10.15am and the atmosphere and good humour was evident, said onlookers.

The congregation had reached 40,000 by the time the Papal Legate, Cardinal MacRory, arrived. The legate praised Liverpool and its Archbishop, Richard Downey. The historic event lasted four hours and during that time 28,000 people stood in the streets. More than 300 people, including Monsignor Godfrey of the English College in Rome, needed medical attention, such was the fervour. The Vatican said the occasion was an arresting act of faith and those who were there can still hear the crowds standing, kneeling and praying on such a joyous day.

Due to financial restrictions, the cathedral plans were abandoned after the construction of the crypt, which remains today.

The present cathedral, designed by Sir Frederick Gibberd, was consecrated in 1967.

*The crowds that gathered for the laying of the cathedral foundation stone were indeed impressive, as these pictures and Echo reports show*

## CEREMONY THEY DID NOT SEE

### Impressive Scene Outside Site

### GAY DECORATIONS

### Blind Pilgrim Who Gave Up Seat

### LAME BOY'S JOURNEY

"ECHO" ARTICLE

The full story of to-day's Catholic

## "The Finest Concert Hall In Europe"

### Liverpool's Great Loss; Hall Mendelssohn Was To Have Opened; Where Jenny Lind Sang; Famous Visitors

The destruction of the Philharmonic Hall last night must have profoundly shocked everyone who has ever been in the building. To those of us who knew it well, the loss seems almost tragic, and to see it, as I did, blazing fiercely against a sunset that filled the western sky gave one a sinking heart, and an uncomfortable feeling that the sunset might be symbolical. It was impossible to see a hall in which one had enjoyed so many of the richest adventures and fullest experiences of the mind crashing in blazing ruins without being genuinely affected.

For the "Phil." despite its anachronisms, was a beautiful hall, "the finest concert hall in Europe," in Richter's phrase. Its acoustics, whether by accident or design I do not know, were unrivalled. Indeed, I should think they were as near perfection as it is possible to achieve, even to-day. The hall had an air about it. To read the names on the boxes was to be irresistably reminded of the old phrase "the nobility and gentry." The boxes themselves with their plush-covered chairs and hangings, their mellow divisions of old wood, their little mirrors and shelves, and the long comfortable couches in the corner ones were a study in themselves. The corridors and crush rooms with their hundreds of autographed photographs were worth an article in their own right. The wide entrance hall, the stairways, with their wrought iron railings cast in symbolic lyres, and the Salon, with its exquisite proportions, suggested, as few things I know did, the spaciousness which the Victorians allowed themselves when they chose. To see them in the intervals on "Phil. nights" was the nearest approach to Covent Garden in the grand season I know, in the atmosphere of elegance, well-being and comfort which was produced.

#### The Green Room

The Green Room, that holy of holies into which no outsider ever strayed without some feeling of...

arranged with Dr. Mendelssohn to superintend the opening of their new concert hall, for which occasion he was about to write a cantata."

The hall opened on August 27, 1849, with a week's festival. The architect who achieved this acoustic gem was John Cunningham. The performers included Halle and Julius Benedict (both subsequently knighted) such famous singers is Grisi, Alboni, Natalia Macfarren, Viardot Garcia, the great Mario, Lablache and the picturesque Sims Reeves, then at the age of thirty, in the first flush of his maturity. Piatti played the 'cello, Bottesini his double bass—names stamped indelibly on the history of instrumental music. The orchestra included a number of violinists from London among whom one notes the name of Van Gruisen.

Tuesday nights were first set apart for Philharmonic concerts in 1850, and so they have remained ever since, except for a brief period during the war. In that year Jenny Lind sang in the hall for the first time. J. L. Hatton, the famous Liverpool song writer, appeared as a singer shortly afterwards, and Patti sang here first in 1861. Sullivan paid his first visit to the hall in 1870 to conduct his "Prodigal Son"; a few years later the uncrowned king of music in England was offered the permanent conductorship, but refused it. In 1871 the composer of "Faust," Charles Gounod, conducted his "St. Cecilia Mass" here, and Max Bruch appeared in 1877, to be made permanent conductor in succession to Sir Julius Benedict in 1880 for a somewhat stormy three years. Halle succeeded him (and started the connection of Manchester instrumentalists in the orchestra, which persists up till the present time), and Sir Frederick Cowen commenced his long tenancy of the post in 1896, resigning in 1910. Since then the "guest" conductors have included practically every conductor of note in the world.

Charles Dickens appeared here, first in 1858, to give his famous readings and later in Lytton's comedy "Not So Bad As We Seem."...

*July 6, 1933*

## Also this year...

ONE of the biggest, if fortunately non-tragic, disasters in Liverpool's history took place at the Philharmonic Hall in 1933, when the city was shocked by a mystery blaze that gutted the whole building and could have dealt a fatal blow to the city's great musical tradition.

The old hall was a place of unrivalled beauty. Opened on August 27, 1849, it enjoyed quite remarkable acoustics.

It was full of extremely fashionable furnishings, with superb boxes lined with silk, chairs covered in plush and little mirrors in unexpected places. A wide entrance hall provided a marvellous greeting on arrival, there were superb wrought iron railings on the stairway and the famous green room was so magnificent that nobody even thought of entering it without permission.

Many famous musicians appeared at the hall and the great writer Charles Dickens gave a memorable performance there.

How fortunate that the famous hall was eventually rebuilt, and continues to be a symbol of Liverpool's great musical history.

---

8     LAST CITY

THE LIVERPOOL ECHO, MO

## To-day's Catholic Cathedral Ceremony ::

### "ARRESTING ACT OF FAITH"

Papal Legate's Impressive Address At Laying Of Foundation Stone

#### MESSAGE DROPPED FROM THE SKIES

Archbishop Downey's Thought For Vast Multitude Of Worshippers

#### IMPRESSIVE SCENES AND CEREMONIALS

In glorious sunshine supremely fitting the sacred occasion, cardinal and archbishops, bishops and humble monks, the Lord Mayor and civic leaders, wealthy pilgrims from overseas, and poor dwellers in the narrow byways that bound the site, to-day assisted at the laying of the foundation stone of the Roman Catholic Liverpool Metropolitan Cathedral.

Long before noon the congregation in the enclosure had reached nearly 40,000. It was announced that, in view of the excessive heat and the broken condition of the ground, the Archbishop would not consider it an irreverence if the people wore their hats and remained seated.

A quarter of an hour before the arrival of the Papal Legate one or two or three aeroplanes which had been flying round the site suddenly swooped down to within a few feet of the top of the Altar and dropped a blue and white parachute with a package attached. The pilot of the machine was Colonel the Master of Sempill and the package was addressed to the Papal Legate. The package was dated "Over Liverpool, 5th June, 1933." The parachute was dropped accurately at the foot of the Legate's throne. It was picked up by attendants and handed to Cardinal MacRory as he took his place.

With solemn and deeply impressive ritual His Grace the Archbishop of Liverpool performed the ceremony of blessing and laying the foundation-stone, following which His Eminence Cardinal MacRory, the Papal Legate, made his address.

The Papal Legate in his address, said: This magnificent Cathedral, the foundation stone of which has just been laid by your brilliant... as it ris...

#### A Little Cooler Than Yesterday

##### 77 Degrees The Highest Reached

| | Monday. | Sunday | Saturday |
|---|---|---|---|
| 8 a.m. | 59 | 65 | 64 |
| 10 a.m. | 64 | 73 | 73 |
| 2 p.m. | 76 | 79 | 76 |

(To-day's holiday story on Page 5.)

##### ANFIELD "HUNDRED" RECORD

##### FASTEST TIME:

#### Laying The Ca

Dr. Downey, Archbishop of Liverp

##### A GENERAL VIE

#### BANK HOLIDAY RA

##### HURST PARK

1 30 NICKEL PLATE at £200, two-year-olds.

thousands of Cathedral flags. A few yards in the rear was Archbishop Downey—a stately, lone, conspicuous figure in his flowing white robes and golden mitre. Loud cheering...

# Metropolitan Cathedral is consecrated

DEDICATED to Christ the King by Pope Pius XII, the consecration of the Metropolitan Cathedral took place on May 14, 1967.

Mass was celebrated at the High Altar on that special Sunday.

Among the 2,000 guests at the ceremony were the Duke of Norfolk, representing HM the Queen, then-Prime Minister Harold Wilson and the leader of the opposition Ted Heath.

There were members of the Church of England, Jewish religion and Free Church.

This was a major event because of new technology – there was a screen outside so the crowds gathered on the street could celebrate too.

And it was a special moment all over the world as the ceremony was also seen by millions on TV.

The Papal Legate at the consecration was Archbishop of Westminster John Carmel Cardinal Heenan.

Pope Paul VI's message was read aloud:

'The new Cathedral soars aloft'.

Down the road in Hope Street, its sister building, the Anglican Cathedral, looked on.

SOUVENIR OF SOLEMN OPENING OF THE METROPOLITAN CATHEDRAL CRYPT LIVERPOOL

The Liverpool Echo and Evening Express, Monday

# A NEW APPR

## Pope Paul's words ring out through new Cathedral

### BY A SPECIAL ECHO REPORTING TEAM

The words of Pope Paul rang out in Liverpool's striking new Cathedral of Christ the King yesterday. They said: "The new cathedral soars aloft and leads the gaze directly to Heaven."

The words came in a message from the Pope, which was read out in a multi-coloured setting for the consecration of the High Altar. The message continued: "It is an approach to harmony and unity. It is a standing religious lesson encouraging men to dedicate their lives to something more than material things."

Only a few hours earlier the Dean of Liverpool, the Very Rev. Edward Patey, had spoken on the theme of harmony and unity at Liverpool Cathedral

Merseyside were among the tightly packed audience who sat watching the giant screen. They were dressed for church, and many were clearly as emotionally involved by what they saw on the screen as if they had been inside the Cathedral itself.

The ceremony began with

#### New spirit in Church

*Left: Archbishop Igino Cardinale, Apostolic Delegate to Great Britian, arrives at the cathedral*

*Right: Rev Mother Ethelreda, Mother of the Sisters of The Sacred Heart of Jesus and Mary (left) and Rev Mother Albina of Allerton Priory chat to Cardinal Heenan, Liverpool Lord Mayor Herbert Allen, Bishop Augustine Harris, the Lady Mayoress and Archbishop George Beck at Allerton garden Priory*

## Guest of the Lord Mayor

Cardinal Heenan was officially welcomed to Liverpool as guest of the Lord Mayor (Alderman Herbert Allen) at the...

*Right: (l-r) Mgr McKenna, Canon G Walsh, Bishop Harris, Father Doran and Canon O'Connor*

## 1,000 at garden party

More than 1,000 people attended a garden party given in honour of Cardinal at Allerton Priory on Saturday, and at a special celebration dinner last night at the Adelphi Hotel, the Lord Mayor told him: "Liverpool is shooting ahead. Plans which have taken a long time are beginning to mature and become bricks and mortar."

The Lord Mayor added that it was hoped that "...Catt...

CH

*Liverpudlians decorate their homes to mark the consecration*

# Liverpool gets its wings at Speke Airport

*A Starways Viscount plane outside the former airport terminal in 1963*

LIVERPOOL Airport was established officially in 1930 but private flying had taken place in the area for several years previously. In 1926 a body was set up to develop a local aerodrome after it had been widely agreed that this would be an advantage to the city.

Sir Alan Cobham, an enthusiastic supporter of flying, was asked to carry out a survey of possible sites.

The city council offered its strong support and in 1928 it purchased 2,000 acres of the old Speke Estate, of which 418 acres were destined to become the new airport.

The first service began on June 18, 1930 with Armstrong Whitworth operating a flight to the Midlands on Argosy aircraft, but it was abandoned after just three months and the place operated only as a flying club until Liverpool Corporation appointed an airport manager in 1932.

The airport was officially opened on July 1, 1933, by the Marquess of Londonderry, Secretary of State for Air, and this was celebrated by a fantastic air pageant involving 246 aircraft, a landing competition and a parachuting event. The first connection with the Armed Forces came with the advent of World War II, when Speke became the destination for hundreds of aircraft including both bombers and fighters.

The home-based 611 Squadron claimed no fewer than 240 aircraft and earned a range of honours that included 10 DFCs and bars, two DFMs and one American Silver Star.

Since the war the airport has continued to develop steadily, especially in recent years, and currently operates a wide range of domestic and European services, with Peel Holdings moving in to effectively take control.

A new terminal building and control tower were completed in 2002 during overall investment of more than £42 million, and millions of passengers now pass through the airport annually.

*Above: Passengers visit customs on arrival at Speke Airport in 1943*

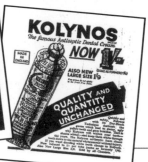

*Left: These adverts show some of the mod-cons on offer to Liverpudlians in 1933*

*Right: Those magnificent men in their flying machines thrilled Echo readers with their display on opening day*

# THRILLING OPENING OF LIVERPOOL AIRPORT

## TWO HUNDRED MACHINES IN GREAT PAGEANT

## AIR SECRETARY ATTENDS TWELVE-HOUR DISPLAY

Crack pilots of the R.A.F. and civil aviation gave wonderful displays at Speke on Saturday to mark the opening of Liverpool Airport, the largest civil aerodrome in the country.

The Secretary of State for Air (the Marquis of Londonderry), who had flown from Hendon to Sealand, was escorted thence to the Airport by a squadron of fighting machines. A huge concourse within and without the aerodrome watched a twelve-hour demonstration.

# LAST TOUCHES AT SPEKE

## YESTERDAY'S 'TRY-OUT' FOR AIR PAGEANT

## HOW TO REACH LIVERPOOL AIRPORT

Given fine weather, the success of the air pageant with which the Liverpool Airport at Speke will be inaugurated to-day, seems certain.

Throughout yesterday the final touches were given to both the arrangements and to the ground itself. While R.A.F. and civilian machines roared overhead, rehearsing to-day's displays, workmen were busy on the ground erecting the last turnstiles and arranging the 5,000 chairs.

## 68 years later...

### The re-naming of Liverpool Airport

IN July 2001 Liverpool took the dramatic step of renaming its airport after Beatle John Lennon and his widow Yoko Ono flew in to perform a spectacular renaming ceremony.

Yoko paid a moving tribute to both Lennon and his native city, unveiling a new airport logo, based on lyrics from John Lennon's song Imagine, which read "Liverpool John Lennon Airport. Above us only sky". Later, a seven-foot bronze image of John Lennon was unveiled to underline his connection and Her Majesty the Queen attended to rename the airport officially. The image was actually created in bronze by Liverpool sculptor Tom Murphy and has since won much praise from many distinguished visitors.

The airport's name change was widely welcomed, and notably by its biggest airline easyJet, who said they thought Lennon's immense sense of fun would be symbolic of both the rapidly expanding airport and the city in general.

*Above: Yoko Ono meets the Queen at the opening of John Lennon Airport in 2001*

# 1934: King George opens the Queensway tunnel

## "This Miracle": His Majesty's Tunnel Tribute

BIRKENHEAD and Liverpool were linked by road for the first time when the Queensway tunnel opened on July 18, 1934.

In Liverpool, crowds filled the streets towards the tunnel and 1,000 children formed a colourful human bouquet on the Liverpool Museum steps, as King George V and Queen Mary arrived in the city for the official opening. Soldiers also stood on top of St George's Hall and signalled the Royal arrival to troops on the Royal Liver buildings.

More than 200,000 people gathered in a three-mile-long crowd at the Old Haymarket on the Birkenhead side, to welcome the King and Queen as they drove through the tunnel.

The construction of the Queensway tunnel had begun on both sides of the water in 1925, with the two parts meeting in 1928.

When it first opened, 60-foot concrete and granite columns stood at each end, but only the column on the Birkenhead side still stands today.

### The King Opens Th

**MILLION PEOPLE LINE CITY'S ROYAL ROUTE**

"This Miracle"—Great Tribute To Merseyside's Feat

**"ENDEAVOURS OF A MULTITUDE"**

Thrilling Reception To Their Majesties Amid Brilliant Pageantry

*"I thank all those whose efforts have achieved this miracle."*

First Public Through T

How Queue Led The Honor

As an anti-climax to the thrill, for the crowds who still lingered, of seeing the first public cars driven through the car drive through the Cars had been jockeyed for hours, but Mr. Brunswick-road, Liverpool, head of the queue when were lined up, under pol along St John's-lane uni There were hundred reminiscences of the long the Liver Buildings where lorry luggage boat. Just before the crowd men in their natty uni ready in their official machines were ready; light which was on a p and on counts the val their bad light was shi had cleared the approa first dozen cars had the

### First Public Cars Through Tunnel

How Queue Leader Lost The Honour

As an anti-climax to the Tunnel tumult andu pageantry there came the thrill, for the crowds who still lingered, of seeing the first public

### SCENES IN THE CITY ITSELF

Six-Figure Crowd Assembles

FINE CEREMONY

Our "Daring Traders & Matchless Seamen"

Here is the story of the Liverpool Tunnel ceremonial, for which a crowd of quite 150,000 to 200,000 had assembled.

Just before the slowly-moving Royal procession came down London-road

*Left: The 1st Battalion of the Lancastrian Volunteers stand by as the Queen's car enters the tunnel*

*Below: The Liverpool Philharmonic Orchestra plays inside the tunnel*

# 1971: Queen Elizabeth II opens the Kingsway tunnel

**ROYAL TUNNEL DAY**

## Her Majesty honours the memory of her father

### By Don McKinlay

It's the — Kingsway. That is the name of the second Mersey Tunnel, the name chosen by the Queen at this afternoon's historic opening.

"My grandfather named the first Mersey Tunnel Queensway in honour of Queen Mary. So in honour of my father it is with the greatest pleasure that I declare the second Mersey Tunnel open and name it Kingsway," said the Queen.

And the name—Liverpool's best kept secret—pleased all. A big burst of cheering followed from the gathering as the long blue curtains at the tunnel entrance released by the button press of the Queen fell aside.

And there above the entrance, carved in beautiful Westmorland green stone was the big 31ft. long name,

Above: The Queen names the tunnel Kingsway, in honour of her father

Left: The Royal party and guests

QUEEN Elizabeth II was welcomed to Merseyside on June 24, 1971, to officially name and open the second road tunnel that was built under the Mersey.

As Her Majesty stood before a crowd of 6,000 Liverpool people at the tunnel, she declared that it was to be named Kingsway, in honour of her father.

This tribute followed King George's decision to name the first tunnel Queensway, in honour of Queen Mary.

Crowds then cheered as curtains were removed to reveal the tunnel's entrance, and a three-foot-long stone with the name spelt out in gold leaf.

During the ceremony, the Queen called the newly built tunnel a "remarkable venture", and she congratulated the Mersey Tunnel Committee and the architects, engineers and contractors involved, for all of their hard work.

# Submarine disaster kills 98

THE tragic loss of the newly built submarine HMS Thetis in June 1939 was one of the worst disasters ever to occur in Liverpool Bay and resulted in the death of 98 people, with only four managing to survive.

She was undergoing sea trials at the time, some 20 miles off the coast by the Great Orme, after being built by famous local shipyard Cammell Laird, and it was always felt quite astonishing that the Royal Navy failed to provide much in the way of support.

For a good 24 hours it seemed likely that the Thetis would be brought back to the surface, but as news spread that most of the crew had been severely affected by chlorine gas, hope soon ran out despite rescue efforts from a number of divers.

A thorough enquiry demanded by the whole country came up with a great deal of valuable information which undoubtedly helped the whole of the submarine fleet during the forthcoming war and a similar tragedy has not happened again.

*Above: Rescuers attempt to reach the crew of the stricken Thetis*

*Right: The Echo reports followed the progress*

*Left: The clock from the Thetis is on display at the Merseyside Maritime Museum*

## Thetis: Divers' Task To-day

### STRONG TIDAL CURRENTS

### Blazing Heat To Intense Cold

### MEMORIAL SERVICES

### To-day's Conference At Admiralty

The British Press, to-day, was at one in demanding that the full inquiry into the loss of the submarine Thetis, announced by the Admiralty as "being held as soon as practicable," should be made public.

Among the questions raised in various quarters were:—

The official reticence towards the Press.

"Delay" in starting rescue operations, the absence of an escort vessel and the emergency equipment at the disposal of the Admiralty.

A call has come from Birkenhead tragic home of the ill-fated Thetis and of many trapped in her mighty hull—that a public inquiry be held there

#### "MUST BE PUBLIC"

"It must be public, and it must be here," demanded Councillor Miles Poland, at an open-air meeting in the town, last night.

"I say this because of the attitude of the Admiralty, which was due to obsolete red tape methods, as shipyard workers know.

"I think the job was bungled, and the work started too late."

He declared, too, that the Press had not been given proper facilities for getting the news for which relatives were waiting.

#### MEMORIAL SERVICES

Memorial services will be held at Portsmouth, Devonport, and Chatham on Wednesday. Should the Thetis not have been raised before then, a memorial service will also be held at the scene of the disaster.

The King, in a cablegram from

### To-day's News Reel

1. A zoo visitor finds the tiger cubs in the mood for petting.
2. The Mayor of Wallasey assists K. Owen (left), senior Victor Luderum, and H. T. L. Jones, junior Victor Luderum, to carry off their cups at Wallasey Grammar School sports.
3. The F.A. team in South Africa doing physical jerks at Cape Town.
4. The 120 yards hurdle race (junior) at the Liverpool and District Secondary Schools championships. R. Faulkner, Holt High School, winner, in centre.

### Appeal Fund For Dependants

#### Merseyside Mayors To Confer

The Mayor of Birkenhead (Ald. H. Beverill) met representatives of the different political parties in Birkenhead, this morning, to discuss the question of issuing an appeal fund for the widows and dependants of the men on board the Thetis.

The meeting was held in the Town Hall and the Mayor presided, those present including Mr. H. Graham White, M.P. for Birkenhead East, Alderman A. W. Baker, deputy leader, and Councillor J. Furness, representing the Conservative Party, Councillor W. H. Egan, leader, and Councillor Charles McVey, deputy leader, representing the Labour Party; Commander C. J. L. Brittlestone, the Admiralty liaison officer, Liverpool, and the Town-clerk (Mr. E. W. Tanie).

Lieutenant-Colonel J. Sandeman Allen, M.P. for Birkenhead West, was detained in London on Parliamentary business.

#### LORD MAYOR'S MOVE

The meeting was held in private, but at the close the Mayor told the Echo that the Lord Mayor of Liverpool (Alderman Sir Sydney Jones) was calling a meeting at Liverpool Town Hall, this afternoon, of the Mayors of the six Merseyside boroughs—Liverpool, Bootle, Birkenhead, Wallasey, Crosby, and Bebington—to consider issuing a joint appeal to Merseyside to raise a fund.

The sum raised by the fund, the Mayor explained, would be remitted to the Mansion House Fund, launched by the Lord Mayor of London (Sir Frank Bowster), for distribution.

The Mayor intimated that he was communicating with the Lord Mayor of London, who, he presumed, would be in agreement with the suggestions

#### CHEQUES ALREADY RECEIVED

"The Admiralty and Messrs Cammell Lairds have assured me," said the Mayor, "that the immediate needs of the widows and dependants are being met by the Admiralty or Messrs. Cammell Lairds.

"Although the fund has not been opened," said the Mayor, "I have already received cheques and contributions."

Referring to memorial services, the Mayor said that the Admiralty's memorial service is to take place on Wednesday at 2 p.m., and if the Thetis has not been salved the service will be held over the spot where she lies. Boats would be provided to take out relatives and friends in the latter case

Simultaneously with this service there will be a memorial service in Birkenhead, but it has not yet been decided where this will take place

# Drama Of 2 a.m. Tappings From Thetis: Women's Grim Vigil!

THE LIVERPOOL ECHO, SATURDAY, JUNE 8, 1939

## LAST-MINUTE RESCUE BID

### Divers' Desperate Efforts

### WEEPING RELATIVES

### Scenes At Shipyard Offices

### SURVIVOR'S STORY

Two hours after hope had been almost abandoned for the men remaining trapped in the submarine Thetis at the bottom of Liverpool Bay, early to-day, a dramatic message which indicated signs of life was issued by the Admiralty.

Divers working feverishly on the hull, heard faint tappings from the interior. Then, at dawn, some hours after it had been estimated that the submarine's air supply, must have been exhausted, a bid began to raise the stern.

Official quarters were not optimistic. However, about averting what would be the worst submarine calamity in his...

## German Ace Crashes In T.T. Practice

### 2-a.m. Operation On Karl Gall

From Our Own Correspondent
DOUGLAS, Saturday.

An operation was completed at 2 a.m. to-day upon Karl Gall, German crack motor-cyclist, who crashed in practice for the T.T. motor-cycle race in the Isle of Man, last night.

His injuries were more serious than at first thought. He is suffering from depressed fracture of the skull, and is now reported to be in a serious condition.

Gall, riding a B.M.W. machine, was approaching Ballaugh Bridge, when his machine got into a skid, and machine and rider both shot into a wall.

Gall, with the rest of the German B.M.W. team, crossed to the island on Thursday, and this was his first practice. Last year a practice crash kept him out of the senior race.

At this morning's practice, 25 riders were on the course.

The fastest were:—

Senior.—Stanley Woods (Velocette), lap time of 25min 42secs.—88.1 m.p.h.
Junior.—L. J. Archer (Velocette), 27min. 58secs.—80.9 m.p.h.
Lightweight.—L. J. Archer (New Imperial), 29min 54secs.—75.73 m.p.h.

## APPLIED FOR THE THETIS

### WAITED FOR CHANCE TO SAIL FROM LIVERPOOL

Left Chief Engine Room Artificer P. F. Jackson (P/MX 46112), who lives at 50 Pitville Avenue, Mossley Hill, is one...

## VIGIL IN LIGHT OF MOON

### Destroyers' Watch Through Night

### SILENCE OF DESPAIR

### Constant Exchange Of Messages

From Our Own Correspondent
CONWAY, Saturday.

In the early hours of to-day a profound silence, which one could sense as despair, hung over the sea at the spot where the Thetis lies submerged.

The brightly-lit destroyers and other vessels standing motionless in a circle the decks of the warships pacing the constant coming and going of speedy launches on patrol indicated that an unceasing watch was being maintained.

A green light flashing at regular intervals somewhere about the centre of the ring of vessels was believed to be marking the position of the Thetis, but despite a full moon and calm sea it was impossible to discern any object near the light.

LIKE GHOSTS...

### Merseyside Men In The Submarine

### Some Other Officers On The Submarine

"HEAVY LOAD"...

## BOOTLE'S DAY OF GAIETY

### 50,000 People See Procession

### THE MAY QUEEN

### Children In Inspiring Spectacle

Bootle to-day was a town transformed from its usual business-like atmosphere, taking on a festive air that only the annual May Day Demonstration could give to it.

Last year about £650 was raised, and this year the elusive £1,000 goal, sought for many years, may come considerably nearer achievement. Bootle General Hospital which is the principal beneficiary stands in need of about £3,000 to complete the appeal for £10,000 spent on improvements.

Commencing from the Town Hall at 1.45 p.m. the procession which was not due to arrive at the North Park, proper, for the crowning of the May Queen, Miss Jean Mackenzie, until 4.15 p.m. was officially estimated to be more than half a mile long.

...lined by something like 50,000 people, who lined the pavements crowds deep throughout the route.

*Reports from the fateful day 98 men lost their lives*

LAST CITY    THE LIVERPOOL ECHO, SATURDAY, JUNE 8, 1939

# "NO HOPE"—THETIS A CHAMBER OF DEATH

## 98 MEN DEAD IN THE WORST SUBMARINE DISASTER

### Men Believed Victims Of Vessel's Escaping Chlorine Gas

### DESPERATE RESCUE WORK FAILS

### Cammell Laird's Statement On What Is Thought To Have Happened

SHORTLY AFTER THREE THIS AFTERNOON AN OFFICIAL OF CAMMELL LAIRDS TOLD WAITING PRESSMEN. "WE HAVE NOW NO HOPE OF SAVING FURTHER LIVES FROM THE THETIS."

"We consider that the men died from chlorine gas. The ship carried a large quantity of chlorine, which we think would escape owing to the angle at which she lay."

It was denied that there was any truth in a suggestion that they were contemplating blowing the vessel up. Now that there was no hope of saving life, the official said, they would attempt to save the vessel.

Ninety-eight men may have lost their lives.

The Admiralty stated this morning that following tappings heard at 2 a.m. there was still hope at 10 a.m. to-day that some of the trapped men might be rescued alive.

Hope, however, faded as the hours sped by with no news that the vessel had been brought to the surface from her position on the seabed 14 miles off the Great Orme's Head.

Then, late this afternoon, an official of Cammell Lairds told the Press that hope was abandoned prior to midnight. He added, concerning the tapping said to have been heard at 2 a.m., that it was now thought to have been due to high compressors working.

### TERRIFIC TASK

A terrific task faced the salvage workers who at dawn began a new attempt to raise the stern of the submarine. The first attempt failed, one hawser parting, and although the workers then realised that the chances of rescuing the trapped men were remote they continued striving desperately to raise the submarine.

Seven additional names of men aboard, announced by the Admiralty to-day, show that there were 102 men on board the Thetis when she made her fatal dive. Four of these escaped, so the number of imprisoned is 98.

Throughout a night of increasing anxiety relatives and friends of the trapped men kept a sad vigil at the Birkenhead offices of Messrs Cammell Lairds, the builders of the Thetis. As time wore on women broke down under the strain and the ambulance staff was called to render first aid.

Two of the four survivors have...

*Before All Hope Had Gone*

*The last that was seen of the submarine before her stern vanished beneath the waves.*

### A.R.P. PROBLEMS

Special pages in the DAILY POST of Monday will deal with air raid precaution problems as they affect both the private person and the employer of labour, and will provide a useful guide to meeting Government requirements and recommendations.

Monday's
## DAILY POST

### DAVIS CUP TENNIS

#### HARE RETIRES IN GAME AGAINST GERMANY

C. E. Hare, showing signs of still suffering from the trouble which earlier made him a doubtful starter, surrendered to Menzel in the Britain v. Germany Davis Cup (European zone) semi-final in Berlin this afternoon.

He played only two sets, losing the first three and the second 6-1 in an exhibition that can only be described as pitiful.

Germany now leads Britain by one match to nil.

#### WIRRAL TENNIS

The Wirral tennis tournament was held at the Hill House courts, Heswall this afternoon. Results:—

OPEN MIXED DOUBLES

MEN'S HANDICAP DOUBLES

WINDSOR RACING RETURNS

## PAYNTER CHECKS DERBYSHIRE

### With A Timely Century

### EARLY "BATS" FAIL

### Oldfield And Iddon Give Their Aid

From Our Own Correspondent
OLD TRAFFORD, Saturday.

Lancashire suffered an early shock in their match with Derbyshire, for without a run being scored they lost Hopwood, caught at square leg.

Paynter obtained the first boundary stroke, a good drive to the sight-screen. The same player scored 14 of the first 22 runs, and then saw Washbrook snapped up as outswinger to Elliott, behind the wicket.

Oldfield and Paynter made a stand, adding 52 in forty minutes.

George Pope had a spell of hostility from the station end, and did his work well. When Copson returned he struck at the made the ball rise sharply.

Oldfield sent one to Alderman at second slip. The partnership had put on 105 at an hour and a half.

Lunch was taken with Lancashire 122 at the board for the loss of three wickets.

Paynter having made his hundred.

Iddon just jump into Lancashire when the game was continued, and one good effort at the expense of A. Pope. Paynter was by no means comfortable, however, though shaking up against a good attack, and came near to giving G. Pope a catch on the leg side when 75.

Warren Mitchell came off his A. Pope's place he escaped 15 in his first over when he went up the 100 when the innings and lunched two and two-quarter hours. Paynter, with the next stroke, drove G. Pope's ball to deep extra.

The slips, reached his second century in the season, after having previously given a chance of stumping at one and Mitchell's service.

## Gordon Richards Takes A Toss

### But Suffers No Ill-Effects

Gordon Richards, the champion jockey, suffered a toss at Windsor to-day, when his mount in the Speedy Two-Year-Old Plate, Petty, slipped up after the field had traversed about a furlong.

Fortunately he suffered no injury, and was able to take the ride on Burytown in the next event, the Castle Handicap.

Arthur Espson was the Salford Borough Handicap, the chief event at Manchester, beating Spliced and Bygone.

MANCHESTER

## DRAMA INSIDE SUBMARINE

### Plan Of Escape For Men

### WATERTIGHT MESSAGES

### In Case First Men Out Were Not Saved

The Echo learns that the drama outside the Thetis was preceded by an even greater drama inside.

After the submarine was found to be in trouble, Captain H. P. K. Oram, Commander of the Fifth Submarine Flotilla, volunteered to take his chance to come to the surface with the Davis apparatus in the hope that he might appraise to him, as there was no news at the time that they had been located.

With Lieutenant Woods he came to the surface, and they had prepared a series of messages, which had been placed in watertight luggings so that these could be picked up if the worst happened.

The messages were to indicate what had happened and the situation inside the submarine.

### CIVILIAN PROBLEM

The presence of civilians on board complicated matters, and it is believed that as soon as they were reported missing, civilians and crew would come up together by means of the Davis apparatus and all divisions had first been exhausted.

In great column H.M.S. Brazen and the Duke Ship's round Vigilant do-corrived on the scene from Captain Oram shot to the two signals...

### WONDERFUL SPIRIT

# Community spirit strong through war years

A RADIO broadcast by then Prime Minister Neville Chamberlain on September 3, 1939 reluctantly revealed that Britain was at war with Germany.

Mr Chamberlain had already been to Munich and was assured by Herr Hitler that war was not imminent.

But when Germany invaded Poland an ultimatum given to Hitler was ignored.

Sirens immediately echoed over Liverpool.

The evacuation of school children had begun, with 56,000 moved out to places such as Cheshire, Wales and Canada. In the first four days of September, millions of British people were evacuated.

Liverpool saw those born here return after just a few months, prepared to endure the endless visits to air raid shelters in order to live in the city they loved.

The spirit of Liverpool was everywhere. It was seen in the never-say-die response to a chilling outbreak of a war that no one wanted, but that would last five years.

## Germany Invades Poland—Full British Mobilisation

*These reports dated September 1, 1939 heralded the beginning of the evacuation process of thousands of Liverpool children, such as those shown, right*

*September 2, 1939*

## Liverpool Echo
### FOOTBALL ED. — FINAL

**Your Problems—**
LEGAL, MEDICAL, GENERAL
GARDEN, POULTRY, BEAUTY
Unique Free Help Bureau
**WEEKLY POST**

NO. 18,603 — SATURDAY, SEPTEMBER 2, 1939 — ONE PENNY

*Join the Younger team* — **WILLIAM YOUNGERS BEER**

# Still Waiting For Hitler's Reply To Britain

**PREMIER'S STATEMENT IN HOUSE OF COMMONS DELAYED**

Germans Claim Capture Of Teschen And Other Towns

**INCREASING AIR ATTACKS**

"Enemy Repulsed Everywhere," Say The Poles

**CABINET CHANGES: CHURCHILL IN?**

Turkey To Stand By Britain And France. To-day's Declaration

**Berlin Says It Is Not War**

**Labour And The War Cabinet**

Decision Not To Join At This Stage

**FOUR TOWNS CAPTURED?**

German - Polish Claims To-day

**ENVOY'S STATEMENT**

"Invaders Repulsed Everywhere"

**Vital Importance Of Blackout**

**Official Warnings To The Public**

**NEW MILITARY BILL**

Debate In The Commons

M.P.'S £5 BETS

His Own View About Bomb Prospects

**THE 18 CLASS**

**LATEST STOP-PRESS**

**CABINET MOVES**

**CHECK YOUR COUPONS**

---

*January 24, 1944*

## Hero of the Atlantic

More than 80,000 people died during the long campaign to thwart German U-Boats in the Atlantic Ocean that threatened to cut off vital supplies to Britain in wartime.

Winston Churchill believed that without this continued effort the Allies would not have won World War II.

The central command for the battle was in Liverpool's Derby Square - often frequented by Churchill himself.

One hero was John Walker, an inspiring commander based at the Gladstone Dock whose 2nd Support Group hunted U-Boats out in the Atlantic. He once sank five U-Boats in ten days.

A statue at the Pier Head commemorates this legendary leader who died in July 1944 - from exhaustion.

### ATLANTIC VICTORY

Sailor's Story Of The Convoy Battle

**LIVERPOOL MAN'S AIR COMBATS**

Yeoman of Signals D. M. Carroll, aged 46, of Paddington, London, yesterday told a story of the recent Atlantic action in which (as announced on Saturday) attempts by strong forces of U-boats and long-range German aircraft equipped with radio-controlled glider bombs to attack an important Atlantic convoy were decisively defeated.

Carroll was serving in the sloop H.M.S. Crane, and saw the entire action, which lasted for four days and three nights. H.M.S. Crane, helped by the frigate H.M.S. Foley, probably destroyed a U-boat.

**Dodged Torpedo**

After telling of an inconclusive attempt to depth-charge a U-boat, Carroll said: "We had a shock when we sighted a torpedo about fifty yards ahead and to starboard. The commanding officer put us hard over to port, and thanks to his fine navigation the torpedo passed

*July 11, 1944*

### Gave His Life To Beat U-Boats

**Captain Frederick John Walker**, four times D.S.O. and commander of sloops which sent at least 17 U-boats to the bottom, and damaged many more, died of a heart attack in a Liverpool hospital. He died, says one naval correspondent, of sheer exhaustion. He was only 47, but in the three years he had spent almost continuously at sea, he had never slept more than two hours in the 24. It

# PART ONE

# LIVERPOOL AT WAR

## Lest we forget...

In 2003, the Echo looked back on the city's war years with a special series entitled Liverpool At War. Readers were able to share their memories of daily life, facing waves of bombings as the Luftwaffe obliterated their surroundings, changing the face of the city forever.

As well as life at home, the Echo remembered those who travelled abroad to fight, showing pictures and reports from the front line.

Looking back it is difficult to see how people managed to cope under such harsh conditions but cope they did, holding on to a spirit of goodwill and ensuring a bright future for Liverpool and generations to come.

# City lies in ruin after May blitz

THROUGHOUT seven nights in May, Liverpool was almost reduced to a pile of rubble after Hitler ordered the Luftwaffe to destroy the city and its port.

The bombing started on May Day and more than 1,450 people were killed across Liverpool, Birkenhead and Wallasey.

Fires burned all over the city and landmarks such as Lewis's store were almost ruined.

Communities were drawn together by sharing air raid shelters that often became homes at night. Many people simply went there every evening to avoid the constant bombs that would devastate parts of the inner city.

On May 5, bombs destroyed all but the outside shell of St Luke's Church on Berry Street, which stands as a memorial today.

The city of Manchester afterwards paid tribute to the strength shown by the people of Liverpool in one of the worst series of attacks outside London.

## The Worst Blitz

### A Big Nazi Armada's Indiscriminate Raid

Business premises, hospitals, working-class tenements and dwellings, and churches, all bore the brunt of Merseyside's most harrowing experience of Nazi barbarism on Saturday night, when for some hours an armada of Nazi bombers made circuits of the area, and dropped great numbers of bombs and incendiaries on Liverpool and surrounding districts.

It was the severest raid Merseyside has yet experienced. Night fighters and a great barrage took record toll of the enemy.

Cultural institutions, a school, and religious buildings, including several churches of various denominations suffered badly as a result of bombs. An old and historic Church of England parish church in a Liverpool suburb was almost completely burnt out while ...

*Anticlockwise from top: The remains of Philip, Son and Nephew bookshop on Church Street; A report from May 5, 1941, told of the devastation; the lord mayor sent his message to the city on May 7 ,1941 ; and the Overhead Railway at the end of James Street was torn apart*

## Lord Mayor's Message

### Pride In The City And Citizens During Their Ordeal

## Defence Services Praised

The Lord Mayor (Alderman Sir Sydney Jones) presiding at Liverpool City Council meeting to-day, referred to the six nights of raiding.

"I think I can say, without boasting but with great pride, that Liverpool has stood up enormously well to its task.

"We need steadfastness, courage, foresight, and we are glad to find those qualities prevailing throughout the city. We still have that unshaken belief in the ultimate victory. I have been amazed at the way in which our citizens have gone about their business during the past few days.

"We deeply deplore that a number of our citizens have lost their lives in the wanton destruction. We shall remember those who have suffered and died. . . .

"We ought to express our gratitude, in our sympathy for others, to all the members of our staffs and forces,

voluntary or otherwise, who have so nobly come forward and played their part. I feel personally very proud to-day for the way in which the city has carried on."

The Lord Mayor accordingly moved the following resolution :

"That this Council desire to place on record its appreciation of the valuable and efficient services rendered by the personnel of all sections of the Civil Defence organisations of the city and neighbouring local authorities, and by voluntary organisations, contractors, and others during the recent heavy enemy air attacks on the city."

The resolution was agreed with acclamation.

Alderman Denton thanked and congratulated the Lord Mayor on behalf of the public for the timely message of encouragement issued through the Press, and expressed his appreciation of the work of the Emergency Committee.

# To The Citizens

The Liverpool Civil Defence Emergency Committee, represented by the Lord Mayor (Alderman Sir Sydney Jones), Alderman A. E. Shennan, and Alderman Luke Hogan, to-day, issued the following communication:—

"Liverpool has passed this, a very serious ordeal, during the last four days and nights. We should like to take this early opportunity of expressing to the citizens our great appreciation of the spirit in which they have met the crisis.

"It was only what was to be expected, but it is a great inspiration to know that Liverpool has not been behind other cities in its realisation of the importance of maintaining the steadiness of our civic life.

"We would like to express our deepest sympathy with those who have been bereaved, with those who have been dispossessed, and with all who have so heroically borne the brunt of the attack

"We wish to assure them that no efforts are being spared to see that all the services which so vitally affect the city and the life of the people at the present time are being maintained to the fullest possible extent."

## LORD MAYOR TO MOTORISTS

The Lord Mayor of Liverpool (Alderman Sir Sydney Jones) appeals to the public to avoid all unnecessary use of motor-cars in the area.

## MANCHESTER PAYS TRIBUTE TO LIVERPOOL

The Daily Dispatch, in a leading article to-day, says:—

"Manchester, as the sister city, is sometimes critical of Liverpool — not maliciously, but frankly, critical, with the interest and the freedom of the close relation But yesterday, as Manchester read of the steadfastness with which the people of Liverpool had met one of the worst aerial attacks of the war, its feelings were of sympathy and pride, sympathy in Liverpool's loss, pride in its courage and endurance.

"The rest of the country, or at least such part of it as has suffered hurt since Hitler's airmen took to scattering fire and high-explosive from the air, will not be far behind in showing similar feelings.

"It is some little comfort to learn that the night-raiding force suffered higher casualties than any of its many predecessors have done on any mission of murder in this country since the war began. Whatever its original size, 16 planes is a considerable loss.

"Liverpool helps to avenge all those other ports which have been among the Luftwaffe's selected targets in recent weeks."

## Our Confidence

### Ready To Meet Middle East Threat

By Edward Kennedy, Associated Press War Correspondent

CAIRO, Monday.

British military leaders, well aware of the threat to Britain's grasp on the Middle East and the vital passageway of the Suez Canal inherent in the presence of the Italo-German Army in the Libyan Desert, and the possibility of a German thrust towards Syria, were to-day confident of meeting the situation.

Reverses in Greece and the events which followed them have brought not fear, but a greater determination to carry on the fight which, with the clean-up of Abyssinia, will enter a defensive

## SWIFT MOVES IN IRAK

### Vital Centres Occupied

Britain's land and air forces in Irak are striking swift, effective blows against Raschid Ali, Irak's pro-Nazi Premier.

British troops have occupied the airport, docks, and power station at Basra, on the Persian Gulf commanding Irak's only seaboard, and the R.A.F. has crippled all the small Iraki Air Force, which, at the outbreak of war, numbered only 50 machines.

A special communiqué issued last night in Cairo stated that bomber aircraft of the R.A.F. carried out a heavy raid on the Iraki aerodrome at Moaschar Raschid.

# Crowded Shelter Drama In Big Mersey Raid

## Golden Wedding Party Tragedy; Newlyweds' Fate; Many Lucky Escapes

Merseyside bore the full brunt of the German attack last night, and while the Air Ministry communiqué this morning said that "casualties may be large," the Echo understands that, happily, they are not so heavy as was feared.

Five German bombers were destroyed during the night, three by night fighters—one over an aerodrome in Northern France—and two by A.A. gunfire.

THE Air Ministry and Ministry of Home Security communiqué said:

"Last night enemy aircraft again attacked the Merseyside area. The attack was heavy and lasted several hours.

"Early reports suggest that the number of casualties may be large and that a substantial amount of damage was done.

"An attack was also made on a town in East Anglia, where a small number of casualties were caused and a considerable number of houses were damaged.

"Bombs were also dropped at other widely-separated points, but these did little damage and caused very few casualties

"Three enemy bombers were destroyed during the night, two by our fighters and one by A.A. gunfire. In addition, another enemy aircraft was shot down by our night fighters over an aerodrome in Northern France, making a total of four enemy aircraft destroyed during the

off the overcoat of the chief warden, Mr. G. E. Edwards."

In the street where Mr. Gordon was on duty, a voluntary fire-watcher, Mr. John Kynaston, aged about 40, of Dorking Grove, Wavertree, was killed outside the premises of his employers

Three voluntary fire-watchers were trapped under the debris of a commercial building. Two were extricated after being buried for about ten hours. They were removed by ambulance to hospital.

### HIT A CEMETERY

Three high explosive bombs and a number of incendiaries fell in a small area. One hit a cemetery, where it made a huge crater, another fell in the adjoining road, and the third struck a garage.

Adjoining property was much damaged and two people were believed to have been buried in the debris of a house which collapsed.

A shelter in a street nearby was badly damaged, and one person is understood to have been killed there, while others were injured

*Top left: Brunswick Street, city centre, looking towards the Pier Head*

*Above: Manchester paid tribute to Liverpool in the Echo on May 5, 1941*

*Left: Echo readers learned the fates of fellow Liverpudlians on May 3, 1941*

# Murder at the movies

ONE of the worst miscarriages of justice in British history occurred in Liverpool in 1950 when two petty criminals, George Kelly and Charles Connolly, were wrongly convicted of murdering the manager of the city's Cameo cinema, Leonard Thomas, and his assistant Bernard Catterall. Some 75,000 people were questioned by detectives, but far too much credit was given to the evidence provided by another petty criminal Robert Graham, who claimed to have overheard comments in Walton Prison by the accused, and prostitute Jacqueline Dixon and her pimp James Northam, who were seeking immunity from prosecution for other offences.

In the first instance the pair were tried together, but a retrial was made necessary by the jury's disagreement, and this time the pair were tried separately, with Kelly sentenced to death by hanging and Connolly sentenced to a lengthy spell of imprisonment.

Since then further investigations have taken place and, in June 2003, both convictions were quashed and Kelly was given a dignified funeral in the Metropolitan Cathedral.

*Right: The Echo revealed the latest developments as the net closed in on the Cameo killer*

*Below: George Kelly, who was hanged for the shooting*

## RING AROUND CINEMA AREA

### Hunt "Cameo" Killer

### LOCAL MAN THEORY

#### Firearms Seized In Houses

Liverpool C.I.D. men investigating the Cameo Cinema murders are understood to have seized a number of firearms in houses in the area they have ringed off as that in which the wanted man may now be hiding.

Their street-by-street search round the Edge Hill and Wavertree areas will probably result in the appearance in court of a number of men on charges of illegal possession of firearms.

As the manhunt progresses—Chief Superintendent T. A. Smith, Liverpool C.I.D. chief, said this morning: "We are much further advanced and very optimistic on an early arrest "— the work of the ballistics experts is becoming of increasing importance

##### BULLETS CHECKED

All firearms seized by the police are being microscopically checked by experts with the calibre of the bullets found in the bodies of the two murdered men.

Since Saturday night, when police were first called to the manager's office of the cinema in Webster Road, Liverpool C.I.D.'s fingerprint squad have been working steadily to identify each set of prints found in the office.

They are gradually eliminating those of the staff and of known visitors to the manager's office. In his panic the gunman may have left fingerprints on furniture in the office, and every square inch of the room is being carefully examined.

*March 22, 1949*

## Police Statement On Cinema Shooting

### Weapon Used May Be A Foreign Type Of Automatic

#### Hundreds Of People Interviewed

LIVERPOOL C.I.D. officers, searching for the masked gunman who on Saturday night shot and killed the manager and assistant manager of the Cameo Cinema, Webster Road, Wavertree, Liverpool, have investigated the possibility of a link between the two shootings and threats to local cinema managers from a gang of youths.

In January, a cinema manager from another part of the city, who was acting as manager of the Cameo Cinema, was attacked by a youth, and had to receive treatment in hospital.

##### TO MANAGERS

The man had previously been warned of the activities of this gang and had been told not to let them in the cinema.

Mr. Leonard Thomas, the murdered manager of the Cameo Cinema, had been threatened by the gang, and threats had been made to the

bullets, is also continuing. The man may have disposed of it in his getaway.

The man followed the cashier, Nellie Jackson, of Pengwern Street, Liverpool, when she took the takings from the pay-box to the manager's office, while the [watching] the film [were] in which there is a [...] incident.

The police believe that he watched the film from a seat in the back stalls, and after the cashier come up the cinema aisle [made] her time to leave the manager's [...] before he left his seat, [...] black silk scarf over the [...] of his face and pulling [...] his hat down low, he w[...] foot of the stairs and c[...] phone connection.

##### STRUGGLE IN O[...]

In the office, Mr. [...] Mr. Catterall, the assista[nt] were counting the d[...] when the gunman [...] They immediately jum[...] one of them went to [...] to shut off the intruder.

There was then [...] struggle, during wh[...] becoming panic stric[...] gun and began to fir[...] surmised.

Mr. Thomas fell f[...] with a bullet in t[...] Catterall, although w[...] bullet through his rig[...] on.

##### FOUR WOUNDS

But the man shot him again in the [...]

Mr. L. Thomas    Mr. J. B. Catterall

*March 21, 1949*

Echo readers followed the story from the courtroom to the gallows

## Kelly Hanged For Cameo Cinema Murder

THE LIVERPOOL ECHO, TUESDAY, MARCH 29, 194

### 600 OUTSIDE WALTON PRISON GATES

#### Rush To Read Notice

##### MOVED BY POLICE

George Kelly, 27-years-old Liverpool labourer, sentenced to death for the Cameo Cinema murder just over a year ago, was hanged at Walton Prison this morning.

From an early hour people waited outside the prison and by a quarter to nine there were at least 600—three-quarters of them women—in Hornby Road, facing the main entrance.

Twenty police officers, under the command of a superintendent, controlled the crowd and kept them on one side of the road. Patrolling outside the prison was a motor-cycle policeman.

##### RUSHED ACROSS ROAD

When the notice of execution was posted on the prison door in the presence of three warders, the crowd rushed across the road. Police officers held them back and then they formed into a queue and filed past the door.

Twenty minutes after th

### RANGER'S NOTES ON SPORT

#### To-morrow's League Games
#### Everton At Home; Liverpool Return To Maine Road

Dave Walsh, Irish international, centre forward of West Bromwich Albion, transferred from Linfield to Swindon Park, West Brom scored 14 League goals for the Throstles this season.

#### TWO "SOUTHS" MEET

If floodlit football has ceased to be a novelty for most people in the South End of the city, the idea itself has certainly proved a big success

##### INCENTIVE FOR SAINTS

### FOOD PROBE BY MINISTRY EXPERTS

#### Fall In Sale Of Rations

##### STOCKS MOUNTING

*March 28, 1949*

## Police Theory In Cinema Deaths

### Gunman May Have Applied For Job

The gunman who shot and killed the manager and his assistant at the Cameo Cinema, Liverpool, last Saturday night, may have applied for a job there three days previously.

In the Liverpool Echo on Thursday, March 17, there appeared this advertisement:—" Cinema. — Smart Foreman; refs.—After 2 p.m. Cameo Cinema, Webster Rd."

Liverpool C.I.D. can find no references at the cinema to applicants for this position, but there may have been some on Friday afternoon, who saw the manager, Mr. Leonard Thomas, or his assistant, Mr. J. B. Catterall.

The C.I.D. are asking any persons who applied to come forward. It is believed that if the gunman was among the applicants the legitimate job-seekers may remember something about a man in a brown tweed overcoat belted all round, trilby hat, with black shoes, about 5ft. 8ins. and full faced, possibly with dark hair

In view of the precise knowledge shown by the gunman of the cinema layout and of the manner in which the cash was taken from the box office to the manager's office, it is possible that it was partly obtained through his applying for the job of foreman.

*March 25, 1949*

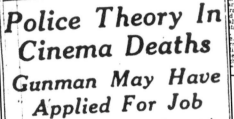

## Profile

**ALBERT PIERREPOINT**

BORN: March 30, 1905 in Bradford, Yorkshire

DIED: July 10, 1992 in Southport, Merseyside

CAREER: Grocer, pub landlord and Britain's last official chief hangman, credited with having executed an estimated 433 men and 17 women in his 24-year career, from 1932-1956

NOTABLE EXECUTIONS: Lord Haw-Haw (William Joyce) in 1946; Acid bath murderer John George Haigh in 1949, Michael Manning, the last person to be hanged in Northern Ireland, in 1954; Ruth Ellis, the last woman to be hanged in Britain, in 1955

FAMILY: Father Henry Pierrepoint and uncle Thomas Pierrepoint were also executioners

LEGACY: A film about Pierrepoint's life was made in 2005, starring Timothy Spall in the title role

# Elizabeth takes the throne

THE Queen's Coronation at Westminster Abbey on June 2, 1953 generated arguably the biggest and most spectacular series of public celebrations ever seen in this country, with an estimated three million people lining the streets of London and more than 20 million elsewhere following the ceremony on BBC Television.

Apart from being a spectacular ceremony, it enabled the Commonwealth to banish memories of World War II and to look forward to what seemed a highly promising future.

Heads of state from all round the world were among the thousands of people in Westminster Abbey who clearly enjoyed a highly spectacular ceremony featuring a lady who had already demonstrated her dedication and belief in service to others.

Many in the huge crowds outside the abbey had camped out overnight and were rewarded with some wonderful entertainment, including the Queen's appearance on the balcony at Buckingham Palace, a spectacular fly-past by the RAF and a magnificent fireworks display over the Victoria embankment.

Similar celebrations were held throughout the country, with people in Liverpool taking the chance to really enjoy themselves.

Typically, Blacklers store sent a loyal message from the whole of the staff to congratulate Her Majesty.

THE LIVERPOOL ECHO, TUESDAY

## Crowds Filled Procession Route Ho

### CORONATION DREAM DR

**EMBLEMS OF COMMONWEALTH**

Historic Gown In English Silk

**TUDOR ROSE THEME**

*Below: Blackler's sent its best wishes to the new Queen*

## Coronation : The

## Surpassing Be

**A HALLOWED SETTING FOR SERVICE OF DEDICATION**

Robes Provide Gorgeous Pattern Of Colour

**THE DUKE'S HOMAGE**

Queen's Stately Entry On A Golden Carpet

INSIDE Westminster Abbey an extraordinary transformation had taken place since the building was closed to allow of preparations for the Crowning.

## Blackler's

## Abbey Spl

## The R

PRINCE CHA
SEES CROW
CEREMON

Brilliant Scer
The Abbe

THUNDEROUS CH

Smiles And Waves A
The Royal Rou

Four-years-old Prince Charles

*Above: Residents enjoy a coronation street party*

*Left: The Queen and Prince Phillip on the happy day*

## Earlier Than Expected

### FOR THE QUEEN

### ...essional Scenes

### ...y Of The Abbey Scene

#### The Queen Had Never Looked More Lovely

##### Radiant Smiles For Cheering Thousands On Route To Her Coronation

*In a scene of fairy tale splendour, the Queen set off from her Palace for her crowning at four minutes before the clock struck half-past ten. There was a smile of great happiness on her face.*

### ...our In Crimson And White

### ...nt Queen's Triumphal Drive

#### THE NATION WELCOMES ITS QUEEN

##### Ninety Minutes Of Rain Drench Waiting Thousands

**ROYAL ROUTE CROWDS**

*Welcoming crowds packed the heart of the Empire this afternoon to cheer the Queen as she drove from her Coronation in Westminster Abbey.*

#### Little Streets Go Gay

##### Showers Fail To Halt The Fun

*The Echo followed the action every step of the way*

---

## Everest: A shining chapter in our history

*Colonel John Hunt, leader of the expedition, with Mr T. D. Bourdillon.*

### Merseyside rejoices

*Dr C. Evans*

ON the eve of the Coronation, the whole of Britain was overcome with excitement at the news that the world's highest mountain, Everest in Nepal, had been conquered by New Zealander Edmund Hillary and Sherpa Tensing.

The news was delivered by Colonel John Hunt, British leader of the Commonwealth expedition, who sent his call just as the public were gathering for the Coronation.

As several of the climbing party had trained in North Wales on the slopes of Snowdon, the news sent waves through the north west.

To the nation's delight, Hillary was immediately knighted.

*Overleaf: Youngsters could collect colour pictures from the expedition in The Echo's Junior Edition, dated March 5, 1955*

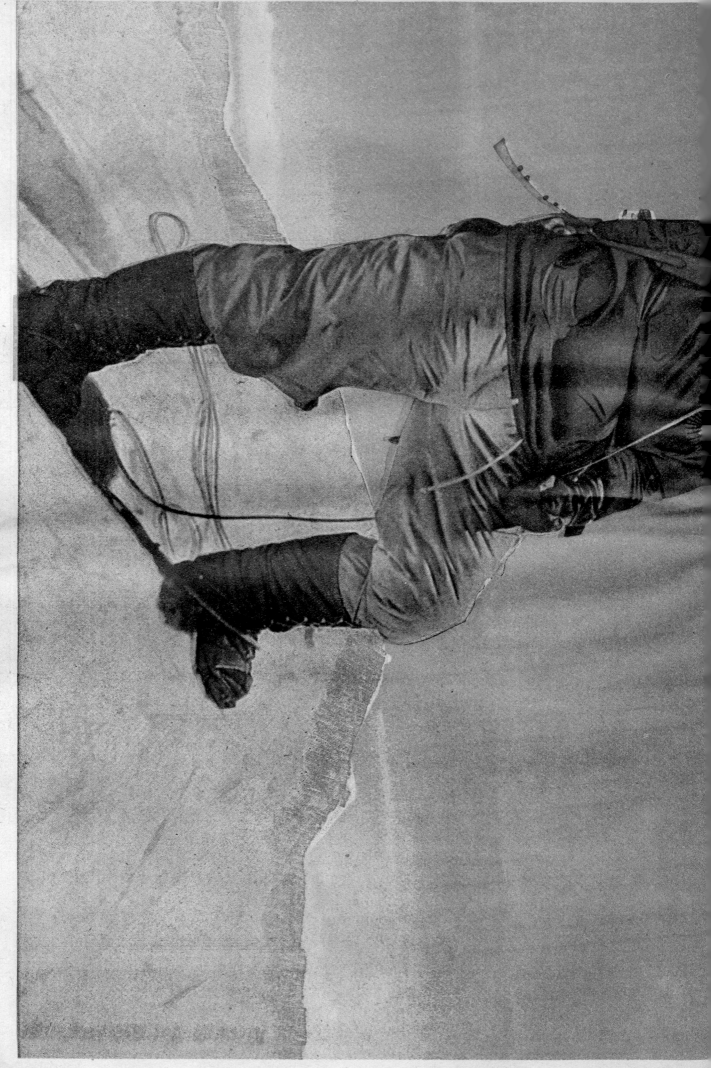

At 11.30 on the morning of May 29, 1953, Hillary and Tensing set foot on the summit of Everest. It must have been an unforgettable moment, and we can only imagine how they felt standing on that small dome of snow, with all the high peaks of the Himalayas stretched out below them; the highest men on earth. It was the fulfilment of the hopes and dreams of two generations of mountaineers. It was for this that we, and those who had gone up before us, had crossed the world and struggled with this great peak, so that now we might be permitted to place two of our number for a brief 15 minutes on the summit of the earth. Tensing, in this now famous picture, with his ice-axe aloft and his flags unfurled, was photographed by Hillary.

—ALFRED GREGORY in The Picture of Everest.

76

# Liverpool Echo

NO. 23,408

SATURDAY, MARCH 5, 1955

TWOPENCE

## JUNIOR EDITION

● **Begin Your Collection Of The Everest Colour Series To-day**

## The SUMMIT of EVEREST

# The end of the line for the Overhead Railway

THE city's Overhead Railway service came to a quiet halt on December 30, 1956.

It ended after the costs of repairs that were necessary on the railway lines proved to be too high to pay.

The lines closed at 10.30pm without any specially organised farewells, when the final trains pulled in at stations in Dingle and Seaforth.

The next day was described by many as a sad occasion, as it was the first time in 63 years that the Overhead trains had not run. Even during the war when parts of the lines were damaged or destroyed, some services managed to keep running.

Over 100 of the railway staff went on to secure jobs with British Railways. However, just under 50 women were left unemployed by the closure.

## First Day Without Overhead

### LINE SHUTS AFTER 63 YEARS

### Small Staff Kept On

### STILL HOPE

By GEORGE EGLIN

This is a sad day on Merseyside. For the first time in 63 years, no train was running on the Liverpool Overhead Railway. The line closed at 10.30 p.m. last night, when the two last trains came to a halt in Dingle and Seaforth stations.

Even during the worst periods of the blitz, when sections of the line were destroyed, some sort of service was kept going. But to-day, after two years of frustration and discussion, the Overhead tracks are deserted, and to thousands of Liverpool did not seem the same. ...ugh the line is

way last night from each end of the line. "Tut" F... Sutcliffe Fawcett... ashamedly as he dr... p.m. out of Dingle.... other end of the ... William Mackey sa... one trip I am not e... driving myself out o... "Tut" is one of ... of the Overhead. ... collecting tickets 38 ... and for years now ... a familiar figure to ...

Mr. Graham Page, M.P. for Crosby, wishing driver Fawcett good luck after the ... had arrived at Seaforth Station

*December 31, 1956*

*Right: A notice of the closure of the Overhead Railway*

LIVERPOOL OVERHEAD RAILWAY COMPANY

Liverpool Overhead Railway Act, 1956

## CESSATION OF SERVICES

NOTICE IS HEREBY GIVEN that under the provisions of the above mentioned Act the Company will after midnight on Sunday, the 30th December, 1956, cease to operate railway services for the use of the public.

DATED this 9th day of November 1956.

BY ORDER OF THE BOARD

HUGH T. NICHOLSON, Secretary.

early meeting of the committee is planned.

### UNDER COVER

To-day Mr. H. M. Rostron, general manager of the Overhead Company, said nothing would be done for the time being that would prevent the line being reopened.

"This is a sad morning indeed," said Mr. Rostron. "We are stabling all the trains under cover with their doors locked. They will be divided between Dingle and Seaforth, and will be ready for driving off to the workshops for overhauling and rebuilding if some way of continuing the line can be found.

"We shall keep a small staff of watchmen and caretakers to take care of the structure and buildings, and nothing at all will be done that might hamper the rebirth of the Overhead."

### STAFF THANKED

This morning Mr. Rostron issued a special message of...

*December 31, 1956*

## NEW JOBS

More than 100 of the Overhead staff started work to-day with British Railways. Drivers became porters, and signalmen of long experience began to wash down carriages — with reductions in their weekly wage packets of up to £4 a week.

Driver William Lavin—he became a porter this morning at Mossley Hill—told me: "You can't pick and choose when you are 62 and have been in the same job for 42 years. I shall be about £3 10s a week worse off. Yet we can't really complain, because it would be unfair to British Railways' own men if chaps from the Overhead went in above their heads.

"They'll tell you that we are getting compensation for our lost jobs, but don't forget we've paid for the compensation. We paid pension contributions, and in 1932, when the Overhead was having a bad time, the staff volunteered to take wage reductions of up to 16 per cent."

There were flowers, handbells and the crashing of detonators

*December 31, 1956*

## QUIET HALT FOR OVERHEAD RAILWAY

### Last Trains On Sunday

### NORMAL SERVICE

Liverpool's Overhead Railway will stop work quietly on Sunday. The last trains will run at 10.3 p.m. —one from Dingle and one from Seaforth Sands as is usual on Sundays.

No special arrangements to see them off have been made, and there are no large scale bookings.

"We are having enough work to keep a normal service running," Mr. H. M. Rostron, general manager of the Overhead said to-day.

"Our staff have been drifting away gradually in the last few months. Our heavy gang is only half its proper strength."

Total staff now is 220 compared with about 250 a year ago.

Bookings this week have been down on previous weeks, although the railway is still carrying a fair amount of traffic. Whether there will be large-scale booking by people wanting to make a last

*December 28, 1956*

## One year later...

THOUSANDS turned up at the Pier Head to say their goodbyes as Liverpool's last tram set off on its final journey on September 14, 1957.

The number 239 tram, built by Liverpool Corporation Transport in 1939, was boarded by the Lord Mayor and Lady Mayoress. This journey heralded the end of Liverpool's tram service that had begun in 1861.

In 1945 Liverpool City Council decided to stop the running of the trams, as damage from World War II had taken its toll on the service and buses began to be a more favoured form of transport.

By 1948 the transition from trams to buses was under way, and it was complete less than a decade later.

*Left: The Echo carried reports of the last tram's final run in the September 16, 1957 edition*

*Below: Liverpool's last tram now resides at the Seashore Trolley Museum in Maine, USA*

Last Tram Was The Most Photographed

It was the most photographed tram in the history of Liverpool transport undertaking. Crowds of amateur photographers were among the thousands who turned out on Saturday to say good-bye to the very last tram of all—seen here at the Pierhead before it started on its journey.

Barbican Plan —£17,000,000 Residential Area

Driver and conductor of the last tram were Mr. T. Webster, who has 38 years... Rodden, 29 years service...

1897 LIVERPOOL'S LAST TRAM 1957

# 1960

# Busy city department store goes up in flames

ELEVEN people died when a blaze destroyed luxury Liverpool department store Henderson's on a bright sunny afternoon on June 22, 1960.

In 100 minutes, the fire, which was started by an electrical fault in the restaurant kitchens, ravaged the £1m store on the corner of Church Street and Whitechapel. Henderson's, which employed 500 people, was packed with customers as it was one of the few big stores to open on Wednesday afternoons. The alarm was raised at 2.23pm and the flames spread through the store with terrifying speed.

Four customers, three of whom were old friends meeting for lunch, five staff and two contractors lost their lives in the fire, described as the worst in Liverpool since the Blitz, and which closed Church Street for three weeks.

Two of the victims, contractor Colin Murphy, 21, and maintenance manager William Terry, 45, died heroes as they tried to control the fire and help others to escape.

*Anticlockwise from top right: Firefighters battle the blaze; The plume of black smoke rises over Liverpool; and The Echo reports the casualties on June 23, 1960*

# HENDERSON'S STORE ABLAZE

## Oil Threat As Fire Havoc Menaces City Centre

### MAN FALLS FROM TOP FLOOR: GIRLS ARE RESCUED

### One Of Staff Is Reported Missing

A member of the staff who stayed in the building to fight the blaze with extinguishers was reported missing when fire had seriously damaged William Henderson's store in Church Street, Liverpool, this afternoon.

The missing man is maintenance manager Mr. Ron Terry, who had not been seen since the fire was discovered. The administration building was searched but Mr. Terry was missing. He was last seen trying to fight the blaze.

Another man who was injured when he plunged from the top storey shortly after the fire started at 2.30 died later in hospital.

The man who died was later identified as Colin Murphy, aged 34, of 18 Turrett Road, Wallasey.

Seven other people were injured—two seriously—and are detained in the Royal Infirmary and Northern Hospital.

Four people—two men and two girls—were rescued from the top of the building by firemen using turn-table ladders.

At the height of the blaze flames spread to the Tatler Cinema in Church Street and Smith's Piano Store in Williamson Street. These were quickly extinguished.

#### New Shop Threat

Flames threatened the new premises of Timothy White's at the corner of White-hape. The opening of ... to-morrow, has been postponed ...

All ...

### SIX KILLED, FOUR HURT IN R.O.F. EXPLOSION

Six men were killed and four injured—one seriously—when an explosion wrecked an underground section of a Royal Ordnance Factory at Bishopton (Renfrewshire), this morning.

The explosion, which occurred in the nitro-glycerine department, demolished three buildings, caused extensive damage to other factory buildings and some damage to private property outside the factory.

The explosion shook an area 10 to 20 miles around the factory, and a huge mushroom cloud of orange-coloured smoke—like an H-bomb explosion—rose high into the air immediately after the blast.

Houses shook violently and workers inside the factory were thrown from their benches. Some sitting outside were blown from a wall.

Fire brigades from Paisley, ... smoking when we arrived. We ... Johnstone, Renfrew and Port had to rool them off." ... Glasgow rushed to the scene. Last Sunday a ... while an emergency call was ... seriously injured when fire ... sent out to Paisley Royal Alex- broke out in the incendiary ... andra Infirmary where surgeons bomb breakdown plant of the ... and nurses stood by to await the explosion factory. ... the arrival of the injured. Since 1952 six men have been ... The factory is on an isolated killed in explosions at the ... site about a mile from Bishop- factory. ... ton Village which is on the ... main coast road from Glasgow ... to Greenock. ... The gates were ...

# SIXTY PER CENT CAN BE RESTORED

## Statement On Hendersons After Complete Inspection

### MR. HUGH FRASER CONFERS WITH C.I.D. CHIEFS

### AINTREE WOMAN NAMED AS ELEVENTH VICTIM

After a complete inspection to-day of Henderson's store, following yesterday's disastrous fire, in which eleven people died, Mr. G. L. Goulden, the Liverpool building surveyor, and Mr. J. W. Beaumont, architect of the new building, said that they considered 60 per cent of the building, mainly the new premises, can be restored.

"The whole of the front, however, which faces on to Church Street and part of the way down Williamson Street, will have to be demolished."

Mr. Goulden said that a heavy crane had already been ordered, and it will be used to take the heavy stonework down from the old part of the premises in Church Street.

Mr. Hugh Fraser, head of the House of Fraser, which controls Henderson's, was in the city for conferences to-day.

He spoke to members of the staff in the canteen opposite the burnt-out building, and also saw C.I.D. officials investigating the cause of the disaster.

Detectives led by Superintendent Harold Welsh began questioning scores of girls who had been working near where the fire began. Superintendent Welsh said: "It's a slow job and may take a few days before we know the real cause of the disaster. We are also having talks with the general manager and Mr. Fraser."

Early this afternoon Mr. Fraser left the company's offices in Williamson Street and with Mr. J. H. Spence, a loss adjuster, made a tour of inspection of the burned-out premises.

The Echo was informed this afternoon that Mr. H. M. ...

*Above: The drama unfolds on June 22*

*Left: Hopes of restoration on June 23, after the flames are put out*

*Onlookers gather round to watch fire crews at work under the skeleton of the collapsed balcony at Henderson's*

## This was the year that...

- Harold Macmillan was British Prime Minister
- Boxing hero Cassius Clay, later Muhammad Ali, won a gold medal in the Rome Olympics
- Lonnie Donegan reached number one in the UK singles chart with My Old Man's A Dustman
- Alfred Hitchcock's Psycho was released at the cinema

# 1957: Liverpool's 750th birthday

Left: A crest is mounted on the Daily Post and Echo building in Victoria Street to mark Liverpool's 750th charter celebrations

Right: Youngsters enjoy cake as Walker Street celebrates

Below: Musicians perform Haydn's Toy Symphony at the charter year's final Prom concert at Liverpool Stadium

Bottom: The 1st Battalion of the Liverpool Scottish (T.A.) parade on Lime Street

Above: A large congregation streams out of the Great West Door of Liverpool Cathedral into the brilliant evening sunshine following the festival service on June 17, 1957 which marked the opening of the city's celebrations

Right: The Lord Mayor of Liverpool, Alderman Frank H Cain, acknowledges a salute as he and the Lady Mayoress arrive at the Town Hall

Below: The charter dinner at the Town Hall, when the Lord Mayor entertained more than 100 guests from the worlds of arts, religion, commerce and industry

# World mourns as president is shot dead

PRESIDENT John Fitzgerald Kennedy was assassinated as he travelled in a presidential motorcade in Dallas on Friday November 22, 1963.

Kennedy was shot twice while travelling with wife Jackie through Dealey Plaza in his campaign for re-election.

Ex-Marine Lee Harvey Oswald was charged with the shooting from a window of the Texas School Book Depository with a 6.5 x 52mm Italian Mannlicher-Carcano rifle.

Oswald was then murdered in front of reporters and TV cameras by Jack Rubinstein, a 52-year-old Dallas nightclub owner, who broke through a strong police guard to shoot Oswald with a revolver.

Prince Philip and Prime Minister Sir Alec Douglas-Home and his wife flew to America for the Washington memorial service and a service was held on November 28, 1963 at Liverpool Cathedral.

## KENNEDY: CHARGED W

### Arrest After Struggle

**CASE WILL GO TO GRAND JURY NEXT WEEK**

A charge of assassinating President Kennedy with a rifle was laid at midnight— 6 a.m. British time—in Dallas, Texas, against Lee Harvey Oswald, 24-years-old ex-Marine and suspected Communist sympath...

---

THE LIVERPOOL ECHO AND EVENING E

## ASSASSIN'S BULLET HAS

### No man ever faced a bigger challenge

When, in January 1961, John Fitzgerald Kennedy, at the early but mature age of 43, became President of the United States, it was a moment in world politics the importance of which was not—could not be— fully appreciated.

Even now, when he is dead, we cannot truly assess the significance of his brief tenure in the highest office

...mous family wealth, a lovely wife, a dynastic family. There was too much Hollywood about the whole set-up.

Every statesman needs a modicum of charm, but young Kennedy surely had a little too much if only he had had more experience.

How very wrong we were, again. We argued: How will he cope with the Pentagon brasshats who, we had heard, had taken unto themselves so much power in the latter days of the Eisenhower regime?

How could he find time for international chess when he has to work so hard to restore confidence and morale among the home checker team?

**KENNEDY SPIRIT**

We did not realise, then, that the Kennedy mind, the Kennedy stamina, the Kennedy spirit could find time for everything—just as in his day, Churchill beat the clock hour after hour, day after day, year after year.

We did not for a moment suppose that he would so quickly back us up with such surprising force his election-time dictum: "The President cannot share his power. He alone is the chief of state."

He himself said, at the outset, that he was in for 'the hell of a revolutionary time' as president—and we thought that that was just talk.

**REVOLUTION**

But revolution there certainly was—and in many ways it was a one-man revolution. John Kennedy was wise enough to listen to his advisers—to the economists and liberal thinkers rather than to the...

**Bigger Load For Premier**

**Added Importance**

President and Mrs. Kennedy with their daughter Caroline

*November 23, 1963*

*Left: The scene on the fateful day Kennedy was shot*

*November 23, 1963*

*John F Kennedy with wife Jackie*

# RMER MARINE
# H MURDER
## Police In A Cinema

**STOP PRESS**

### PREMIER AND PRINCE FLYING TO AMERICA

Prince Philip, Prime Minister and Lady Douglas-Home flying to America for the memorial service for President Kennedy in Washington on Monday. Travelling by BOAC charter aircraft, they leave London Airport at 5 p.m. to-morrow.

### BODY OF PRESIDENT AT WHITE HOUSE
### Lying In Repose

A guard of honour watched over President Kennedy's flag-draped coffin when it was taken in a blue naval ambulance to the White House to-day to lie in repose in the East Room from 10 a.m. (3 p.m. G.M.T.) until 6 p.m. (11 p.m. G.M.T.) Troops of the three Armed

**RACING**

# T HISTORY SHORT

## BRITAIN MOURNS THE PRESIDENT'S DEATH

*November 25, 1963*

# WORLD'S LAST TRIBUTE TO KENNEDY
## Sixty Countries Pay Homage At Funeral Of Murdered President

**STOP PRESS**

THE LIVERPOOL ECHO AND EVENING EXPRESS, MONDAY, NOVEMBER 25, 1963

## Kennedy Bullet Map Was Found In Oswald's Room, Says Dallas Report

### FRIENDS ASK FOR JACK RUBY TO BE GIVEN BAIL

### F.B.I. Launch Full-Scale Probe Into Shooting

### PRESIDENT'S REQUEST

The Dallas Morning News said to-day that officers who searched Lee Harvey Oswald's room found a map, with a line marking the path of the bullet which killed President Kennedy.

The newspaper quoted a reliable source as saying that Oswald had placed three or four marks at major intersections on the motorcade route.

"There was also a line from the Texas school - book depository building to Elm Street—the trajectory for the bullets which struck the President and Governor Connally."

The paper said that police

### City Lights Off For Mourning

As a mark of respect on this day of mourning for President Kennedy, the Liverpool Christmas Lights Committee have arranged that the festive lights in Bold Street, Church Street, and

believed that Oswald had marked the other intersections while considering spots from which a sniper could get a good shot.

**BIZARRE**

F.B.I. agents to-day launched an investigation into the bizarre murder of Oswald as friend's of Oswald's killer pressed for his release on bail.

Lawyers for 52-years-old Dallas night club owner Jack Ruby announced they would seek a writ of habeas corpus to end his detention in the same maximum security cell as his victim, on a charge of murdering Oswald.

The corpulent Ruby, whose real name is Rubinstein, broke through a strong police guard yesterday and shot the 24-years-old ex-Marine with a revolver before reporters and a battery of TV cameras in the basement of Dallas police HQ.

The F.B.I. intervened at the direct request of President Lyndon Johnson as a wave of criticism built up against Dallas police and an air of unreality developed the oil and cattle city.

**"ABOUT JACKIE"**

Mrs. Eva Grant, 53-year-old sister of Jack Ruby, said Dallas

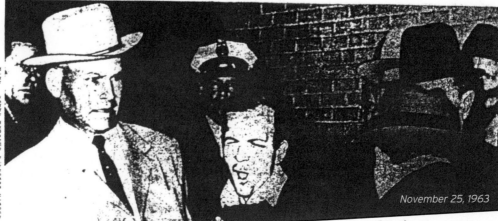
*November 25, 1963*

**LAWYERS HAVE A BRIEF FOR**

**Britax**
**TEXTLENE**
**safety belts**
Keep your seat and save your life

# Liverpool Echo
*Evening Express*

NO. 26,115

TUESDAY, NOVEMBER 26, 1963

**CARPETS! CARPETS! CARPETS!**
TOP QUALITY ★ CUT PRICES ★ GREEN SHIELD STAMPS

**SHAWS** CARPET WAREHOUSE

# GUNMAN SEEN ON WASHINGTON ROOF

*November 26, 1963*

# Hundreds of fans flock to see Fab Four

BEATLEMANIA swept Liverpool once again on July 11, as the Fab Four returned to the city for the charity premiere of their film A Hard Day's Night at the Odeon.

The sell-out premiere was accompanied by the Beatles' plans to arrive at Liverpool Airport and then make their way to the Town Hall for a special appearance on the balcony.

Hundreds of fans flocked to both locations just to get a glimpse of their idols, with many camping on the Town Hall steps hours before, to be guaranteed the best spots behind the crash barriers.

The four superstars were at the height of their fame and popularity at this time, with companies all around the city being desperate to associate their products and services with the band that could provoke such a huge reaction from their fans.

*Left: Advertisers jumped at the chance to promote their services*

*Right: Cuttings show the excitement of the day*

*Below: The Fab Four on the set of A Hard Day's Night*

**BEATLES' FILM IS A BOX-OFFICE SELL-OUT**

**Fans Line-Up Early At Town Hall And Airport**

The charity premiere to-night of The Beatles' film "A Hard Day's Night" is a sell-out.

A spokesman at the Odeon Cinema said this morning that the box office had been inundated with last minute requests for tickets.

"All the seats were sold early yesterday and we have just had to turn people away," he said.

Charities benefiting from the premiere are the Liverpool Boys' Association, who will get 75 per cent of the takings, and the Gordonstoun Scholarship Foundation which will receive the remaining quarter.

**SAFETY MEASURES**

Just across the road from the Town Hall this morning workmen were erecting hardboard sheets over the windows of Martins Bank building at the corner of Water Street.

The idea is to keep the crowd from standing on the window ledges, said Mr ... the joiner who was fixing the sheets. "You see they might topple backwards and fall right through the windows."

service this morning, and taking into account extra accommodation required as a result of the London Airport strike to-day. British Eagle announced that the Beatles would be travelling in a Britannia.

The first-class compartment—16 seats—will accommodate the Beatles' party. Flight take-off was to be at 4.15 p.m., with touchdown at Liverpool, as planned. The Britannia will carry about 100 passengers, and after calling at Liverpool, will continue to Glasgow.

**60 Fans At The Airport**

By lunchtime only 60 young Beatle fans—nearly all of them schoolgirls—had gathered at Liverpool Airport to wait for the group's arrival.

Extra police were on duty but they had little work to do as the fans basked in the sunshine on the upper balcony of the terminal buildings. Many of the girls said they had played truant from school in order to get a good spot on the balcony.

**TEA RELAYS**

One of the first teenagers to arrive at the Town Hall was 15 - years - old Hazel Kellett, of 108 Moss Lane, Litherland. She was taking no chances with the weather and was well wrapped in a duffle coat, slacks, and sweater.

"I have lots of sandwiches for my dinner and my friends and I will be going to the Pier Head for cups of tea in relays," Hazel said.

"We have a fourteen-foot long banner with "Welcome home lads" painted on it. We did want to put it up on the balcony of the Town Hall, but they wouldn't let us," said Hazel.

## Liverpool Echo
### BEATLES 8-PAGE SOUVENIR

## Liverpool, Here We Come!

# Liverpool Echo
*and Evening Express*

NO. 36,307     FRIDAY, JULY 10, 1964    3d

**BLACKLERS**
**MEN'S CASUAL SHIRTS**
Men's cotton knit, Casual Shirts; attractive colours;
Long or short sleeves; some slight subs **12/11**

**HARFORDS** THE CLOTH SPECIALISTS

# YOUNGSTERS BOOK BEATLE SPOTS
## Nine-Hour Wait Begins On The Steps Of Liverpool Town Hall

### FANS GATHER FOR BIG AIRPORT WELCOME
*By Echo Reporters*

Nine hours before the Beatles were due to make their triumphant appearance on the balcony of Liverpool Town Hall to-night, scores of teenagers were camping on the steps of the building.

Early arrivals were guaranteed the best places behind the crush barriers when John, Paul, George and Ringo arrive.

Police told them that eventually they would have to move from the Town Hall steps, but good vantage points would be provided for them.

Organisers of the Northern charity premiere of the Beatles' film, " A Hard Day's Night," at the Odeon to-day, revealed that more than £6,000 had already been raised by the sale of tickets and advertising space in the souvenir programme.

By three o'clock this afternoon about 300 fans had arrived at the airport and were lining the outside balcony.

#### CANADIANS IN CROWD
By 3.45 p.m. the crowd outside the Liverpool Town Hall had grown to about 200 strong. Police were keeping the crowds confined to the crush barrier area on either side of Castle Street, and

### Beatles H.Q. Raided
West End detectives were investigating to-day a night raid on the offices of Beatles manager Brian Epstein, in Sutherland House, Argyle Street, Mayfair.

aged 22, both of Victoria, British Columbia. Said Joan " We are hitchhiking through the British Isles and are making our way down to Dover to-morrow, but we thought we had better stop off in Liverpool to see the Beatles..."

*Beatle fans lined up outside Liverpool Town Hall this afternoon ready for their arrival from the Airport.*

*Wilfrid Brambell signing autographs on arrival at Lime Street Station this afternoon.*

### Queues For Autographs
"Beatles' Special"
### Beat The Clock

### De Courcy Must Pay £4,750
#### Towards Costs Of His Appeal

### Scoutmaster Is Gaoled
#### Assaulted Boy After Threat

### POSTMEN WALK OUT TO ATTEND RALLY
#### 5,000 Go On 1-Day Strike
#### PAY DISPUTE

### They Were On The Spot
#### Off-Duty Firemen Fight Blaze

### GREAT THIRD-ROUND RECOVERY GIVES LEMA BIG LEAD IN OPEN
Nicklaus Equals Record, But Is Still 7 Strokes Behind
### LEADER RETURNS 68

### STOP PRESS

### PAY DEMAND REJECTED

### FORTH BRIDGE TRAGEDY

*Above, top: Beatles fans cheer their heroes as they return to Liverpool for the premiere*

*Above: Echo reporters joined the front line at the airport*

*Right: John, Ringo, Paul and George on the balcony of Liverpool Town Hall with the Alderman Louis Caplan and Lady Mayoress Fanny Bodeker*

# A small step for man, big news for the Echo

MANKIND'S first historic landing on the moon was eagerly followed by millions across the world as Neil Armstrong and Edwin 'Buzz' Aldrin took their first tentative steps out of the Eagle lunar module.

The Apollo 11 landing on July 21, 1969 saw Commander Armstrong utter the now legendary words, "That is one small step for man, one giant leap for mankind" as he stepped out onto the moon's surface.

The pair walked around for two hours before planting the American flag and unveiling a plaque. The return to Earth marked another dangerous and epic chapter in their adventure before the team landed safely in the Pacific, near Hawaii.

## THE ECHO SAYS..

Columbus set out for the New World, when men scaled Everest and plumbed the depths of the oceans. They were there when Edison recorded sound, when Faraday's inventions heralded the era of electricity, and when the pioneers of flight, radio and television gradually changed everyday life for millions.

None of these men as they pondered and acted could have predicted how their single-mindedness, their sense of adventure and inventive curiosity would affect the future.

So it is with the three men who today challenge the perils of the universe.

Where will their historic mission lead? What will it mean? None can say for sure.

All that is certain is that another momentous step has been taken. Human endeavour and scientific skill have achieved a voyage beyond our dreams of only years ago.

Problems, a multitude of problems— social, political and moral — still need solution on earth. Yet man has always reached for the stars.

Let us remember this day and salute the three men — Armstrong, Aldrin and Collins — who so deserve their place in history.

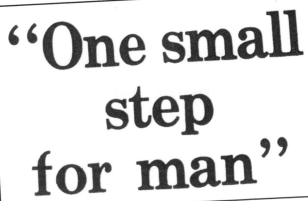

## "One small step for man"

*Clockwise from left: Astronaut Buzz Aldrin on the moon; The Echo comment on the moon landing; The news has a big impact on the front page; Apollo 11 blasts off; and a TV schedule for the space mission*

# Liverpool Echo

*LAST CITY*

IT PAYS T
ADVERTI
SEE PAGE

MONDAY, JULY 21, 1969  5d

## ...LUTE TO A ...W WORLD

## Now moon men face blast-off peril

**America's two men on the moon faced another crisis point in their epic adventure this evening.**

Their task: to blast their landing module Eagle off the lunar surface for a reunion with their mother spaceship orbiting miles above them.

As the countdown began the world was still buzzing over the televised exploits of Neil Armstrong and Edwin "Buzz" Aldrin.

Earlier, Armstrong and Aldrin had settled down to sleep after their epic walk on the moon.

At 1855 B.S.T. if the flight plan is adhered to — Armstrong and Aldrin will fire their ascent engine to lift off from the moon's surface and dock with Columbia.

Then, at 0557 B.S.T to-morrow, all being well, they will fire the main engine to start their journey back to earth.

Eagle landed on the moon at 2117 B.S.T. yesterday, 102 hours, 45 minutes and 40 seconds after blast-off from Cape Kennedy on Wednesday.

### 'Eagle has landed'

After Eagle pilot Aldrin had delicately manoeuvred the space craft by manual control past craters into a level spot on the moon, Apollo 11 commander Armstrong became the first man to speak...

*lunar module listening to the words of President Nixon. Between them they planted on the moon's surface.*

## Apollo at a glance

**B.B.C.-1:**
5.50, 6.20,
8.0, 8.50,
10.25.

**B.B.C.-2:**
7.0, 10.50.

**ITV:** 5.50,
6.30, 10.0.

---

RUSSIAN Earth satellite Sputnik was seen on its launch on October 4, 1957, as the first step to the moon.

The 180lb sphere was the first in a series of satellites, which first passed 560 miles over Britain on Monday October 7 at 7.07am.

The Echo followed its progress as it made flights round the Earth every 95 minutes.

Critics at first thought that the satellite would re-enter the Earth's atmosphere and burn up but the theory was soon proved unfounded.

A Russian astronomer said that the next step from the orbiting satellite was to fly a rocket around the moon and, although they did put the first man into space, American astronauts pipped them to the post and were the first men to walk on the moon 12 years later.

*October 8, 1957*

## B.B.C. PICK UP SIGNALS AGAIN AFTER SILENCE

### Satellite's Morning Orbits Go Unheard By Engineers

## POOR RADIO CONDITIONS

After being unable to hear any signals from the Russian satellite on several of its orbits this morning, B.B.C. engineers at Tatsfield picked up the "bleep" again at 11...

Radio conditions were poor this morning and account for the... pick up earlier sign...

Earlier, an engineer... The last definite... picked up was at 7... heard it every time...

At 8.47 a.m. the... weak signal. We a... was from the satel... was the time it... heard. There wer... 10.15 a.m. or 11.4...

The Italian ra... Monza said to... reception of si... artificial moon b... during the nigh... 03.20 G.M.T. to-...

Technicians... some irregula... ...me about 22 (...

...the signals became more frequent—from 23 every ten seconds they increased to 30 and even 40.

The technicians thought the "silence" was due to exhaus... ...battery on the radio... ...changes.

## Satellite Is Still Going Strong

### It Will Be Over Liverpool At 10-50 To-night

RUSSIA'S earth-circling satellite, which Moscow Radio says will be over Liverpool at 10.50 to-night—and over Melbourne, Australia, 42 minutes later—"called" over Britain just after 5.30 a.m. to-day.

It was scheduled to be over London at 5.32, and scientists taking its pulse beats reported it to be dead on time—as usual.

At the Cambridge University Mullard Radio Astronomy Field Station it was reported to be "still going strongly, and emitting signals at about the usual strength."

### SIX TIMES IN NIGHT

Scientists at Cambridge, who recorded the satellite six times during the night, have defined its orbit—going down to about...

...tory, said: "It was a completely clear sky in Edinburgh, yet we failed to see either the rocket or the satellite. We did expect to see the rocket. It means that either we missed it, which is a possibility, or its trajectory has changed.

When the satellite passed over the radio astronomy station at Jodrell Bank, Cheshire, last night, B.B.C. television viewers saw a very jagged line on a piece of graph paper as an indication of the signals. One of the scientists said the satellite was rotating slowly— a few times a minute.

### ROCKET ROUND MOON

In Moscow, a Soviet astronomer writing in *Pravda* said that man-made satellites...

*October 11, 1957*

# 1971

# D Day as new pennies drop

DECIMAL currency was introduced on February 15, 1971, a day that became known as 'D Day'.

This change of money system meant that the old £sd was being swapped for the new £p.

While pounds remained the same, 'coppers' including the new one penny, the new two penny and the new halfpenny were brought in, as well as the silver five pence, ten pence and 50 pence coins.

The changeover became a confusing time for people as the full transition took weeks beyond D Day.

Banks closed for five days before so that they could stock up on new coins, while after the day, shops needed time to adjust their cash registers. This resulted in some shops using new currency, while others still used old.

Public transport also encountered difficulties during the change. February was seen as the most convenient month for this change as it was the slackest financial time of year.

*January 15, 1971*

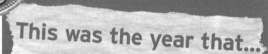

## This was the year that...

- The first students signed up to the Open University

- Apollo 14 landed on the moon

- Filming began on The Godfather

- Charles Manson was imprisoned for conspiracy to commit murder

- 500,000 people in Washington DC and 125,000 in San Francisco marched against the Vietnam War

- Norway began oil production in the North Sea

- Doors lead singer Jim Morrison was found dead in his Paris apartment

- Walt Disney World opened in Florida

- A bomb exploded at the top of the Post Office Tower in London

February 10, 1971

10 The Liverpool Echo, Wednesday, February 10, 1971

● Britain goes decimal on Monday—and to-day Page 10 presents a detailed look at how decimalisation will affect Merseyside. Don't forget that the banks close to-night until Monday to prepare for the big change-over, and British Railways will be going decimal on Sunday. The Post Office have issued their plans for decimalisation, and our reporters have also been taking a look at how the big switch will affect schools, motorists, telephones, buses, etc.

## It's D-Day plus six for the buses

The Merseyside Passenger Transport Executive, in common with the rest of the bus industry, will not be going decimal until Sunday, February 21—six days after D-Day.

This is because they wish to avoid the difficulties which are likely to arise from the limited numbers of the new bronze decimal coins which will be in circulation.

Conductors will, of course, accept the new decimal currency during this first week, but change will be given in old coinage. After February 21, both currencies can be used, but change will be given in decimal currency.

The M.P.T.E. started training their staff six weeks ago and by D-Day every one of over 2,500 conductors and driver-operators in Liverpool and on the Wirral will have received at least four hours decimal training.

M.P.T.E. joint decimalisation officer, Mr. Harold Crick, said: "We want to ensure that a good relationship exists between contractors and the public and we are trying to anticipate the problems which are likely to arise so that our staff can handle them efficiently with the least delay to passengers."

Fares will be rounded to the nearest decimal equivalent.

Crosville and Ribble also say that between February 15 and 21, they will be accepting either type of coins and calculating their fares in old pence. From then on they will continue accepting all coins, but for decimal fares.

Both companies have prepared posters, charts and stickers giving fare conversions, details and hints.

Both also have their ticket machines ready for conversion.

| | | 1 | 2 | 3 | 4 | 5 | 6 | 7 | 8 | 9 | 10 | 11 |
|---|---|---|---|---|---|---|---|---|---|---|---|---|
| | 0 | ½ | 1 | 1 | 1½ | 2 | 2½ | 3 | 3½ | 4 | 4 | 4½ |
| 1/- | 5 | 5½ | 6 | 6 | 6½ | 7 | 7½ | 8 | 8½ | 9 | 9 | 9½ |
| 2/- | 10 | 10½ | 11 | 11 | 11½ | 12 | 12½ | 13 | 13½ | 14 | 14 | 14½ |
| 3/- | 15 | 15½ | 16 | 16 | 16½ | 17 | 17½ | 18 | 18½ | 19 | 19 | 19½ |
| 4/- | 20 | 20½ | 21 | 21 | 21½ | 22 | 22½ | 23 | 23½ | 24 | 24 | 24½ |
| 5/- | 25 | 25½ | 26 | 26 | 26½ | 27 | 27½ | 28 | 28½ | 29 | 29 | 29½ |
| 6/- | 30 | 30½ | 31 | 31 | 31½ | 32 | 32½ | 33 | 33½ | 34 | 34 | 34½ |
| 7/- | 35 | 35½ | 36 | 36 | 36½ | 37 | 37½ | 38 | 38½ | 39 | 39 | 39½ |
| 8/- | 40 | 40½ | 41 | 41 | 41½ | 42 | 42½ | 43 | 43½ | 44 | 44 | 44½ |
| 9/- | 45 | 45½ | 46 | 46 | 46½ | 47 | 47½ | 48 | 48½ | 49 | 49 | 49½ |

● Your quick-check guide to decimal shopping. Remember, 10s equals 50p.

# Stores smooth the way to decimal shopping

**Trouble-free shopping is guaranteed at Liverpool's major city stores after Decimalisation Day—thanks to the homework put in by store personnel.**

Focus on
D-Day

FEBRUARY 15

By Eileen Senior and Keith Ely

Without exception all the major stores will be using decimal currency system as soon as D-day arrives.

But up to closing time on Saturday, February 13, all cash transactions will be in £ s d.

After D-day customers offering the old currency will be given change in new pence, and every day the old coins will be returned to the banks.

To ensure a smooth transition, stores like Lewis's, Owen Owen, T. J. Hughes and George Henry Lee will have skeleton staffs working over the week-end to alter price tickets.

### Tear-off

Hendersons are using dual £ s d/decimal price tags, and after closing time on February 13, it will just be a case of tearing off the old price.

Blacklers will gradually change their price tickets during the first week of decimalisation.

Said Miss Nora L. Arthurson, chairman of the Liverpool Stores' Committee: "The public will find the staff are thoroughly trained and able to help them.

"They have been trained, not only to deal with the new currency, but to be patient and helpful to the public.

### Courses

"Every staff member of the large stores from the chairmen downwards has been trained.

"Most attended courses some time ago and have recently been on refreshers.

"Conversion tables will be on display in all stores."

Problem-free shopping is also assured at W. H. Smith's shops after decimalisation . . . that is the promise issued in the million copies of which have been distributed to all customers in W.H.S. shops.

The promise is backed by the intensive training programme which has been given to their staff during the past year.

### Birkenhead sets lead

Birkenhead Technical College was the first in the North-West to provide courses in decimalisation. It has become one of the country's leading centres and has had inquiries from as far away as John O' Groats.

The college is the regional decimalisation training centre for the Hotel and Catering Industry Training Board and has been used as a training centre by many commercial giants.

It has been responsible for training 150 "trainers" who in turn have instructed hundreds of people.

In recent months there has been a great demand from smaller tradesmen and about 400 have completed courses there.

### Housewives go to school

Bootle housewives are so keen to learn about decimalisation that an extra course has had to be laid on for them at Bootle College of Further Education.

The housewives' course had been arranged for Thursday evenings from 7 p.m. to 9 p.m. But it proved so popular that the class became full, and another course has been provided.

This started on Wednesday, February 3 and will continue on February 10 and 17 at 1.30 p.m.

## Post Office advise . . .

# Go early for your pensions

**Although the strike has caused a set-back to its decimalisation plans, the Post Office will go decimal on Monday, which is also the day when higher postal tariffs, announced last September, come into operation.**

D-Day was chosen for the tariff increase following the findings of the Post Office Users National Council, which made its views known to the Government.

The Council is the public's own "watchdog" on the Post Office, and it felt it would be better for the increase charges to come into operation on D-Day.

Second class mail will cost 2½ NEW PENCE (6d) and first class mail, 3 new pence—just over 7d.

"The increases are nothing to do with decimalisation, but are merely being introduced on D-Day on the advice of the public's own organisation on post spokesman for the North Western region of the Post Office.

● Sub-post Offices will close on Friday from 1 p.m. and will not re-open until Monday, February 15. Customers normally drawing pensions and allowances on Friday or Saturday should do so before then to avoid last-minute pressure.

● "When another business is run in conjunction with a sub-post office, as they so often are, it may well be that this will be open, but the post office side of the shop will certainly close," said the spokesman.

● Main post offices in the North West were due to close at the same time, but because of the strike these offices, staffed by volunteers provided by the postmen's union, will again be open on Friday for pensions and allowances, providing volunteers come forward.

● When the strike is over it will take some time to go decimal, and main post offices will not be open for two or three days so that stocks can be changed over. Further announcements by the Post Office about the closure of these main offices will be made when the position becomes clear.

Sub-post offices will not be affected; they will have already gone decimal.

Leaflets explaining decimalisation in the Post Office and the new charges are available from sub-post offices and any main post office which is open normally.

To make it easier for customers, the Post Office has mounted what is probably its most concentrated point-of-sale campaign.

### Some tips to help with those sums

The Decimal Currency Board say you should "think decimal," and that way you don't have to put up with the mental contortions of conversion.

But, no matter how often you are told that decimals simple matter, you can't help worrying when the shopkeeper says something like: "That'll be 73 new pence, less your discount of 2½ new pence."

There are a couple of tips worth bearing in mind to help you solve those tricky conversions.

A simple way to convert new pence to the approximate old pence value, goes like this:

Say, for instance, you see an item priced 23p, double the figure, making 46. Think of this as shillings and pence and you have the approximate answer—4s 6d. Your answers will always be within 2d of the exact figure.

To convert shillings and pence to their approximate decimal equivalent this is what you do:

If the pence part of the price is between 3d and 9d (inclusive) deduct one penny. So, 8s 5d would become 8s 4d. Drop the "s" and "d", which give you 84. Divide by two, which gives you 42, which is how many new pence there are in 8s 5d.

If the pence amount is 11d or 10d, you have to deduct 2d. And if it is 0d, 1d or 2d you do not deduct anything.

### Boost for UVO fund

**Decimalisation is going to give an unexpected boost to the finances of the United Voluntary Organisation which helps to support 44 member charities on Merseyside**

**Until now most people have been donating a penny a week but many have agreed to give three new pence or even five new pence out of the wages once decimalisation starts.**

### All part of the service

Some of Liverpool's old folk are learning about the new decimal currency over a cup of tea and a meal.

When the city's Women's Royal Voluntary Service members call on old folk with meals on wheels they are telling pensioners about the change-over and showing them the new coins.

## How it will affect Corporation charges

All Liverpool Corporation's charges will be rounded to the nearest new halfpenny as advised by the Decimal Currency Board, says Mr. D. Robinson, the Corporation's Decimal Conversion Officer.

This means that the number of charges which go up fractionally will be counter-balanced by those which go down.

Conversion has been quite a lengthy process for the local authority.

Mr. Robinson has spent the past two years co-ordinating the activities of various Corporation departments as they prepare to go over to decimals.

Now, everything is ready for D-Day and the Corporation will be switching over immediately on February 15. However, payments in old sixpenny units will still be accepted.

### Weekly check

**Weekly price checks are to be made in shops throughout Britain both before and after D-Day by the Consumers' Association, to see what effect the change-over has on the housewife's grocery bill.**

## INFORMATION BOX

### BANKS

Banks and many building societies on Merseyside in keeping with those throughout the country, will be closed from to-night to prepare for D-Day.

An estimated 6,000,000 cheques will be presented to banks all over the country before they close, and special plans have been made to clear those before February 15.

In total, of course, they will remain closed for four days — including the week-end — before the decimal system comes into operation. When they open again all transactions will be carried out in decimal currency.

Booklets explaining the new system are available at all banks and building societies. All cheques dated before D-Day must be in £sd currency. But after that date the law requires all cheques and deposits to be written in £p.

A banking and accounting table should be used for conversions between the two currencies. This is a table which converts the old system into whole new penny amounts. It does not use the new halfpenny because these will be ignored in bank accounting. Amounts are rounded up and down to give a fair result. Your bank will convert the shillings and pence in your bank balance and standing orders according to this table.

### TRAINS

British Railways, who will be going decimal one day early—on Sunday February 14—will be distributing leaflets to passengers asking them to renew their weekly season ticket before D-Day.

"We are making this appeal to try and avoid longer queues at stations on the morning of D-Day—the day of the week when most of our customers normally renew their weekly tickets," said a B.R. spokesman.

The leaflets will also be available at stations to enable customers to check the decimal prices of rail tickets.

The change-over will make no difference to season ticket rates or to full fares for long-distance travel.

Short-distance fares may be subject to very slight "ups or downs," but the difference in value will never be more than just over the existing penny, and will usually be less.

To balance the increases and decreases, all even shilling prices ending in 6d will be rounded down, and all odd shilling prices ending in 6d will be rounded up—both to whole new pence.

Although all ticket office staff have undergone training for D Day, it was decided to go decimal a day earlier for a sort of rehearsal. Both currencies will be accepted, but the old currency in sixpenny-worth units only.

### MOTORISTS

Linked with the more complicated problems of metric conversion, decimalisation could present some tricky calculations for the motorist.

Fortunately metrication is not due to be fully implemented until 1975, giving the motorist a fair chance to master the decimal system beforehand.

But the two systems combined, do represent a complicated task ahead for drivers and petrol retailers. Most filling stations already have the new decimal scales on display.

It has not been possible to convert all petrol grade prices to exact decimal equivalents, and rour‑ ‑ up or down has bee Necessary—but only slightly because the petrol industry uses one-tenth of a new penny units, making actual increases or decreases of only around 0.67 per cent.

The R.A.C. have asked Mr. Anthony Barber, the Chancellor of the Exchequer, to ensure that efforts to "save the sixpence" will not be frustrated by restriction of supplies after Decimal Day.

An R.A.C. spokesman said statements by the Decimal Currency Board that the majority of sixpences "will be sent back to the Mint and melted down" indicated that the supply may become inadequate to meet public demand.

In a letter to Mr. Barber, R.A.C. chairman Mr. Wilfred Andrews said abolition of the sixpence would adversely affect motoring costs, particularly by causing increases in parking charges.

### INSURANCE OFFICES

It will be business as usual at Liverpool insurance offices for the rest of this week which will see the culmination of several years of preparation.

One leading group set up a decimal currency committee as far back as 1967 and staff have undergone thorough training.

Internal transactions will be carried out in decimal currency after Thursday morning. But old currency will be accepted after D-Day.

### HOSPITALS

On the evening before decimalisation is introduced, Mr. David Burrows, a member of the Oswestry Orthopaedic Hospital League of Friends, with 30 helpers, will go round the wards of the hospital changing all pennies and threepenny bits belonging to the patients, to decimal coins.

### TAXIS

**Decimalisation means new meters for Liverpool cab-drivers. And it is cor'ing some of them £100.**

**The 300 members of the Liverpool Taxi Owners' Association have started having new meters fitted and all should be ready for February 15.**

**But one meter company, who have allowed taxi-men to rent their meters, say they have to buy new ones at about £100 each.**

### SCHOOLS

Schools on Merseyside are taking decimalisation day in their stride.

For most of them, the count-down began two years ago, since when most of them have been slowly replacing their old books and equipment with up-to-date material.

Liverpool Education Department have made an allocation of 2s a head to help with the replacement of books and rulers, etc. Money has also been provided for changing equipment in workshops in secondary schools.

Courses have been arranged to help teachers prepare for the complete change-over.

Birkenhead Education Committee have made an allocation to schools to cover most of the cost of the change-over.

And at Bootle, schools are buying things as and when they need them within their limited capitation.

Lancashire County Council have provided Crosby Education Department with an extra allowance to cover conversion costs.

Said Wallasey's Director of Education: "Quite honestly, decimalisation does not provide any problems. Children and teachers have known it was coming for a long time.

"What has been more difficult has been the shortage of appropriate text books in some cases."

daffodil
tulip 2p
crocus 3p
snowdrop
huacint

Daily shopping trips to their Spring Garden shop are an adventure in decimalisation to infants at Fonthill Road School, Kirkdale.

They shop for their spring bulbs in decimal coins. And when their bulbs start to shoot, they measure their weekly growth with metric rulers.

Since they started school last autumn they have been learning to count money in decimal currency. And for all their measuring they use the metric system.

In fact they are probably much better acquainted with the decimal system than many adults!

Pictured are six-year-olds (left to right) Marie Nester, Kevin Carter, Mandy Yates, Sharon Matthews and Frank Hargreaves.

### PHONES

Telephone coin boxes are to be converted to take 2p and 10p within a few weeks of D-Day. But until this adaptation takes place, £sd charges will continue.

People with private phones will receive their bills in £p.

## How the Stock Exchange will make the switch

by Simon Proctor

Like the banks, the Stock Exchange will close its doors to-morrow and on Friday to allow stockbrokers time to change over to decimal currency.

You won't be able to buy and sell the shares of any United Kingdom companies during those two days — but you may be able to persuade your broker to deal in the shares of any overseas company.

Not that you'll win any prizes for popularity with your broker. But if the present slide in Australian shares induces you to pull out of Poseidon, then your broker is allowed to ring his correspondent in Australia and get rid of the shares for you. He can't, however, sell them to a U.K. jobber or broker.

The present account period ends to-day and dealings in £ s d cease.

When the settlement day for this account period arrives on February 23 — the day your broker sends you a cheque or a bill for the shares traded — you will find things expressed in new pence.

You can still buy and sell shares in U.K. companies to-day. But you will be doing so for the account period which starts on February 15, and that account will be in new pence.

Your brokers will be not too pleased if you do want to sell overseas shares during the two days the exchange is closed, mainly because his staff are going to be very busy.

Unlike the banks, stockbrokers don't have to concern themselves with carting about huge crates of the new money, but they do have their ledgers, accounts and machines to convert, just like any other business.

The Stock Exchange has tried to make the change-over go as smoothly as possible by sending out about 250,000 leaflets to member firms and to the provincial exchanges. They, in turn, have sent these to their larger customers.

If you want a copy, give your broker a ring.

From Monday, Gilt-edged stocks, debentures and other fixed-interest securities, now priced on a per cent. basis, will continue to be priced in pounds and fractions of pounds.

For instance, Unilever's 4 per cent. debenture stock 1960-80 will continue to appear as 62¼.

But shares now priced on a unit basis will be quoted in new pence and fractions of new pence. For example, I.C.I. shares now priced at 44s 9d will next week be 223¾p. Shell Transport at 72s 6d becomes 362½p.

Those over 1,000p or £10 will be expressed in pounds and fractions of pounds.

There is a very specialised currency used for some American and Canadian shares called the dummy or London dollar. This way of treating shares which involves pricing them on the basis of fiv dummy dollars to the £ (instead of $2.40 to £) st to-day.

From Monday these securities will be quo the same fashion as other stocks.

The nominal or face value of shares changed, says the Government, when the chooses. Since this aspect of the change-over some time — and it is really only a forma Stock Exchange's official list is going to nominal values in decimals from next Mon

Any shares involved in probate proce be calculated in the old currency if they w before D-Day. The totals will then be co decimals.

For unit trusts, the Association of U Managers has advised its members to quote in new pence and decimals of new pence decimal place after the change-over.

If you haven't been buying or selling recently, you won't, of course, get contract no accounts in the new currency. But eventually e one's account will be converted — and by then yo everyday affairs will have got you thinking in terms of new pence.

# 1974

# Surprise retirement is end of an era for Reds

BILL Shankly took the people of Liverpool and the football world by surprise when he retired as manager of Liverpool Football Club on a July day in 1974.

Shankly, then 60, had been Reds manager for 15 years and turned them from a struggling Second Division outfit into one of the greatest clubs in Europe.

Shankly, born in a poor mining village in Scotland, had been a talented player in his time but it as manager at Liverpool that his name acquired the legendary status it now commands. Shankly was greatly admired by the fans because he shared their passion for football and for success.

Never a man for understatement, at his final press conference when he told the world he was retiring, he said: "This decision has been the most difficult thing in the world and when I went to the chairman to tell him, it was like walking to the electric chair."

*Above: Bill Shankly celebrates with The Kop as Liverpool win the Football League Championship after a draw with Leicester City on April 27, 1973*

**"When I went to the chairman to tell him, it was like walking to the electric chair"**
**Bill Shankly**

*Right: The Echo breaks the news of Bill Shankly's retirement*

## 'It was like walking to the electric chair'

# SOCCER BOMBSHELL —SHANKLY RETIRES

### By ALEX GOODMAN and ALF GREEN

**On other pages**

The decision was his, says Nessie.
—Page Seven.

Incredible Mr. Shankly! Echo Comment:
—Page 35.

Who's the next boss?
—Back Page.

Reds to sign Ray Kennedy?
—Back Page.

Liverpool F.C. manager Bill Shankly, in charge at Anfield for 15 years, to-day stunned the soccer world by announcing his retirement.

Mr. Shankly, who has made Liverpool into one of the top clubs in the world and led them to countless successes, told of his shock decision at a packed Press conference at Anfield.

Mr. Shankly, aged 60, said: "This decision has been the most difficult thing in the world and when I went to the chairman to tell him it was like walking to the electric chair."

He added: "This has not been a decision that has been taken quickly. It has been on my mind for the last 12 months, but my wife and I both feel that we want a rest from the game which we have served for 43 years so that we can charge up our batteries again."

The club chairman, Mr. John Smith, said the board had to announce with "great regret" that Mr. Shankly wanted to retire.

He said: "It is with extreme reluctance that we accept this and we want to place on record our great appreciation of the magnificent job he has done for us."

Mr. Smith added : "He has agreed to give every assistance to the club for as long as necessary."

Mr. Shankly's decision is the biggest sensation in soccer since Sir Alf Ramsey was sacked as England team manager.

The King of the Kop was in sparkling form as he held court for the last time in the main lounge at Anfield, flanked by seven directors.

Asked if he thought whether he could survive without football, Mr. Shankly replied: "I can't

really answer that question—yet. I'll have to wait and see. Some people say that I will be bored. I'll have to risk that.

"This is a big game. There are many things one can do."

Asked if this implied that he might turn to coaching, scouting or even managing elsewhere, Mr. Shankly said: "I am leaving the Liverpool club for retirement. There is absolutely no animosity between the directors and myself. There is all the goodwill in the world.

"My intentions have been kept secret for five weeks during which the directors have been bartering and putting all sorts of propositions in my way, propositions that even Paul Getty might have been tempted to take."

Asked about the future, Mr. Smith said the board would be giving every consideration to the future at a meeting to be held shortly. "We realise the size of the task ahead," he added.

Mr. Shankly said that he and his wife intended to continue to live in Liverpool.

Asked where he would be on Monday morning, Mr. Shankly replied: "Here, at Anfield. I will be giving them every help and assistance until a successor is appointed."

Mr. Shankly gives the shock news at the Anfield Press conference. Left to right: Mr. Jack Cross (vice-chairman), Mr. Shankly, Mr. John Smith (chairman), and Mr. T. V. Williams (president).

### Dead PC and 'rotten society'

Constable John Scholfield died when he "came up aganst a member of that small, rotten part of society", Surrey Chief Constable Mr. Peter Matthews said at the murdered policemen's funeral in Caterham to-day.

And the Rev. David Frayne, rector of St. Mary's, described the murder as a "squalid exhibition of evil."

After the funeral, Mrs. Geraldine Scholfield broke down and wept.

### Smash and grab

A tape recorder worth £35 was stolen in a smash and grab raid at an electrical shop in Mount Pleasant, Waterloo.

### Thousands watch the Orangemen

Over 20,000 sightseers lined the streets of Southport town centre to-day to watch the traditional Orange Lodge parade.

The ranks of the Merseyside lodges were swelled to over 25,000 in Southport by contingents from as far as Scotland and South-East England. See also Page Five

# Third Grand National win for superstar racehorse

THE Grand National at Aintree is described as the world's greatest steeplechase, and forever linked with it is surely the world's greatest Grand National horse Red Rum.

Rummie, as he was affectionately known, is the only horse to win the gruelling race three times. He galloped into the record books when he won the race in 1977, capping his wins in 1973 and 1974.

Owned by Southport man Noel le Mare and famously trained on the sands at Birkdale by Ginger McCain, Red Rum was 12 when he won the four-and-a-half mile race for the third time and some commentators had feared he was too old. But as he romped home, his jockey on the day, Tommy Stack, said: "He is so intelligent, always looks for the open places and is always on the alert for loose horses."

After retirement, Red Rum became something of a celebrity, appearing at charity events and supermarket openings.

**"Bloody marvellous! He's a very exceptional horse and he'll be back next year for the National"**

**Ginger McCain**

*Ginger McCain with record racehorse Red Rum*

# FOOTBALL ECHO

Saturday, April 2, 1977 8p

**National day headline makers**

Gordon Lee—who sent on Pearson.

**Gordon's tactical switch pays off**

David Fairclough — vital goal

**Fairclough magic inspires a fine Reds' victory**

● For all today's Anfield action plus match pictures, see Back Page.

**RES SER**

● Just magic . . . a hat-trick of wins for Red Rum and a jubilant Tommy Stack salutes the crowd as they race past the winning post.

# WHAT A HORSE!

## Super Red Rum, 9-1 romps to victory and Aintree history

Red Rum proved himself the greatest Grand National horse of all time, when he gained a record - shattering third victory in the big Aintree race to-day, writes Captain Becher.

He won by an astonishing 25 lengths from Churchtown Boy with Eyecatcher in third and The Pilgarlic fourth to notch another great success for Southport trainer Ginger McCain, whose confident pre-race optimism was more than matched by what Red Rum did on the track.

In a race of many fallers Red Rum came into his own at Becher's on the second circuit when he took over at the front from Andy Pandy, the 15-2 favourite, who had been going well in the lead but suffered a crashing tumble.

From that point, Red Rum and jockey Tommy Stack were never headed, despite the fact that it looked at one stage as if Churchtown Boy, who had won the Topham 'Chase over the big Aintree fences only two days ago, was going to present a real challenge.

But in the end nothing could live with Red Rum, second in the race for the

2. **Churchtown Boy** ......... 20-1
3. **Eyecatcher** ... 18-1
4. **The Pilgarlic** 40-1

past two years and the winner in 1973 and 1974.

Red Rum, who won the pre-race prize for the best turned-out horse, was way back when the cavalry charge of 42 runners went off, nearly 10 minutes late. But he was kept clear of the trouble which started at the very first obstacle, where Duffle Coat, Spittin Image and Willy What all came down.

Boom Docker led at this point, from Collingwood and Brown Admiral, and stayed there until the third, when the big Irish hope, Gold Cup winner Davy Lad, came down along with Burrator, Royal Thrust and Inycarra.

Sebastian V was showing the way from Boom Docker and Hidden Value, but the leader came down at Becher's, as did Winter Rain and Castleruddery.

This left Boom Docker clear, and as they swept out over the Canal Turn and Valentine's, he opened up a considerable gap. War Bonnet went out of the race at Valentine's, as did Pengrail, with Prince Rock disappearing shortly afterwards.

Boom Docker, out on his own, led to the Chair, which claimed Sage Mer-

lin. By now Red Rum had crept up to fifth.

Over the water, Boom Docker led from Andy Pandy, Hidden Value and Red Rum. What A Buck came into the picture, but at Becher's on the second circuit Andy Pandy, when fully 10 lengths clear, came down, as did Nereo and Brown Admiral — leaving Red Rum to take over. Sir Garnet fell at the Canal Turn, but it was now Red Rum all the way, cheered on by the biggest Aintree crowd for years as he stormed to the line leaving the rest trailing in his wake.

Charlotte Brew, who carried the hopes of house-wives everywhere, had a marvellous ride on Barony Fort, until her mount refused at the final fence after always promising to complete the course.

Breathless Tommy Stack, who once trained the horse, said: "He is the most tremendous horse round Aintree.

"I am just glad to be part of this horse. He won it. Not me. I had a good run all the way round, staying back for the first part. The only tricky moment was at Becher's, second time round, when the leader, Andy Pandy, fell in front of us. But Red Rum jumps like a cat. He swerved his way round Andy Pandy and another loose horse which was bothering us.

"The only trouble on the run-in was two loose horses, so I took him around them and it was all over after that."

Trainer McCain said: "Bloody marvellous! He's a very exceptional horse, and he'll be back next year for the National."

Red Rum's three National victories took his overall winnings to a jump record of £114,000 for his Southport owner, octogenarian Mr. Noel le Mare.

Only 11 horses completed the course. What A Buck finished sixth, Happy Ranger seventh, Carroll Street eighth, Collingwood ninth, Hidden Value tenth, and last past the post was one of the two mares in the race, Saucy Belle.

One punter who collected £39,000 after Red Rum's win was Formby restaurant owner Mr. Tony Stannard.

Mr. Stannard aged 43, who owns the Tree Tops Hotel and restaurant, stuck an ante-post £200 win double on the National and the Cheltenham Gold Cup. Irish-trained Davy Lad did the trick for him in the Gold Cup.

Aintree course managers, Ladbrokes, reported losses of £250,000 but

**ROBSON DOUBLE SNATCHES POINT FROM EVERTON**

### West Ham 2, Everton 2

Continued from Back Page.

Lawson, as he flung himself to his left to touch the ball away.

Then Brooking was involved after 50 minutes with a cross-goal pass aimed for Radford only for Latchford to get back and end the danger.

But after all the Hammers' pressure, it was Everton who went ahead again after 58 minutes. PEARSON took a pass from Hamilton, got past Lock and cut into the penalty area before driving the ball low past Day.

McNaught and Dobson combined to stop the next West Ham attack, and then Everton moved forward, with Darracott going down the right. The ball was headed away from his cross though as West Ham survived.

There were more attacking ideas from Everton now, but Bonds and Taylor combined to stop Goodlass when he tried to work the ball down the left.

Brooking was the main inspiration behind the majority of the West Ham attacks, and he took on Jones and Darracott in one run down the left only for the ball to rebound off him and over for a goal kick when he tried to centre.

A timely tackle by Darracott halted Brooking as

he put the ball behind his centre.

The West Ham pressure paid off with an equaliser from ROBSON after minutes.

Jennings set it up with good run down the left, a cross into the middle where Robson was waiting and his firm header the ball flying Lawson.

West Ham threw everything one forward as they chased the winner and they forced two corners in succession. But Lyall ended the danger from the second with a back pass to Lawson.

Attendance: 22,518.

### Paisley's reward

Liverpool's dramatic drive towards a record breaking treble brought national acclaim for the architect of it all, manager Bob Paisley, writes Michael Charters.

Mr. Paisley, manager in one year for 1976 after League and U.E.F.A. double last season, is named to-day as Manager of the Month for March. He was a clear winner in the voting by the panel of sports writers throughout the country.

injury at halftime, bringing on Harrower as replacement. But this did not stop them from continuing to have the better of things against a Waterloo side

Airdrie ... 2 0
Half-time
Clydebnk 2 h
Half-time
East Fife 1 A

**We have a great big warehouse full of beautiful furniture just for you**

Here is just a small

### DIVISION 1

| | |
|---|---|
| Arsenal ..3 l | icester 0 |
| Half-time | |
| Birmgham 1 N | stle 2 |
| Half-time | |
| Bristol C. 0 A | ton V. |
| Half-time | |
| Coventry 1 T | o |
| Half-time | ttenham 1 |
| Derby ... 2 5 | o |
| Half-time | |
| .'POOL .. 3 l | o |
| Half-time | eds |
| Man. City 2 1 | |
| Half-time | wich 1 |
| Norwich.. 2 N | o |
| Half-time | a. Utd. 1 |
| Sund'land 1 C | e |
| Half-time | P.R. 0 |
| W. Brom.. 2 N | iddlsbro 1 |
| Half-time | |
| W. Ham 2 B | |

| | P | W |
|---|---|---|
| L'pool | 33 | 19 |
| Ipswich | 33 | 1 |
| Man. C. | 32 | 1 |
| Newcastle | 33 | 1 |
| W.B.A. | 33 | 1 |
| Man Utd. | 30 | 14 |
| Leicester | 34 | 1 |
| Aston V. | 28 | 1 |
| Leeds | 31 | 1 |
| Middboro | 33 | 1 |
| Arsenal | 33 | 1 |
| Norwich | 33 | 1 |
| Everton | 38 | 1 |
| Birmgham | 32 | 1 |
| Stoke | 31 | |
| Q.P.R. | 28 | |
| Coventry | 29 | |
| Totnham | 33 | |
| Derby | 30 | |
| Bristol C. | 30 | |
| Snderland | 33 | |
| W Ham | 30 | |

**DIVISION**

# The Queen visits in Silver Jubilee year

*Queen Elizabeth II greets her fans on her jubilee year visit to Liverpool in 1977*

*Above: The Queen and Prince Philip wave to the crowds at Liverpool's Pier Head*

Children on Northcote Road gather for a party

*Above: A Jubilee gathering in full swing on Hardy Street*

**Liverpool Echo**

We print (almost) except money

SOUTHPORT PRINTERS LTD

No. 30,283    WEDNESDAY, JUNE 22, 1977

**A glittering farewell to a Royal day on Merseyside...**

## The sunshine Queen whose smile never faded

*Tribute to the pageant children*

By CHRIS OSWICK

THE QUEEN started her visit to North Wales to-day after a dazzling Jubilee farewell from Merseyside.

Bonfires and flashing headlights saluted the departing Britannia from the banks of the Mersey in a festival of light as the sun finally set on Merseyside's big day.

The Royal Yacht "winked" back with a flashing searchlight.

But the Queen and Duke left Lime Street in the Royal train for North Wales.

And Merseyside was left with the memory of the "sunshine" Queen whose smile never faded.

Police estimated that more than 500,000 people took to the streets to line the 18-mile Royal route.

By NICK SKIDMORE and IAN CRAIG

The 17,000 Liverpool children who took part in yesterday's unique musical pageant before the Queen received a massive pat on the back to-day.

"They were a credit to themselves, to their schools and to the city," added Mr. Kenneth Antcliffe, Liverpool's Director of Education.

"I express the thanks of all in the authority's education service to those who participated in the musical pageant.

"Also to the parents, friends, relatives and supporters whose presence in Hope Street so greatly helped to create a festive atmosphere for the performers.

"I hope they felt, as I did, that the children of Liverpool were a credit to themselves, to their schools and to the city," added Mr. Antcliffe.

The Queen and the Duke of Edinburgh leave Lime Street Station.

**AND ONLY HOURS AFTER THE PAGEANTRY...**

## CATHEDRAL'S

**T'S JUBI-GLEE ALL THE WAY...**

**OYAL REIGN SHINES THROUGH THE RAIN**

### Nothing was going to stop this party

By Charles Nevin

# The murder of a musical hero

FANS across Merseyside, and all over the world, were shocked and saddened to hear about the murder of Liverpool music icon John Lennon. On December 8, 1980, the 40-year-old former Beatle was killed by crazed fan Mark Chapman outside New York's Dakota building, where he shared an apartment with his wife Yoko Ono. Chapman was said to have stalked Lennon for several days before the murder took place. Tributes poured in for the Liverpudlian rock superstar, who had died in the arms of his wife after three bullets tore through his left lung, and another through a bone in his shoulder. Many said that Lennon's death brought the loss of an amazing talent, while they also mourned his witty and rebellious nature, as well as his longing for world peace.

## 'I love New York—it's a 24-hour city... nobody bothers you, that's what I like'

● Lennon's ironic quote on the city where he met his shock death.

*Anticlockwise from left: John Lennon; The Echo's opinion on his tragic death; An excerpt from the front page that broke the news; Lennon's killer Mark Chapman who remains in jail; One of the Echo's follow-up stories; and the infamous front page in full*

### ECHO COMMENT

" 'Paul's the nice guy. I'm the one they love to hate.''

The quote is from John Lennon, of course. And it was to sum up an attitude from authority and some of the public which prevailed right to his death.

He was frequently the centre of controversy. His antics with Yoko in the early days of their partnership shocked many.

He had to fight to stay in the United States. It was a country that suited his temperament.

He liked New York because "You can do anything you want here. Nobody bothers you. That's what I like.'

That's what John Lennon was about above all else—doing his own thing. Public reaction never worried him.

He was the withdrawn one even in the earliest days of the Beatles, The one that could be difficult.

But the image he sometimes earned was unfair. To those who knew him he was a warm man, a man of great generosity and kindness. He was also an astute man; he foresaw that a Beatles reunion could not redapture the magic and might even spoil the legend.

He chose in these last years to live as a virtual recluse. He wanted to be with his family. He was, as always, doing what he felt was right for that period of his life.

His death robs the international music world of a great talent and a vibrant personality.

Liverpool especially owes him a debt. Might it now be appropriate to provide a permanent tribute to him—and to the three of the Fab Four—by a memorial, perhaps not of stone but in some way marking those heady years of the sixties when it was all happening.

**JOHN LENNON**, leader of the legendary Liverpool pop group, The Beatles, was shot dead in New York to-day by a crazed gunman.

After a man police described as "a local screwball" pumped five bullets into Lennon, he yelled "I'm shot" and staggered up a few steps into the apartment building where he lived.

And as the 40-years-old superstar lay dying in the arms of his wife, Yoko Ono, he whispered "Help me," according to neighbour Carrie Rouse.

The Liverpool Echo, Wednesday, December 10, 1980

**DIAMONDS and GOLD**

DIAMOND GIFTS
DIAMOND EARRINGS from ........ £35-£1,800
DIAMOND BRACELETS from ....... £29.50-£3,900
DIAMOND NECKLETS & PENDANTS from ..£42.50-£850
TOP PRICES PAID FOR YOUR OLD GOLD

**O'HARES** 59 FROST RD, LIVERPOOL L56 6QX TEL. 051-709 2262

**Liverpo**

No. 31,322   WEDNESDAY, D

## REVEALED

## JOHN'S KIL

A BIZARRE picture of the man who gunned down ex-Beatle John Lennon in a New York street was being put together by police to-day.

By Martin Dunn and Fred ... in New York

● Page 6: Lennon, the ... Page 7: Liverpool's lament...

### Woman's body found

Murder Squad detectives were alerted in Dewsbury, West Yorkshire today, after a woman's body was found.

Two of the county's top officers, Mr Peter Gilrast, former head of the Ripper Squad and Det. Supt Tony Hickey were at the scene.

A police spokesman said: Early indications suggest that this is not a Ripper killing—but we will not know until after a post-mortem.

### Hall-marked

A flag was flying over Liverpool Town Hall today to commemorate the 30th anniversary of the signing of the Universal Declaration of Human Rights by the United Nations.

### Jobless plea

Eight church leaders from the steel town of Consett, County Durham, hit hard by the recession, have written to Premier Margaret Thatcher appealing for "real understanding and maximum help" for the unemployed.

### Appeal upheld

A Department of Health and Social Security has won an appeal in the House of Lords in a legal battle over the role of nurses and midwives in medically-induced abor...

Dakota apartments, where the singer lived, and began reading "Catcher in the Rye" by J. D. Salinger, said police.

Salinger's novel is about a rebellious youth who tells, in authentic teenage language, his flight from the "phony" adult world, his search for innocence and truth and his final collapse on a psychiatrist's couch.

Three bullets tore through his left lung and one shoulder...

tered a... accord...

For assassin (40), fortun years expecte Attica up with York...

He batten his ha hurry might...

If guilty, nation sentenc...

Lennon's killer

## Chapman 'marked for life

Mark Chapman charged with the second degree brown-haired Hawaiian murder of John Lennon was stared by a police spokesman to be "marked for the rest of his life. Wherever he goes there will be someone who has it in for him''.

But the whereabouts of the 25-years-old unemployed security guard...

being arrested the tanned, resident was taken to Manhattan Criminal Court and put in a solitary cell to protect him from retaliation from other prisoners.

Correction Department spokesman Ed Hershey said: "We still remember Lee Harvey Oswald.

The alleged assassin of...

sure that that doesn't happen here," he said.

The switchboard of the court was busy all night with threats from hate-filled fans of the rock star.

After a brief court appearance Chapman was placed under a three-man suicide watch and was later reported to be in the prison wing of the Gener...

# Liverpool Echo

**A SPORTS** STARTS THURSDAY 11th DEC. AT 10.00 A.M. EVERY GARMENT IS REDUCED LF PRICE & LESS BOLD STREET, LIVERPOOL 1.

**NEWS FROM** Binns TOY DEPARTMENT SUPER INTERNATIONAL TYPEWRITER FROM PETITE. Usually £18.95. Now for only **£13.25**

No. 31,521 TUESDAY, DECEMBER 9, 1980 10p

## *Crazed gunman charged*

RUSH
NEW YORK, MONDAY — FORMER BEATLE JOHN LENNON WAS SHOT AND KILLED TONIGHT AT HIS HOME IN NEW YORK CITY, POLICE SAID.
REUTER 0453

● How the news was broken in the world.

# JOHN LENNON SHOT DEAD

JOHN LENNON, leader of the legendary Liverpool pop group, The Beatles, was shot dead in New York to-day by a crazed gunman.

After a man police described as "a local screwball" pumped five bullets into Lennon, he yelled "I'm shot" and staggered up a few steps into the apartment building where he lived.

And as the 40-years-old superstar lay dying in the arms of his wife, Yoko Ono, he whispered "Help me," according to neighbour Carrie Rouse.

But his final pleas for help in the courtyard of the plush Dakota building were drowned by the sound of late night revellery dancing to his latest music in bars on Manhattan's upper West side.

Carrie Rouse said: "Yoko screamed 'He's been shot, he's been shot. Somebody come quickly.'

"He was hysterical.

"He was bleeding heavily. His eyes were closed. Then he slowly rolled over."

Lennon died in his wife's arms in the back seat of a Manhattan police car speeding him to hospital.

Police officer John Morgan said Lennon was conscious and moaning when he was put into the back seat of the police car.

"I asked him 'Do you know who you are?'" the officer Morgan said. "And he replied: 'Yes, John Lennon.'"

No more than a couple of minutes later he was...

...and illegal possession of a firearm.

Chapman stood on the courtyard and dropped the empty gun. The doorman kicked it away and an elevator operator picked it up. The fat police on the scene took Chapman into custody, police said.

Chapman, who were wearing tinted sunglasses of a freelance photographer, his was carrying a copy of Lennon's latest album — "Double Fantasy" — which the ex-Beatle had autographed for him. He offered no motive for the killing.

Legions of fans who kept vigil outside the plush Dakota building where Lennon lived and died called for Chapman's blood.

They ignored police appeals to leave the scene. From her secret hideout in New York where she is mourning her husband's sudden and violent death, Yoko Ono asked for his fans' prayers.

Chapman is a Texan who moved to Hawaii three years ago.

### THE MAGIC OF JOHN LENNON

**Starts in the Echo tomorrow**

Police said that six weeks ago Chapman applied for a permit to buy a gun. As he had no criminal record, he was granted.

Lennon and his wife had been at the Record Plant recording studio earlier in the evening and had left before at 10.30 p.m. New York time.

Lennon told studio technicians that he and his wife were going out for a bite and then returning.

Asking why Chapman was allowed to hang around the Dakota for six hours, Sullivan said — "That's not common at the Dakota. A lot of celebrities live...

**FACE OF GRIEF ... Yoko Ono is comforted by police as she leaves Roosevelt Hospital in New York.**

## *Grief-stricken fans at Mathew Street shrine*

The people of Liverpool were stunned today by the shock news of John Lennon's death.

Grief-stricken fans gathered in the cold of Mathew Street.

They sat at the Cavern, where Brotherhausis was born, has quickly become a shrine to his memory.

"Four lads who shook the world," goes the message under the special street sign, but it was just the death of one that caused the shock waves of grief.

Oona Keating, at 15, was too young to have seen the Beatles in their heyday, but she could hardly speak for tears.

"I was sick," she said "for everyone to know him. As soon as I heard the news, I knew I had to come here.

"I thought I would feel closer to him again. They say it doesn't matter so much because the other three are left, but it really...

**TEARFUL MEMORIES as Julie Fisher, of Raleigh Road, Leasowe, and Elaine Royle, of Merton Close, Little Neston, lay a wreath on the site of the former Cavern the Beatles this afternoon. Scarcely old enough to remember the Beatles' music in their heyday, they were introduced to the Beatles' music at an early age and have remained fans ever since.**

### A GREAT LOSS TO WORLD —PAUL

The surviving member of Britain's most famous contemporary song-writing team was visibly upset by the news of his former partner's death to-day.

Paul McCartney, who now has his own group Wings, said: "I can't take it in at the moment," as he drove away from his Sussex cottage in a red Mercedes.

At the gate in the drive which leads through a Forestry Commission land, The Waterfall Cottage, he said: "John was a great guy. He is going to be missed by the whole world."

### It's tragic says former wife Cynthia

John Lennon's former wife Cynthia, said to-day that his death was tragic.

Cynthia, now Mrs. John Twist, issued a statement within minutes of returning to her home in Ruthin, North Wales, which she shares with her third husband and son by John Lennon, 17-year-old Julian.

She and her husband now run a restaurant in a former manor house in the town centre.

Mrs. Twist, who arrived by car from London with Maureen, the former wife of Ringo Starr, said in her statement: "I would like to say how terribly upset we are at the sudden and tragic death of John Lennon.

"Julian, of course, is particularly upset about it. It came so suddenly."

---

Echo 10p

**NEWS FROM** Binns INDIAN COLLECTION
Dresses, suits, skirts and waistcoats in new prints. Choose your size from a range of exciting colours.
Eg. Wrap over style skirts **£7.99**

# THE MIND OF ...ER

...sources. He would then move into the YMCA.

On his last visit to the courtyard and asked a shop assistant, who told him how much he wanted to meet Lennon. Last week he arrived in New York again, stayed at the YMCA, on Saturday night before checking into the Sheraton Centre Hotel at £40 a night.

His belongings were still there last night.

Two days before the murder, he had breakfast with the Lennons' girl baby sitter at a local diner, said police. She thought him a "nice guy."

Chapman was married. With his wife Gloria he lived in Honolulu and worked in a hospital print shop as a security guard. Then he left for a similar job as an unarmed guard for a Waikiki condominium building until resigning on October 23.

"On the day he left, he signed the log sheet 'John Lennon' instead of 'Mark Chapman,'" manager Joe Bustamente said today.

On October 27, he bought a .38 calibre "Charter Arms Undercover" short barrelled revolver from a company called J. & S. Enterprises in Honolulu, near a police station. It was a model used by many American police forces.

He paid £75 for it and the weapon which killed Lennon, police said.

The famous and the humble ... Tears from two people who prayed for John Lennon at Liverpool Parish Church in the city centre today, while former Beatle Ringo Starr and his fiancee Barbara Bach were too upset to say anything after visiting John's widow, Yoko.

### Peace theme at city service

The message "peace be with you" had a special ring at Liverpool Parish Church's daily lunchtime eucharist in the city centre today, as a tribute was...

...end against nation.

Before the service, attended by about 70 people, the Rev. Donald Gray said: "Like everybody else, I was very...

...violent hand. It seems to be the pattern of the world."

Among the mourners were two Liverpool University students, Louise, Professor...

### A GREAT LOSS TO WORLD —PAUL

# Workers stage sit-in as axe falls at Meccano

WHEN 900 people lost their jobs in Liverpool with the closure of the Meccano factory in Binns Road, Edge Hill, in 1980, it was the end of the city's connection with a story that had begun on an inventor's kitchen table. In 1901 Frank Hornby created a construction kit to entertain his children and Mechanics Made Easy was born, soon to become Meccano. Sales grew and with the advent of Hornby train sets and Dinky toys, production led eventually to Binns Road.

But just before Christmas 1979 workers were told the then owners had decided to close the factory. A three-month sit-in was ended by High Court bailiffs one morning at 5am and Day 102 of the workers' fight for their jobs ended in defeat.

While the factory closed, the Meccano name lived on, being made in France and China and latterly owned by a Japanese toy company; a long way from Binns Road.

**SPECIAL JACKETS** oose from shades of blue. £29.95 Floor

**Liverpo**

TUESDAY, MAR

Convener Frank Bloor found time for a joke with police outside the M

## BAILIFFS S MECCANO

**Meccano battle after closure shock hits 900**

## TOY WORKERS' SIT-IN FIGHT TO SAVE JOBS

A **PRE-DAWN** swoop by High Court bailiffs gained Meccano management access to their Liverpool factory today for the first time in three months.

The bailiffs turned up at the occupied toy factory shortly after five o'clock this morning and smashed their way through a locked door.

**By TONY MARTIN**

*MP Eric Ogden meets some of the workers staging the sit-in*

### Motoring law review may bring new deal

The Government's review of motoring laws could be far reaching and offer a new deal for motorists in the 1980's, said Transport Minister Mr. Norman Fowler, this afternoon.

He told a conference of road safety experts at the RAC's London headquarters that he was against additional motoring laws, and was looking for simpler systems to lighten the load on magistrates' courts.

He said the present totting-up procedure was a blunt instrument. Endorsement for a minor offence such as having a defective stop-lamp weighed equally with an endorsement for a hit-and-run offence.

A points system, similar to that in use in other countries, would represent a more flexible approach in distinguishing levels of seriousness.

Mr. Fowler said he was

### Bouncing car hits man

*Below: The Meccano sit-in comes to an end*

# Echo

10p

...ce to-day. Picture: Eddie Barford.

## ...ASH

## ...T-IN

...rail

...ts

...ead

**Chain dem...**

Women medical dressed as suf... chained themselves... ings in protest at t... ble closure of the... ing school during... strong demonstra... London to-day.

The girls were fro... Royal Free Hospi... School of Medicine, stead, one of the... earmarked for c...

...l services, ... given the Transport ...uce costs

**CRAIG**

...ncillor Mrs. ...d no rail or ...s to be cut ... but she ...would be ...ous services ...ered in a

...wen Con- ...tested that ...Newton-le- ...ffering at ...the city

...ayers we ...he outer ...value for ...he asked, ...are being ...of money ...at Mersey- ...which is

---

# TATE'S AXE REFINERY —1,570 CITY JOBS GO

22 JAN 1981    22 JAN 1981    22 JAN 1981

*By Peter Phelps, Colin Wright and John Shaughnessy*

Sugar giant Tate and Lyle is to close its Liverpool refinery with the loss of 1,570 jobs.

This new hammer blow to Merseyside's economy was confirmed today.

The news came on the day the company announced it's profits had gone up by £4,500,000 to £30,700,000. Shareholders are to get larger dividend for every share they held during the year.

Company chairman Lord Jellicoe said: "Because of its grave employment implications, the board has taken the decision only with the greatest reluctance."

"The board is, however, determined to put Tate back on a sound footing, and to do this it has to cure the long-standing structural weaknesses of the company's UK sugar refining business."

He said the refinery had been "victim of E.E.C. membership."

The closure decision had been "exceptionally unpalatable" because the company had links with Liverpool for a very long

## March will highlight plight of jobless

The TUC is planning a national march from Liverpool to London to "draw attention of the country to the urgent plight of the unemployed."

The march is to begin on May 1 and on the weekend of May 29/30.

An appeal is being sent to all Labour movement organisation, MPs, churches

and voluntary organisations asking them to sponsor marchers.

Mr. Colin Barnett, secretary of the North West region of the TUC, said: "I am delighted this major event has been planned in the North West as a follow-up to the Labour Party: TUC demonstration on November 29.

time—some families being involved for two or three generations.

"We have done everything in our power to avert this closure," he said.

For the last seven years, the company had put its case on sugar quotas "almost ad-nauseum.

"But each 100,000 tons of over-capacity cost the company between £3 million and £4 million a year.

"We cannot afford to carry these costs any longer. We have squarely faced our problems," he added.

Managing director Mr. Frank Tomlinson expanded on the Liverpool losses.

Last year, Liverpool lost £1,500,000, and the cost of carrying surplus capacity

at the two other refineries added a further £7.5m to losses.

"If we carried on with the same excess capacity this year, the losses would have been over £10,000,000," he said. "We have got to do something."

He said he was "personally devoted" to Liverpool. But, taking into account the plant's capacity and also its distance from the docks, the sugar was more expensive per ton to refine than at the London or Greenock, Scotland, refineries.

For example, if the London refinery cost £40 per ton, and the Scottish refinery £51 per ton, the Liverpool refinery would cost £60 per ton.

We had no choice what-

soever," he said. "It is going to be terribly difficult for our chaps up there (Liverpool) but we have to look at the good of the whole company."

Shop stewards from the Love Lane refinery were called to a special meeting at Liverpool Centre Hotel, where they were given news of the closure by Mr. Charles Runge the company's chief executive from London.

It took him 10 minutes to tell the 70 stewards that the axe was to fall.

As he left the hotel, Mr. Runge he was once worked as transport manager at the Love Lane refinery — said: "I am very sad at the decision that has been announced today."

For today's meeting, the Tate and Lyle shop stewards were joined by at least one senior full time union official — Regional Officer of the G.M.W.U. Mr. Tony Humphries whose union has 1,000 members at the refinery.

Mr. Humphries said: "It is a shattering blow to Merseyside, and has special implications peculiar to the Love Lane site.

"It is not just a question of putting men out of work. This is going to wipe out whole families."

He said the refinery had an ageing work force and, if the company's decision was accepted, most of the men would have to face the fact that they would never work again...

THE MOMENT The Blow Fell . . . A solemn Mr. Albert Sloane, chairman of the Tate and Lyle North West Union Committee outside the Love Lane factory to-day.

*Tate's shock announcement*

---

# Doors close at sugar factory

THE closure of the Tate and Lyle sugar refinery in January 1981 was a massive setback to Liverpool and a shattering blow for the 1,570 people who lost their jobs. The harsh facts of economics and the EEC were blamed for the closure but for the workers and their families it was the end of a way of life.

Many lived near the Love Lane site on the edge of the city centre, where the Eldonian Village now stands, and generations had worked in the factory during its 112-year history.

Henry Tate, of Tate and Lyle, had built the large sugar refinery in Liverpool's Vauxhall area. He later founded the Tate gallery.

Despite the century of history in Liverpool, when the decision came it took the company's London chief executive only 10 minutes in a city hotel room to tell the factory's 70 union shop stewards that the axe was to fall.

## Tate workers' sad farewell

16 APR 1981

WORKERS at Liverpool's Tate & Lyle sugar refinery were this afternoon saying their farewells at the doomed Love Lane factory.

Just a skeleton staff will    The original closure date return after the Easter    the end of the 90 days'

*Workers on their way to a mass meeting after learning of the closure*

---

# Riots break out in Toxteth

AN explosion of tension between police and youths resulted in riots that devastated areas of Toxteth in one weekend in July 1981. Although many at the time blamed race relations, it is alleged that the riots were started when police used excessive force when trying to arrest a motorcyclist on Friday 3 July. A group of black youths retaliated and police turned out on the streets of Toxteth in force after reports of a planned 'bloodbath' for Saturday night.

Overnight a battle raged around Upper Parliament Street with police lines hit with petrol bombs and bricks. The streets were left littered with burning cars and rubble, bus

shelters were flattened, and burned out shops were looted.

More than 2,000 policemen were drafted in to arrest hundreds of people. It took over seven hours to regain control although Toxteth was still classed as 'no-go' territory.

The riots are believed to be the first time CS gas flares were used in Britain.

TOXTETH'S NIGHTMARE—SUNDAY/MONDAY

## Aftermath of terror
### Cold light of day shows the ruins

*Police patrol Toxteth as the dust settles*

## Ordeal for the fleeing patients

As the 100-year-old Racquet Club was engulfed by flames at the height of last night's rioting 102 elderly patients at the Princes Park geriatric hospital in Toxteth were evacuated.

Flames were ripping through the building next door as a fleet of 12 ambulances arrived to ferry the patients to other hospitals around Liverpool.

A wall of policemen ensured a passageway for the ambulances as staff organised the old folk—

### Children

Miss Dorothy Houghton (81), said: "I was too angry to be afraid, I could see children, no more than 12 or 13, throwing bottles and stones. One even hit [an] ambulance as we were [to] the hospital.

[M]any of the patients [we]re terrified, al[though t]he staff at the [hospital, the] police and the [firem]en can't be [rated] highly enough. [Th]ere eight of us [carry]ing into the ambu[lance]s in and the am[bul]an tried to get a [...] going to keep [...] up.

[...] of folk at the [...]ark Hospital had [...] witnessed the [...] Saturday night's [...]njured police[...] brought into the [...] while they [...] ambulances to [...]n to casualty de[...]s elsewhere.

[...]night more [...] young officers [...] arriving just [...]dnight. One and [...]urs later all the [...]tients were told [...] their beds and get [...] be evacuated as [...]reatened the hos-

[...]uld smell the [...]d when we got [...]he Racquet Club [...]ing from top to

many already confused and totally bewildered by last night's occurrences— as they emptied the three-storeys of the hospital.

One of the elderly patients said today: "I didn't even think the blitz was as bad as what happened last night. But there was a reason for the blitz, that was war."

bottom," added Houghton.

"Both sides of Parliament Stree[t were] burning. It was a[maz]ing. I never though[t any]thing like this [could] happen."

People in Toxteth [came out] and help during the [height] of the riots. "I sav[e some] women, at least, [crawling] across to our hospit[al vol]unteering to help," [said] Miss Houghton.

And like the othe[r pa]tients 79-year-old Mis[s Edith] Roberts had to flee [with] just a cardigan and w[hat]ever other belonging[s they] could clutch before [being] evacuated. Many of th[e old] folk were forced to l[eave] without money and [even] their false teeth.

"The whole place aro[und] was on fire. It gave [me a] terrific shock," she sa[id.]

### Five detained

Thirty-seven patie[nts] were transferred [to] Walton Hospital. The s[taff] at Walton also had to c[ope] with 12 police casual[ties] and five were kept in h[os]pital.

All 20 day-beds [at] Walton were to-day [oc]cupied by old folk from [the] Princes Park Hospital. [To-] day's day admissions [to] Walton were cancelled.

### 1,000 years

The Isle of Man — t[he] oldest self-governing p[art] of the Commonwea[lth] celebrates its indepen[d]ence today with the 1,00[0] year-old Tynwald cere[mony] at which the island[s] new Governor Rear Adm[i]ral Sir Nigel Cecil, w[ill] preside.

## Heffer slams riot leaflet

### By Tom Utley

Walton Labour M.P. Eric Heffer to-day spoke out against the controversial Young Socialist leaflet circulated during the Toxteth riots.

And he has launched an investigation into how the leaflet, which calls for the dropping of all charges against those arrested during the rioting, came to bear the address of Labour's Liverpool H.Q.

Mr. Heffer told the Echo: "There are one or two things in the leaflet which I certainly would not have formulated in that way. But the party is not responsible for that.

"The Young Socialists are the youth movement of the party. They have their own ideas, which are not necessarily acceptable to the adult wing of the party.

"I want to know why the [le]aflet h[...]

Edge Hill Liberal M.P. Mr. David Alton condemned the leaflet during yesterday's Commons inquest on the weekend rioting. He asked Home Secretary William Whitelaw what action he would take against those responsible for it.

Mr. Whitelaw said it was not a matter for him, but that others should face up to their responsibilities.

Mr. Whitelaw said that all claims for compensation would be dealt with under the Riots Damages Act of 1866.

Under the Act, police authorities are required to pay compensation for all houses, shops or buildings destroyed and all property spoiled or stolen by "persons riotously and tumultuously assembled together".

Meanwhile, Merseyside Young Socialists to-day stood by their pamphlet

*The effects of the riots were felt far and wide*

# TOXTETH: 11.17 p.m

## And now Whitelaw sees for himself

**27 JUL 1981**

HOME SECRETARY William Whitelaw was this afternoon on his way to Liverpool to see for himself the aftermath of the Liverpool 8 riots.

His visit was being surrounded by a big police security operation. Mr. Whitelaw was meeting senior police officers to discuss the three nights of street violence and looting.

His journey to Merseyside was prompted during talks in London yesterday with Chief Constable Mr. Ken Oxford.

Apart from the devastated Upper Parliament Street and Lodge Lane areas, the Home Secretary will visit Park Road, Toxteth, scene of rioting and looting last night.

Police arrested 75 during the disturbances, 21 of whom were juveniles. The alleged offences are mainly connected with looting.

Meanwhile, 2,000 officers drafted in from all parts of the country were resting to-day, and will be on stand-by again to-night.

Last night's fresh outbreak of violence involved a mob of white youths.

The news quickly spread that Park Road had been singled out for the new night of violence, and the uneasy calm was shattered at 9 p.m.

Then, windows were smashed at the Ethel Austin clothing shop. Police mounted a charge — and the looters fled.

Moments later came new onslaughts. Targets were ... warehouse ...

**By Brian Roberts and Larry Neild**

Then came another half of stone-throwing. And while this was going on, bystanders gathered up cigarettes, canned beer and food which had been scattered across the street by the looters.

Police made several appeals for people to go ...

visors sealed off Park Road and the surrounding streets.

No petrol bombs were thrown, but some officers carried fire extinguishers as a precaution.

Police had asked all-night garages to stop petrol sales until daylight, so that fuel could not be obtained to make bombs.

An AA spokesman said the call had got 100 per cent backing.

At the height of last night's troubles, three clergymen from a multi-ceremonial Christian centre in Toxteth toured the trouble spot, pleading with youngsters to end the trouble and looting.

But the clergymen's van was stoned and had all its ... smashed.

Lewis's in Renshaw Street, and others wearing riot helmets patrolled Lime Street.

The one police casualty was a constable who suffered leg injuries.

Ambulance chief Albert Guinney made a heartfelt plea on behalf of old people evacuated from Princes Park Hospital at the weekend.

In an appeal to looters, he said: "You have taken everything they possess.

This was the scene in Park Road, Toxteth, at 11.17 last night. Teenagers stand on a pavement strewn with broken glass while, right, a youngster prepares to duck into the wines and spirits section.

## Business as usual!

**By Diana Pulson**

If it wasn't business as usual in Liverpool's Lodge Lane to-day, it was as near to it as local shopkeepers could manage.

With smoke and debris still swirling round the devastated scene of the weekend riots, and the majority of shops gutted and empty, a gallant handful managed to open to provide food and services for shoppers.

You couldn't have a sweat at the baths because there was no electricity, but the public library opened at 10 o'clock and ...

... at the lower end of the street violence and attacks on the police of the last few days, and she will condemn the riots strongly.

... books and selling stamps, while at Snips the unisex hairdressers you could get your hair done— a grey-haired lady was having a trim at 9 a.m.

Charlie the Mynah Bird, a favourite with Toxteth children, was not ... Mac's pet shop ...

---

ALIVE to the sound of music—these schoolchildren from Toxteth and Dingle danced and sang at South Liverpool Festival of Arts in the Phoenix Adult Education Centre, Toxteth.

## Toxteth revival hope after riots ordeal

LIVERPOOL'S Roman Catholic Archbishop says, he hopes Toxteth will rise like a phoenix from the ashes" of last weekend's rioting.

The Most Rev. Derek Worlock appealed for genuine long-term consultation over the area's future.

"The most hopeful sign is the apparent desire of those responsible for the life of our city to listen to the voice of the community.

"It has a right to be heard about its own future, its relationships and the conditions on which its members live, work and raise their families.

"To listen to the voice must not be mere lip service, brought about by the present emergency, said the Archbishop.

"I appeal to all political parties, offices and institutions which have part in the life of our city, for genuine long-term consultation with the community.

The Archbishop urged that the young unemployed in Liverpool be given a chance to take part in the building of their future homes and destiny.

● A Labour Party public meeting about the Toxteth troubles, due to have been held at Paddington Comprehensive School last night, was cancelled by the authorities.

The chairman of the city's Education Committee, Councillor Mike Storey, refused to let the meeting take place and was supported by the chairman of the school governors, Labour Councillor Mrs. Margaret Simey, who is also chairman of the Police Committee.

Councillor Mrs. Simey said: "The reason was that such a meeting might create trouble and the police, in my opinion, are already heavily over-burdened. So I asked them to cancel the meeting."

Handed out before the group dispersed were Labour leaflets, which said the police have used the looting in Toxteth as an excuse to "harass and persecute young people in the area even more."

● Massive cash injections to help distressed inner

city areas like Toxteth have been ruled out by Environment Secretary Michael Heseltine.

Commenting on a TUC call for aid to inner cities to be quadrupled to £700 million, Mr. Heseltine said the money could only be raised through cuts or borrowing.

The group, led by Council Labour leader, Councillor Jim Stuart-Cole, had sought restoration of cash lost through the Government's replacement of the previous Rate Support Grant with a block grant system.

● The Communist Party has called for a local inquiry into the Toxteth riots. A spokesman for the party's Merseyside area committee said the decision to extend the Scarman inquiry will not satisfy people of Liverpool 8.

● A special peace service for the Toxteth neighbourhood will be held at Princes Park Christian Centre on Sunday at 11 a.m.

---

*Liverpool Echo, Friday, July 10, 1981* 3

## Fury at Maggie 'slur on city'

Premier Margaret Thatcher was at the centre of a new row over allegations she had slurred the people of Liverpool.

Speaking on the Toxteth riots, she said in the Commons: "In that particular area the history of labour relations does not encourage firms to go there."

And she told M.P.s she agreed with the verdict of one newspaper that the mob violence in Liverpool had nothing to do with bad housing or unemployment, but was "a spree of naked greed".

Liverpool Walton M.P. Eric Heffer shouted: "Stupid woman."

And the row continued for nearly eight minutes with the irate Left Winger accusing Mrs. Thatcher of having attacked Liverpool and its people.

Speaker Mr. George Thomas, however, insisted this was not a point of order, but Mr. Heffer, getting more angry every minute, protested that not one Liverpool M.P. had been called during the 15 minutes of Prime Minister's question-time to refute her charges.

Mr. Heffer continued the attack outside the chamber. "Like so many other people, Mrs. Thatcher has said that industrial relations in Liverpool are responsible for our problems," he said.

"But those industrial relations are no better or worse than any other city in the country."

Ormskirk Labour M.P. Robert Kilroy-Silk said this was confirmed by the Government's own statistics.

---

## Maggie's grim warning to the riot gangs

PRIME MINISTER Mrs. Margaret Thatcher will go on television to-night and bluntly tell the rioters who have devastated areas of Liverpool, London and Manchester: "There is no excuse for what you are doing."

Her political broadcast is likely to be dominated by economic issues and the Government's grim determination to hold to its present course.

She is expected to express her deep concern over mounting unemployment, especially among the young.

But she will insist that this in no way justifies the street violence and attacks on the police of the last few days, and she will condemn the riots strongly.

In particular, she may warn of the threat of violence the rioters pose to law and order and the authorities of Parliament.

She will point out the dangers they represent to traditional British values and stress to parents the duty they have in preventing their children breaking the law.

Ministers will soon be discussing what further measures should be taken to combat unemployment.

And the Government is almost certain to give the go-ahead for an extra £93 million for the Youth Opportunities programme to fulfil the commitment to provide every child who

● **PAGE 3: Night of friendship**

● **PAGE 6: Out of the sun into the riots**

leaves school with training or work experience by Christmas.

A massive police contingent again flooded Liverpool's Toxteth district last night, but only on one occasion were they needed — to disperse about 200 youths who congregated around the Dingle area of the city.

No incidents of looting, arson or stoning, were reported, but 28 people, eight of whom were juveniles were arrested.

Officers are hopeful the situation is now cooling down in the Toxteth area and have praised the community leaders for getting the message accross to people to behave.

However, Mr. Oxford said he was adamant that 2,000 men were still being made available to his force

for any potential outbreaks.

Meanwhile, Tory Party chairman Lord Thorneycroft this afternoon accused left-wingers of exploiting the problems of Toxteth

He told a Party meeting in London: "There are to-day active forces far beyond the confines of the House of Commons which challenge authority.

"This challenge is to be seen in the squalid happenings at Brixton and Toxteth.

"The challenge to the authority of law and order and to Parliament itself is now increasingly apparent."

---

*Overleaf: The front page of the Echo on July 6, 1981 showed the devastation*

were made for public order and looting offences.

Eight hundred policemen were used to combat rampaging gangs, totalling about 500, last night and senior officers said today that even more police would be on duty to-night.

C.S. gas canisters would again be available for use.

Mr. Wright described the violence as being at 'a level beyond my experience.'

He said last night's violence began at 7.45, when youths broke into a dairy and removed floats. Police were attacked and police reinforcements ambushed, rocks, iron bars, petrol had.

"In the end, we were forced to use about 25 C.S. gas canisters."

The police chief said he was satisfied with the way his officers handled the riot.

"We deployed our resources to the main area of threat, which in our opinion was Upper Parliament Street. The conclusions that some people draw that the police could have done something in Lodge Lane, but didn't, is totally wrong," he said.

He said police were not happy with the incidents in Lodge Lane and the situa-

... volved in the riots lived in Toxteth and did not seem to be under the contol of their parents.

Senior police officers were meeting today to see what lessons could be learned form the weekend riots.

"But if police are faced with attack from 500 people, we are very limited in our choice of tactics," said Mr. Wright.

"The injuries being suffered by our officers last night were such that the use of C.S. gas was right. "I have no knowledge of C. S. gas being used before on the mainland in a public order situation.

"We cannot allow our officers to suffer brutality without some means to reducd the level of attack. We know there are rubber bullets available. Whether we use them on Merseyside is a judgement we will have to take later."

Police Federation chairman, Mr. Jim Jardine said: "We must have better protection, even if that means the loss of the traditional look of policemen in situations of crowd dusturbance."

He called for crash helmets to prevent head injuries, as well as protective clothing and urged that police should wade in and arrest ringleaders in flare-ups.

BATTLEGROUND . . . the devastation in Toxteth To-day's aerial picture by Eddie Barford. The burnt-out Rialto; NatWest Bank; the unscathed Princes Park Hospital; the ruins of the Racquet Club.

# Mercy men face gangs and bricks

SCORES of ambulancemen called into Liverpool from all over Merseyside to ferry casualties to hospital, were faced with a virtual "no-go" area during the height of last night's riots.

Throughout the disturbances mercy crews braved stone-throwing gangs to tend the hundreds of injured.

One ambulanceman was hit by a brick. An ambulance full of elderly patients evacuated from a Toxteth hospital threatened by flames from a burning building next door even became a target for missiles.

But many calls for help had to go unanswered. "It was a free-for-all. And there were some horrific things happened last night," said Merseyside's Chief Ambulance Officer Mr. Albert Guinney.

"A young baby was choking and yet we couldn't get near it. The father ran 150 yards through everything to get the beby to us.

"One woman was screaming down the phone for an ambulance after her child was injured, but we couldn't get there. People were having coronaries and we could do nothing for a time.

"I wonder if the people responsible for last night realise what they were doing to their own people, perhaps even to their own relatives?"

So busy was the Merseyside Ambulance Service control room last night, that all attempts to monitor calls and keep a tally of patients moved had to be abandoned as empty beds in Liverpool's hospitals began to be filled by the evening's casualties.

"It was bloody terrible, there's no other way of describing it," said Mr. Guinney.

The ambulance chief added: "The men did a fantastic job. They knew the job had to be done and they did it. We had men on duty who just wouldn't go home. They worked on.

"The control room staff too did a really magnificent job

## ECHO COMMENT

**Urban deprivation, Police harassment, high unemployment, racial discrimination . . . reasons behind Toxteth's nights of rioting and looting are being advanced from many quarters.**

**Without doubt, almost every factor being blamed will have played some part in creating a situation out of which such violence and lawlessness have erupted.**

**It is vital that the cause and pattern of events should be established by an inquiry, and a major effort made to bring changes in the crucial areas, whether they are of human relationships or environmental conditions.**

**The immediate task however, is to restore order. What we have seen is a breakdown in law and order unprecedented in this city. Despite the considerable courage of police officers ill-equipped to face such mob violence—and the scale of injuries they have suffered bears testimony to this—looting, burning and wrecking of vehicles has continued, creating scenes reminiscent of Northern Ireland.**

**While the Chief Constable has been asserting that there would be no no-go areas, citizens in some parts, often elderly and living alone, have felt themselves totally unprotected and in a state of extreme fear as mobs have run amok around them.**

**The police policy has been one of containment; that must be abandoned in favour of a more positive approach.**

**There is also strong evidence that extremists from outside have been exploiting the situation. They must be stopped from coming in.**

**New methods may have to be used, methods—like the tear-gas which has proved effective—which no one wishes to employ, and which will no doubt be condemned by some critics.**

**But this situation must not be allowed to continue, and it is not only the duty of the police but the responsibility of every citizen to join ranks until the normal writ of law runs again in all parts of this city.**

... Carr, said he was summon... ing a special meeting of the city council on Friday to discuss the riots.

## STOP PRESS
NEWS DESK 227 2000

**£115,000 DAMAGES:** University graduate Susan Evans, now 27, of Friskney, near Boston, Lincs, whose life was wrecked in car crash five years ago, awarded £115,000 agreed damages in High Court in London. She was left paralysed from the waist down and will be confined to wheel-chair for life.

**WHITELAW REPORT** (See this page): Home Secretary Mr. William Whitelaw to make full report on Toxteth rioting to Commons later to-day.

**MURDER CHARGE:** Two youths appeared at Liverpool Magistrates' Court charged with murder of Police Constable Raymond Davenport. Jeffrey Jaycock (19), of Charlton Road, and Mark Anthony Kelly (20), of Ringcroft Road, both of Wavertree, remanded in custody for seven days until July 13.

**MENACES CHARGE:** Hospital porter, Thomas William Grainger, 31, of Juliet Avenue, Bebington, remanded in custody for seven days by Wirral magistrates charged with making unwarranted demand with menaces for £15,000 from widow, Betty Kirkham, at Rock Ferry, on Friday, and second charge of causing £20,000 damage by fire to wooden pallets at Rock Ferry firm owned by Mrs. Kirkham on June 28.

**MOSCOW'S 'NO':** Soviet Union told Lord Carrington that Common Market proposals for international conference on Afghanistan "not realistic", British sources said in Moscow. But Foreign Minister Andrei Gromyko did not reject it out of hand.

**TEST:** Australia 257-7 (Marsh lbw b Dilley 47)

# Liverpool Echo

31,493    MONDAY, JULY 6, 1981    12p

# DEVASTATED!

## Toxteth landmarks in ruins

THE devastated Toxteth area of Liverpool was to-day counting the multi-million pound cost of a second night of rioting, which left 200 policemen injured and scores of shops wrecked and looted.

Police regained control after seven hours of bloody street battles, during which they were under constant attack by mobs of rampaging youths—and at one stage were forced to use CS gas to fight back the rioters.

To-day, the Toxteth area was scarred with burnt-out vehicles, flattened bus shelters and lamp-posts, and broken glass and rubble.

In Lodge Lane, shop-keepers were clearing up damage—and some claimed they had to arm themselves against what they described as "organised" gangs of looters brandishing machetes and cleavers.

And, at a Press conference to-day at Merseyside Police Headquarters, Deputy Chief Constable

### Inside

Page 3: Aftermath of terror

Pages 6/7: Night of terror

Page 8: Tragic battle

Page 9: Why did it happen?

tion may be handled differently if there was a similar outbreak.

Mr. Wright said it was feared to-night could see a repetition of the violence. There would probably be more uniformed officers available from neighbouring forces.

But the possibility of troops being brought in has been ruled out, he added.

He appealed to parents to keep their children at home.

Mr. Wright said police equipment against the ... bombs and vehicles were ...

## Stay off the street plea

The chairman of Liverpool's Community Relations Council today appealed to the people of Toxteth to stay off the streets.

"We are deeply shocked by the scale of the violence and destruction of last night and the whole weekend," said Mr. Wally Brown.

"I urge everybody in Liverpool 8 to keep off the streets tonight because, otherwise, we are in danger of destroying our community."

Mr. Brown said he thought it was wrong of some politicians and public figures to blame outside agitators for the troubles.

"It became clear last night that these terrible events are a question not only of race, but of young people, both black and white, expressing their resentment against the police.

"Unless the authorities accept this, they will block

The Rialto

NatWest Bank

Princes Park Geriatric Hospital

105

# Thousands line streets to greet Pope John Paul II

IN 1982 Pope John Paul II spent 15 memorable hours in Liverpool.

A simple man with an extraordinary personality and charisma, the visit of the Pilgrim of Peace was one that brought a lifetime of memories for all who saw him.

On Sunday May 30, there were 150,000 people to greet him at Speke airport and crowds cheered his Popemobile on the six miles into the city centre. The Pope went first and most memorably to the city's magnificent Anglican Cathedral then made his way along Hope Street to the modern Catholic Cathedral, Paddy's Wigwam, where he celebrated Mass with his old friend and much-loved city churchman Derek Worlock. Massive crowds who had waited patiently in temperatures of 75°F were greeted with a papal walkabout. The Pope spent the night at the Archbishop's Woolton home before crowds bade him a fond and tearful farewell as he boarded his helicopter at Speke to continue his six-day UK tour.

*Above: Bishop David Sheppard speaks to the Pope*

*Above right: The Order of Mass for celebration at Speke Airport*

*Right: The Pope in Liverpool*

# WEEKEND ECHO

No. 31,767     Weekend Echo, May 29/30, 1982     14p

POPE JOHN PAUL II BRITISH VISIT 1982

## The Pope on Merseyside
12-Page guide for those who want to see him

- The Mass at Speke
- Travel details
- The Pope as a person

# PILGRIM FROM THE VATICAN

## Pope bridges the 500-year gulf

*The Pope and Prince Charles chat privately before entering the cathedral for the service.*

POPE John Paul II today told an old gulf when he made a heartfelt plea for Christian unity during a historic address from the pulpit of Canterbury Cathedral.

Earlier, the Pope's helicopter emerged from the summer blue sky and hovered for many seconds over its landing area before touching down safely—the beginning of an historic pilgrimage.

It was 1,000 years ago that the Romans had built the first church on the site of Canterbury Cathedral. Now, the head of the Church of Rome had arrived.

He emerged from the helicopter to the warm applause of the expectant crowds and made his way down the steps to be warmly embraced by the Archbishop of Canterbury, Dr Robert Runcie.

He was introduced to a welcoming party including the Lord Mayor and his wife and the Chief Constable.

The Pope had smiles and warm words for them all. Cheering crowds lined the route all the way to the cathedral.

The cavalcade made its way into the hotly-viewed St Peter's Place, where he was given a flag-waving reception.

Waving and smiling all the way, the Pope was obviously charmed by the ancient city, and moved by his sincere welcome to Canterbury, the cradle of English Christianity.

As he arrived at the cathedral, he spent some time gazing in admiration towards the building which has seen so many historic events but never, until now, the visit of a reigning Pope.

Shaking hands warmly, the Pope was heard to recall his meeting with "your mother" yesterday—when he spent half an hour with the Queen at Buckingham Palace.

### Division

He said to the Anglicans in the congregation: "My dear brothers and sisters of the Anglican Communion whom I love and long for.

"How happy I am to be able to speak directly to you today in this great cathedral. The building itself is an eloquent witness both to our long years of common inheritance and to the sad years of division that followed."

He recalled the history of the Catholic and Anglican faiths, then added: "I appeal to you in this holy place, all my fellow Christians and especially the members of the Church of England and the members of the Anglican Communion throughout the world, to accept the commitment to which Archbishop Runcie and I pledge ourselves anew before you today."

The Pope spoke of the time before Henry VIII broke away from the Church of Rome and set himself up as head of the Church of England.

He said his own predecessor, Gregory, sent a servant of God called Augustine and several monks to preach the word of God to the English race.

Augustine became the first Archbishop of Canterbury.

He told the congregation: "On this first visit of a Pope to Canterbury I come to you in love."

He added: "With me I bring to you, beloved brothers and sisters of the Anglican Communion, the hopes and the desires, the prayers and the goodwill of all who are united with the Church of Rome."

His visit to the cathedral was, he said a day "which centuries and generations have awaited".

*Pope John Paul...*

## Troops march on after battle

BRITISH troops were poised for the final assault to win back the Falklands after recapturing the settlements of Darwin and Goose Green.

**By Ian Craig**

Argentine forces, dug in around the capital Port Stanley, face attack from both North and South in a pincer movement that will now be progressively tightened.

Paratroops stormed the two settlements, capturing hundreds of Argentine prisoners and the vital air strip at Goose Green, which will now be used as a base for Harrier jump jets.

A number of Argentine soldiers were reported to have been wounded in yesterday's battle, but British casualties are thought to have been light.

Overnight an Argentine Pucara plane was shot down and British warships kept up a steady bombardment of Port Stanley.

Men of the 2nd Battalion of the Parachute Regiment, the Red Devils, took Darwin and Goose Green, the Argentine's second biggest stronghold, with 1,000 troops, after striking out South from the bridgehead at Port San Carlos, 20 miles away.

### Progress

Thousands of Marines and other paratroops are now moving East towards Port Stanley, the key to the Falklands, supported by tanks and artillery.

But Marines and Paras have also made progress along the Northern routes, above the capital, overwhelming Douglas station and Teal Inlet.

In addition to this pincer movement, the land forces can call on the 3,000 troops now believed to be transferred from the QE2 into landing craft. They are likely to disembark on the Eastern edge of the island.

So the massive Argentine garrison is hemmed in.

*A Scorpion light tank.*

And the Governor of the Falklands, Mr. Rex Hunt, has told islanders in a radio broadcast that his bags are packed ready for a swift return.

But it seems certain that sometimes have artillery and missiles posing the high ground along the road to the Falklands capital.

The storming of Darwin and Goose Green, south of the San Carlos beach-head, was done using helicopter-borne troops and Scorpion tanks after tough trials.

The Ministry of Defence said to-day that it was awaiting further reports "on the engagements announced last night at Darwin and Goose Green."

The number of British troops and sailors killed or missing in the Falklands battle has now risen to 114.

The toll was expected to rise to-day when more details were released of the fierce fighting during the recapture by paratroops of Goose Green and Darwin.

The next bout of activity on the island came yesterday from Ministry of Defence spokesman Ian McDonald when he announced that offensive land operations were in progress. Then, dramatically, a statement last night announced baldly that the parachute regiment had recaptured Darwin and Goose Green.

First indications were that the Argentine troops had "fought well".

### Star found dead

*Granada showed coverage of John Paul II's visit to Liverpool*

*The Echo dedicated its front page to the Pope's visit and also issued a Big Picture souvenir edition (below)*

ECHO BIG PICTURE SOUVENIR

# A Pope among us
### JOHN PAUL II ON MERSEYSIDE

A FULL-SCALE air rescue search launched to-day... man who fell overc... from a fishing boat... Formby.

A helicopter crew... R.A.F. Valley and the shore life-boat crew... New Brighton have... sweeping the area... Formby light-buoy for... missing man.

The fisherman was... board the Glenda, be... to have sailed from... pool, when the acc... happened.

"He weather is... lest at the moment,"... spokesman for the... post Coastguard... dinating the hunt. "We only assume at this... that he must have fall...

The water is still... cold and it isn't possi... survive for long...

## 140 jobs axed

A BIRKENHEAD f... run by R.H.M. Agricu... division of Rank... McDougall, is to cl... autumn with the... about 140 jobs.

The company is p... to set up a new distr... centre at Ilmeton,... Warrington.

Announcing the... down, Mr. A. W. Jon... aging director, sai... Birkenhead mill is cl... and has become v... economic.

"We looked long... at ways of improving... operation here, but... decided to close th... move to the distri... centre...

## WE WELCOME YOU WITH A FULL HEART...

# Victory in the Falklands

ARGENTINA invaded the Falkland Islands without warning on April 2, 1982.

The tiny islands in the South Atlantic with just 1,800 inhabitants are 380 miles from Argentina, yet became the focus of world news for ten dramatic weeks with newspaper and TV reports capturing every development.

This British Dependency, since 1833, had been over-run by an Argentinian naval task force who called the Islands Las Malvinas. British Prime Minister Margaret Thatcher immediately fought to reclaim the islands. She sent our own task force to the South Atlantic - 8,000 miles away.

Mrs Thatcher's resolve won her popularity with not only the Forces chiefs but her loyal supporters in Britain.

The Argentinians surrendered on June 14, 1982.

The Falklands War had been fought on land, sea and sky.

The crisis saw 255 British servicemen die - mostly sailors - and 655 Argentine servicemen lost their lives in the conflict.

*June 19, 1982*

*Left: The frigate Antelope is silhouetted by a devastating fireball that ripped through her heart after she was hit by a 1,000lb bomb*

*Overleaf: An Echo special, in aid of the South Atlantic Fund, marked the victory*

*June 15, 1982*

The Liverpool Echo, Tuesday, June 15, 1982

B

**VICTORY IN THE FALKLANDS!**
Special pages inside

# Liverpool Echo

31,780 TUESDAY, June 15, 1982 14p

ELS
FURNITURE & CARPET SUPERSTORE
PARK ROAD LIVERPOOL 8
Telephone: (051) 727 1903

# 11,000 Argentine troops in the bag

THE British flag was today flying over the Governor's house in the Falklands capital Port Stanley with 11,000 Argentine prisoners in the bag.

Victory has brought new problems for the British commander Major-General Jeremy Moore—many of the Argentines captured at Port Stanley are said to be "in a bad way" suffering from exposure, exhaustion and frostbite.

The number of Argentines captured has astonished the Ministery of Defence.

Sources believe the Hercules reinforcement flights have been secretly landing nightly with more and more troops for the "last bullet last man" defence General Menendez promised, but failed to deliver.

The total number of Argentine troops involved in the islands is thought to have totalled 14,000—6,000 more than the entire British land force.

A supply ship has also been found in Stanley Harbour, which had slipped through the Navy cordon enforcing the 200 miles total exclusion zone around the islands.

Once the Argentines have had their names, ranks, and numbers recorded, and been shipped out of the islands, special runway repair teams already on the Falklands will work 24 hours a day to get Stanley airfield working again.

Despite the constant and ferocious air and naval bombardment of the runway and facilities, it is believed in London the airfield could be operational again in just two days.

There is speculation in London that two squadrons of Phantom air defence aircraft may be flown to Stanley, being refuelled at Ascension Island and then from Victor air-to-air tankers, to provide a potent force against possible Argentine air attacks.

It still seems too early to assume that the Falklands war is completely over.

Reports from Buenos Aires suggest the military junta may continue to launch hit-and-run air raids by Mirage and Skyhawk fighter bombers in a face-saving operation to keep up the Argentine claim to the Falklands.

### Death toll

● The civilian death-toll in the Falklands has risen to three, according to a pooled despatch from reporter Max Hastings.

Recent reports said that Mrs. Sue Whitley and Mrs. Doreen Bonner had been killed during a British naval bombardment of Port Stanley.

But Mrs. Mary Godwin (82), has also died.

She was sheltering with the two others in a house hit by a single shell.

Falklands executive councillor Mr. Bill Luxton, who was deported from the islands at the beginning of the conflict, was shattered to hear of another death.

He said Mrs. Goodwin, although elderly, had been in fairly good health and had lived on the islands all her life.

● The Queen was "delighted and relieved" when she received news of the ceasefire in the Falklands. Her Press secretary, Mr. Michael Shea, said to-day she was given the news at Windsor.

At a Press conference in Edinburgh on the royal visit to Scotland he said: "In view of the news, I would like to say that the Queen, who was immediately informed, is delighted and relieved.

"She is very pleased and proud of the courage, determination and professionalism of the servicemen and all those involved down there."

☐ The end of the 75-day conflict was signalled in this dramatic message from Major-General Jeremy Moore, the land force commander:

"In Port Stanley at 9 p.m. Falkland time to-night, June 14, Major-General Menendez surrendered all Argentine armed forces in East and West Falklands, together with their impediments.

"Arrangements are in hand to assemble the men for return to Argentina, to gather in their arms and equipment and to mark and make safe their munitions.

"The Falkland Islands are once more under the government desired by their inhabitants.

"God Save the Queen."

Signed J. Moore."

## ...and from Port Stanley, the heartfelt message

# 'BY GOD, YOU'RE SO WELCOME!'

BRITISH forces are in Port Stanley.

At 5.45 p.m. British time, as men of the Parachute Regiment halted on the outskirts at the end of their magnificent drive on the capital. I walked through the Argentinian lines with my hands in the air and met the town's civilian population.

"By God, you are welcome," said Monsignor Daniel Spraggon, Stanley's catholic priest, with delighted fervour as I told him of the British forces, a few hundred yards behind me.

"It's bloody marvellous as far as I'm concerned," said Ian Stewart, local manager of Cable and Wireless.

As we talked, hundreds—perhaps thousands—of dejected Argentine troups marched in columns past us down the main street to prepare to surrender. I walked to the Argentine civil admin. building, and met their senior colonel on the steps.

"Are you ready to surrender West as well as East Falklands?" I asked. "I think so," he said, "but it is best to wait until your general meets general Mendendez."

This story really begins last night, when men of the Guards, the Gurkhas and the Parachute Regiment launched a major attack supported by a overwhelming British bombardment upon the last line of enemy positions on the high ground above Stanley.

The enemy responded with massive artillery fire. Civilians told me this afternoon that they had been firing from the very houses of Stanley, and indeed while I was under fire with the attacking Parachute Battalion, they were told repeatedly on the radio that our guns could not shoot directly upon the enemy batteries because these were in the midst of the capital.

Three civilians died in

> ● In Denmark a top newspaper said: "Politically and psychologically, Margaret Thatcher has won an outstanding personal victory . . . the junta was allowed far too long to believe that its recklessness would be rewarded."

**● From Max Hastings and David Norris with the Parachute Regiment in Port Stanley.**

British counter-battery fire the night before last, as far as we know the only civilian casualties of the war.

At first light to-day, the paras were preparing to renew their attack in a few hours after seizing all their objectives on Wireless Ridge under fierce shell and mortar fire.

Suddenly, word came that enemy troops could be seen fleeing for their lives in all directions around Port Stanley. They had evidently had enough. The decision was taken to press on immediately to complete their collapse.

Spearheaded by a company of the Parachute Regiment commanded by Major Dare Farrar-Hockley, son of the regiment's colonel, British forces began a headlong dash down the rocky hills for honour of being first into Stanley.

I marched with Major Farrar-Hockley through the ruins of the former Royal Marine base at Moody Brook, then past the smoking remains of buildings and strongpoints destroyed by our shelling and bombing.

Our route was littered with the debris of the enemy's utter defeat—clothing ammunition, vehicles, weapons, food, shell and bomb craters.

We were already past the first houses of the town, indeed up to the war memorial beside the sea, when the order came through to halt, pending negotiations, and to fire only in self-defence.

The paras stopped on the racecourse, where they raised their flag and we listened to the last shell and machine gun fire from the hills above where the Guards and Gurkhas were mopping up.

The men, desperately tired after three nights without sleep, exhulted like schoolboys in this great moment of victory.

Blackened, shaggy, unshaven, bent under mud-coated equipment and ammunition belts, they knew that this was their achievement.

Major Farrar-Hockley ordered off helmets, on red berets. Some men showed their sadness for those who hadn't made it all the way, who had died even during the last night of bitter fighting.

As the road ahead stretched empty, I stripped off my military equipment and combat clothes, and walked into Stanley in a blue civilian anorak with my hands high in the air.

The Argentinians made no hostile movement as I moved past the apparently undamaged but heavily bunkered Government House to Port Stanley's famous hotel, the Upland Goose.

There I met one of the few audiences in my life willing to clap and cheer my coming, under false pretences, since it was really the men of the British forces to whom they wanted to pay homage.

They offered me a drink and began to talk about all that had happened in the past three months.

> ● Another Falklands singalong organised by Huyton housewife Audrey Wilson is to be held to-morrow night at Liverpool's Pier Head to mark the British victory and pay tribute to servicemen who lost their lives.

It was like liberating a pub, or a community, in East Surrery or Kent. The Falklanders, as I suppose I must call them, though they might have been any saloon bar group in England, said the Argentinians did not behave intolerably badly towards them, although there were moments when they were pushing civilians hither and thither at the point of sub-machine guns.

"The last few days were the worst," said the owner of the Upland Goose, Desmond King. The 600 civilians left in Stanley had been compelled to listen to the continuous roar of gunfire from the hills, apprehensive that the battle would soon be in their own streets.

They revealed that the Argentinians had been beating the British blockade until the very end. Hercules aircraft had been flying onto the airfield as late as last night, and much more serious, the huge container ship Formosa had beaten the blockade around May 1 to unload huge quantities of food and ammunition.

The civilians rejoiced freely in the British triumph: "Never for a moment did we doubt that British forces would come," said Mr. King.

In another pooled despatch, David Norris writes:

I walked into the liberated capital with the Second Battalion, the Parachute Regiment, the soldiers I have accompanied throughout the Falklands Campaign.

It was a Two Para Sergeant Major, Dave Fenwick, who raised the Union Flag over Stanley Racecourse, watched by his commanding officer, Lieutenant Colonel David Chaundler.

Lieutenant Colonel Chaundler, who took over command after the death of Colonel "H" Jones at the battle of Goose Green, told me: "It has been the most amazing two weeks of my life. My feeling now is one of relief — a feeling that at the end of the day, the British can't be kicked around."

Two Para, came down from Wireless Ridge, the enemy position they had captured in the freezing darkness of the night, to file down the hillside onto the narrow, paved road into Stanley.

Through the night, enemy guns had pounded us. I crouched in a shallow "shell scrape" trench with three sergeants as mortars crashed into the frost-covered field around us.

Spearhead companies of Two Para were attacking the enemy trenches' in front of us, on Wireless Ridge. Artillery fire from both sides thundered above us, lighting up the night sky.

At first light the news was "they are running." A pathetic group of 13 Argentinian prisoners told us they had been without food for three days. Their officers had fled during the fighting.

We walked up to the abandoned Wireless Ridge position — and looked down over Stanley.

A para sergeant handed me a flask of whisky and said: "They've jacked — it's all over." He had been keeping the Scotch for just that occasion.

It has been a long and bitter campaign, during which I have walked — or in Para Parlance "tabbed it" from one end of East Falklands to the other, sleeping in muddy trenches, or sometimes in the comparative luxury of a wool shed. I would not have missed it.

Staff Sergeant Peter Harbuirn summed it up: "This is a great day for the Parachute Regiment.

# Britain salutes Maggie

Victory . . . Bur the strain and relief shows on the face of Mrs. Thatcher as she faces an enthusiastic reception from well-wishers outside No. 10 Downing Street.

CONGRATULATIONS were pouring into Downing Street to-day as Prime Minister Mrs. Thatcher gave to give M.P.s full details of the surrender of the Argentine garrison on the Falklands.

She spelled out the massive problems of handling thousands of Argentine prisoners, desperately short of food and accommodation.

In the aftermath of today's surrender the Government faces enormous administrative difficulties in preparing the prisoners for an eventual return to Argentina.

But first, Mrs. Thatcher is insisting that all hostilities end — and that includes air attacks from the Artentine mainland.

The Government does not have to hand the prisoners over immediately.

Mrs. Thatcher was due to fly tonight to a United Nations meeting in New York, but she may delay the flight because of circumstances.

Meanwhile, the future of the Falkland Islands has to be decided.

The Port Stanley airport runway has to be extended by several thousand feet. And this will be supervised in the short-term by Major General Moore.

Bringing life back to normal will be aided by the engineers who have all the necessary equipment for, for instance, repairing the runway, building roads and bridges, and restoring water and sewerage supplies.

Mrs. Thatcher is expected soon to announce that she will visit the Falklands, in the aftermath of the war. And Lord Shackleton's report on its future development is expected to land on her desk soon.

# 'Final bullet' hits heartbreak family

**By Mark Thomas**

THE "final bullet" for a heart-broken Liverpool family dropped through their letterbox to-day on the first day of peace in the Falklands.

The news they had dreaded, that their Army medic son was dead, came after an agonising weekend of waiting and praying.

Lance Corporal Ian Farrell, (22), of Hodder Place, Everton, was one of the dead from the Argentine attack on the Sir Galahad.

His family were warned he was missing on Friday and on Saturday evening were told he must be presumed dead.

Weeping as he held the brief Ministry of Defence letter in his hand, his father, Raymond (46), said: "We got the final bullet this morning."

Ian, a keen fisherman, with four sisters and one brother, joined the Army two and a half years ago.

"It was sheer boredom after he was unemployed," said Mrs. Farrell. "He was full of energy and kept saying it was a great life."

### Dumps

Ian had been bitterly disappointed when most of his unit sailed for the Falkland Islands aboard QE2 and he was one of the men left behind.

"He was really down in the dumps because he wasn't going," said Mr. Farrell.

"Then he was told he was going to be flown to Ascension Island to join the Task Force. It was what he had been trained to do and he was pleased

The couple both spoke of their pride that Ian died fighting for his country.

"For the little bit of real estate involved, it doesn't seem worth it," said Mr. Farrell.

"But the principle behind it was right — and we are proud of him."

## STOP PRESS

NEWS DESK 227 2000

**WEATHER:** Merseyside: Light rain in places later. Outlook: Warme,r but unsettled. Rain or showers, some heavy. Liverpool Bay: Winds south-east, forces 3 or less, becoming southerly, force 4. Visibility good, moderate in rain. Sea slight. High water: 18.25, 7.5 metres. To-morrow: 06.54, 7.9 metres; 19.35, 7.7 metres. Lighting-up: 22.15 to 04.12.

**NO ALL-OUT STRIKE:** Confederation of Health Service Employees' conference in Bridlington rejected calls for all-out strikes in Health Service. Delegates backed union's national executive in calling for more selective withdrawals by key groups of staff.

**BODY FOUND:** Murder hunt launched after woman's body found in Garden Field Lane, Thurmaston, Leicester. She had been stabbed in throat.

**WATER APPEAL:** Save water appeal to householders on Merseyside and North-West made by Regional Water Authority. Officials concerned over drop in levels of many reservoirs.

**BLANEY GUILTY:** Michael Blaney convicted by Liverpool magistrates of wasting police time. Sentenced to six months' imprisonment, suspended for two years. See page 3.

**ULSTER SHOOTING:** Part-time UDR man shot dead in Stranbane, Co. Tyrone.

**THIRSK**

**2.15:** Charlottes Dunce 1, Shabnam 2, Orange Rose 3; 12-1, 2-1 fav, 6-1.

**ASCOT**

**2.30:** Mr. Flourocarbon 1, Noalcoholic 2, Spanish Pool 3; 3-1 jt fav, 33-1, 8-1, Beiteo Earl jnt fav.

QUALITY BUILT IN

● We manufacture
● We install (no subcontractors)
● We Guarantee

St. Helens Glass
ALUMINIUM WINDOWS, DOORS AND PATIOS

£10 deposit AND NO MORE TO PAY FOR 6 months

Home Improvement Loan typical APR 18.3. Written quotation on request.
Tel: St Helens (0744) 53332

SHG Co Ltd St. Helens Glass
Freepost, St. Helens WA10 1BR
Name
Address
Tel.
I am interested in:
☐ Aluminium Patio Doors
☐ Aluminium Replacement Windows
☐ Aluminium Doors
☐ Aluminium Bays
☐ Porches
LE 156

## Help us help the South Atlantic Fund

THE people of the Falklands are free again thanks to the heroism and the sacrifice of the men of the Task Force

Now, as a permanent record of a campaign unique in the annals of British military history and as a tangible expression of gratitude to our fighting men, the Liverpool Echo is to publish a special edition "Victory in the Falklands."

All the proceeds will go to the South Atlantic Fund.

The Liverpool Echo with help from some of its suppliers is providing all the production facilities, newsprint and materials. We are asking our friends the newsagents to co-operate to ensure that the entire 14p cover price goes to help the families of the servicemen who have been killed or wounded in the fight for freedom.

The business community of Merseyside is being asked to place advertisements in the publication. All those proceeds, too, will go to the fund.

"Victory in the Falklands" will be on sale this week. Please remember—all the proceeds will go to the South Atlantic Fund.

A TRIBUTE
TO ALL
BRITONS
IN THE
FALKLANDS
CONFLICT

ECHO special in aid of the South Atlantic Fund

# VICTORY
## IN THE FALKLANDS

Saturday, June 19, 1982

14p

# TV drama as Brookside bursts onto soap scene

THE first episode of soap opera Brookside, set in fictional Liverpool cul-de-sac Brookside Close, was screened on Channel Four's launch night on November 2.

Created by Phil Redmond and his Mersey TV company, the show caused controversy right from the start as it was criticised for its violent scenes and language that was slightly more colourful than expected in a prime-time soap.

Brookside helped to shoot many well-known personalities to fame, including Ricky Tomlinson, Claire Sweeney, Jennifer Ellison and Anna Friel.

Based around families such as the Dixons, the Corkhills, the Shadwicks and the Grants, the soap featured an array of gripping storylines involving everything from murders and drug-dealing to love affairs and bullying.

Following ratings slumps and schedule changes to late-night slots, Brookside ended its impressive 21-year run in the early hours of November 5 2003, and storylines in the final episode were as explosive as ever.

The Echo TV editor gives his report on the build-up to Brookside

## All set for new style Coronation Street

ALL eyes will be on Channel 4 tonight as the viewing public at last finds out what all the fuss is about.

And the programme creating most curiosity on Merseyside is Brookside (8.00), the new Liverpool-based soap opera that puts the emphasis on realism.

It's said that Brookside families even watch Coronation Street — so in theory that must mean they could even switch over and watch themselves!

The opening episode shows the new neighbours just starting to move into their houses on the smart little cul-de-sac on the edge of the huge Croxteth Park estate.

The Collins family who come from a big house on Wirral and regard their move to

● Roger Walker: Squadron, BBC-1.

### By Roy West
### TV Editor

Brookside as coming down in the world find themselves straight away facing confrontation with the more down-to-earth Grants, a family who're buying their first house after living on a council estate.

A lot of hopes are riding on Brookside, which is being shot on location in real houses and around various parts of Merseyside. The first year's budget is nearly £3.5 million and Channel 4 see it as one of their chances of winning a big popular audience.

As for the rest of the Channel 4 evening it's an odd mixture.

The real heavyweight offering is a film drama called Walter, a grim but moving account of the life of a mentally handicapped man.

Ian McKellen takes the title role in a story that has some nightmare moments but stresses Channel 4's commitment to "caring" programme-making.

One of the best programmes of the night could well be In The Pink (10.45), a lively revue that puts the woman's viewpoint without ever preaching.

More way-out is The Comic Strip Presents . . . Five Go Mad in Dorset (10.15) — a distinctly irreverent spoof on Enid Blyton's Famous Five, that features Crossroads star Ronnie Allen (alias David Hunter) as an outrageous homosexual and portrays the children's aunt Fanny as an alcoholic nymphomaniac.

*Main image: Brookside was explosive, controversial but always memorable, as this special Echo montage shows*

*Right: Roy West's review of Brookside, which debuted on Channel Four's opening night*

*Below: Roy's verdict on the rest of the shows on the launch night of Channel Four*

Wednesday, October 30, 2002    **BROOKSIDE SPECIAL**    www.icliverpool.co.uk    Page **15**

OKSIDE CLOSE

## A bold debut, of sorts

CHANNEL FOUR is good for you ... that seemed to be the message judging by the choice of programmes for the opening night. Rather like a certain brand of stout, you might say. Except that a night on the Guinness is a lot more fun.

As promised, it started quietly enough. Just a quick welcome, then straight into a quiz called Countdown that must have fascinated Scrabble fans who love mental arithmetic but must have lost most people.

Having sharpened our minds they then turned to our bodies with half an hour of dancing to music, presumably designed to get you in shape to tackle the rest of the evening's programmes.

If by now you were feeling relaxed there was a special reason. Instead of adverts every quarter of an hour, along came a musical interlude, thanks to a union dispute settled too late to save the commercials.

Trying hard to look relaxed were C4's casually dressed presenters including a lady called Olga, sporting a vivid yellow scarf and an affected manner, I will charitably put down to first night nerves.

Brookside is not the kind of soap you allow to wash over you. Rather it's the new improved biological brand that tackles the deep-seated social problems other soaps fail to reach.

## Brookside kicks off with a rumpus

*George Spenton-Foster — quit after three months.*

CONTROVERSY enveloped Brookside, the new Liverpool soap opera to-day, after its top director quit in a row over bad language and violence.

George Spenton-Foster quit after he had worked for just three months on Brookside, created by Liverpool's Phil Redmond and set in a city cul-de-sac. "It's full of language I would not use in front of my own children with an unacceptable degree of physical violence," he said.

To-day Phil Redmond, who also created the controversial B.B.C. series Grange Hill, refused to comment on Spenton-Foster's resignation other than to say, via a secretary: "The question of language and violence is one of interpretation. Anyone who knows me and my reputation will realise I know how far to go."

Mr. Spenton-Foster (55) said he was washing his hands of Brookside after months of trying to get the series cleaned up.

### Tough

Spenton-Foster claimed Redmond wanted the scripts to be very tough and very vulgar. The row developed when Redmond implied he was softening the impact by the way he directed.

Spenton-Foster revealed that a lot of the swearing in the original scripts had been toned down. His greatest objection was to the series being repeated at Saturday tea-time, when lots of small children would be watching.

### By Roy West
### TV Editor

seemed appropriate to the characters.

Out of three families from a neighbouring road on the Croxteth estate who watched the episode for a special Echo feature (See Page Six) not one person took exception to the swear words.

### Reputation

The cast themselves celebrated the screening of the first episode at a party in the city.

Ricky Tomlinson, who plays shop steward Bobby Grant, said: "The atmosphere was something like what you would expect at the first night of a big London show. We watched the show, but, unfortunately, I didn't see it, if you know what I mean. I was concentrating too much on my performance ... looking at ways it could be improved."

On the subject of language used in the first episode Ricky said it was no different than one could hear any day in Liverpool.

"Phil Redmond has put his reputation on the line with Brookside. If he is prepared to take a chance then we should be prepared to back him to the

# Queen Elizabeth opens city Garden Festival

QUEEN Elizabeth opened the first International Garden Festival held in Great Britain at a purpose built site alongside the Mersey on May 2, 1984. Accompanied by Prince Philip, the Queen was greeted at Lime Street station by crowds of well wishers before spending four-and-a-half hours taking in the sights of the festival.

Finishing touches were still being made to the displays when the Royal party arrived but preparations had taken almost two-and-a half years to transform the area from a derelict dock to a spectacular 250-acre garden.

A rousing welcome was given to the Queen, who stood on a colourful Royal podium, surrounded by British flowers, while she listened to the traditional song 'In My Liverpool Home'.

The Queen also opened the £35.5m Queen Elizabeth II Law Courts complex later that same day.

*Clockwise from top: An Echo royal souvenir from the garden festival; Queen Elizabeth II enjoys a stroll around the gardens, meeting some famous faces along the way; and the full extent of the garden festival site*

*Left: A sculpture in the Liverpool Quiz Garden, sponsored by the Echo*

"Some people have probably wondered about the relevance of a garden festival in a derelict area of Liverpool but I think it is most appropriate. The wonderful feature of nature is its powers of renewal. Plants wither and die but with the coming of spring growth begins again. The gardens and exhibitions blooming on the site are symbolic of what we all wish for Liverpool"

Queen Elizabeth II

## Some of the attractions

- A giant dragon slide, which was thought up by 14-year-old Theodore Gayer-Anderson who won a Blue Peter competition to design a fantasy garden

- Toxteth-based Diggers community project produced a mini Scouseland for the Liverpool Quiz Garden, which was sponsored by the Echo. It featured pieces of Merseyside history, cartoons by Bill Tidy and sculptures from Liverpool Polytechnic

- A glasshouse featuring semi-tropical and tropical plants sent specially by countries such as India, Singapore and Sri Lanka

- A Japanese garden, featuring a small pool, wooden pavilion and moon-view platform

- A 1,000ft-long tiered Esplanade which ran from Riverside's old Herculaneum Dock to the Britannia Inn pub

- Red steam engine Samson which pulled visitors around two miles of miniature railway track

- The festival hall, which held the main horticultural shows and some of the permanent exhibits. It was longer than a football pitch

- A huge Yellow Submarine dominated the Beatles maze. Narrow winding paths led visitors through lily-filled pools in the shape of the famous half-apple symbol into the belly of the sub, there to see the Octopus's Garden and hear the Fab Four's music

## FAST FACTS

- The 12-month reclamation of the land undertaken by the Merseyside Development Corporation cost 12.5 million and employed around 500 workers

- More than 3.5 million tons of rubbish and earth were moved from a site that was once a derelict dock, three fuel container farms and a civic rubbish tip

- The giant Festival Hall was heated by methane gas produced by the decaying rubbish under the festival throughout the 23-week event

- The sunburst display of tulips, covering 1.925sqm, was the largest in Europe

- There were around 5,000 different species of plants on display

- The system of streams, waterfalls and rapids around the display used 2.5 million gallons of water

# 1986

# Blues meet Reds in FA Cup Final

*The Pink Football Echo covered all the action from the all-Merseyside cup final*

THE first and only all Merseyside FA Cup Final took Liverpool and Everton to Wembley on May 10, 1986.

Kenny Dalglish, crowned manager of the year, built up the suspense to the cup clash by not announcing his injury-struck Liverpool side until after the team had reached Wembley. Steve McMahon was given the substitute spot in the side making him the only Englishman and the only Merseysider in the squad. Everton fielded their strongest possible team with the exception of injured goalkeeper, Neville Southall.

Liverpool won the game 3-1 being only the third team of the century to walk away with the league and FA cup double.

The 1986 Merseyside FA Cup Final was replayed for the Marina Dalglish appeal in May 2006 at Anfield.

# Football ECHO

## The VOICE of Mersey Sport

32,968

SATURDAY MAY 10, 1986

16p

**Gary Gillespie**

# KENNY'S KINGS DOUBLE TOPS

## Virus keeps out Gary

KENNY Dalglish had his Wembley selection problems solved for him today when it was found that Gary Gillespie had not recovered from a virus complaint which has been troubling him for the last two days.

His absence meant a recall for the experienced Mark Lawrenson, with Kevin MacDonald continuing in the midfield spot that he has filled so capably during the last five games of the championship.

The substitute's spot went to Steve McMahon, who was playing against his old club and was not only the only Englishman but the only Merseysider in the Liverpool 12.

There was better news for Everton with centre back Derek Mountfield showing no ill effects from the knee injury that has been bothering him all week.

Mountfield had not been able to train normally and was a major doubt but he was put through a tough workout this morning and came through without any discomfort.

Consequently, Everton fielded their strongest possible team, with the obvious exception of Neville Southall, naming Adrian Heath as substitute.

It was Mountfield's third Cup Final in succession and his presence gave Everton additional scoring power as well as strengthening the defence.

Dalglish, crowned manager of the year yesterday, did not announce his team until after the party had reached Wembley. He said: "It is very bad luck for Gillespie, but it is bad luck also for Paul Walsh and Sammy Lee. They have all played a part in our championship and Cup successes and it was very difficult to leave them out."

## Rush and Johnston sink Blues

by Ken Rogers

### Everton 1, Liverpool 3

LIVERPOOL came storming back at Wembley this afternoon, wiping out a Gary Lineker opener and becoming only the third team this century to claim a League and F.A.Cup double - Ian Rush with two and Craig Johnston scoring the second half goals that destroyed Everton's dreams.

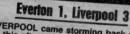

**LINE-UP**

**Everton:** Mimms; Stevens, Mountfield, Ratcliffe, Van Den Hauwe; Steven, Reid, Bracewell, Sheedy; Lineker, Sharp. Sub. Heath.

**Liverpool:** Grobbelaar; Nicol, Lawrenson, Hansen, Beglin; Johnston, Molby, MacDonald, Whelan; Dalglish, Rush. Sub. McMahon.

An end to end first half was significant for two things - a loud Graeme Sharp penalty appeal and Gary Lineker's opening goal - secured in dramatic fashion after 29 minutes.

Sharp was furious when referee Alan Robinson denied him that early spot kick after the Scot appeared to be pushed in the back by Steve Nicol.

But Everton's disappointment on that score turned to elation when Lineker's pace took him powering into the box to beat Bruce Grobbelaar on the rebound and make the breakthrough.

Liverpool made a shaky start to the second half, but they suddenly exploded into life when Rush cashed in on a Gary Stevens error to round Bobby Mimms and equalise. Craig Johnston then sent the Liverpudlians wild with delight when he slotted home in front of the posts after 62 minutes to turn the game on its head and give his side the lead - a remarkable turnaround to a thoroughly entertaining final.

Kenny Dalglish, the first player-manager at Wembley, led his team proudly into the sunshine alongside Howard Kendall. The 105th F.A.Cup Final - such an historic occasion for Merseyside - was about to unfold. The players looked relaxed as they were introduced to Her Royal Highness, The Duchess of Kent, dressed suitably in neutral green.

But there was nothing neutral about Bruce Grobbelaar - the colourful Anfield keeper was sporting a bright red cap.

It was the Blues who had the first chance to threaten when Hansen pushed Sharp just outside the box to concede a free kick. The fans expected a Sheedy bender around the defensive wall, but Stevens stepped up to shoot high over the top.

Continued on Back Page

Blues for Reds! Gary Lineker puts Everton ahead after Grobbelaar had saved his initial shot.

**Inside: Super pictures of historic occasion**

**Have we spotted you in crowd? — see inside**

# City in shock as fans are crushed at Hillsborough

NINETY-SIX Liverpool FC fans died and hundreds were injured in Britain's worst ever football disaster on April 16, 1989.

The FA Cup semi final between Liverpool and Nottingham Forest took place at Hillsborough, the home of Sheffield Wednesday.

Both teams had played in the semi final at the same ground the previous year with no problems.

Many factors contributed to the tragedy. Due to traffic problems, Liverpool fans were arriving late leading to thousands of them being left standing outside the Leppings Lane turnstiles.

South Yorkshire Police, fearing a crush, opened gates leading to a narrow tunnel at the rear of the terrace. Fans streamed down into the central section and supporters at the front were pushed against steel fencing.

Many tried to climb over the fences, others were being pulled up by supporters into the upper tier.

The city of Liverpool and soccer fans everywhere were in shock. Eyewitnesses said the pitch had resembled a battlefield, as the victims were rushed from the stadium on stretchers and advertising hoardings.

One 17-year-old survivor said: "A human wave surged forward crushing people against the fencing at the front. There was nothing they could do, and nowhere they could go. I shall never go to another football match in my life."

The Echo published a 28-page disaster edition revealing the full horrors of Hillsborough

# 28-page disaster edition

## Sunday ECHO

33,870

SUNDAY, APRIL 16, 1989

20p

# OUR DAY OF TEARS

## The toll

# 93 DEAD, OVER 200 INJURED (SEE BACK PAGE)

INSIDE: The full horror of Hillsborough in words and dramatic pictures

Liverpool Echo, Sunday, April 16, 1989    13

☐ Stunned ... grim-faced Liverpool manager Kenny Dalglish looks on as the disaster unfolds

# 'FOOTBALL IS IRRELEVANT — IT'S THE FANS THAT COUNT . . .'

REDS' MANAGER Kenny Dalglish said: "The thing that is most upsetting is that there was no animosity there — it was just sheer volume of numbers that caused it.

"There is not a lot we can do. We can only sympathise with people that have had fatalities and friends and relatives who have unfortunately been injured."

Asked about Heysel he said: "There are different circumstances. There is no comparison whatsoever between the two.

"I am sure that there will be people accusing certain bodies of irresponsibility, but at the end of the day that is irrelevant at the moment.

### By Bob Burns

"The only thing we could do at the end of incident was to try to help the people out there and ensure that the numbers of people involved and dying were going to be minimal.

"It is a family club that we have got. There were a lot of people there who knew each other. They may have not gone to the game with the persons who died but they have known them.

"Football is irrelevant when something like that happens. Nobody has bothered to ask the scores nobody even wants to know the scores."

Nottingham Forest coach L. O'Kane said: "We're devastated too ... came to play football and a lot of people have lost their lives."

**We came to play football now a lot of people have lost their lives**

—Liam O'Kane

## Heysel agony – Page 17

# Liverpool ECHO

OUTLOOK:
Cold,
with rain.
★★ ★

35,269          FRIDAY★★★★OCTOBER 15, 1993          26p

## Damages for MP Bob

BOB PARRY was one of three MPs who accepted a public apology and undisclosed libel damages today.

They sued over a newspaper article listing them among politicians who had "failed to shine" in Parliament.

Tories David Atkinson and Sir Fergus Montgomery and Labour's Mr Parry (Riverside) were featured in a full-page article entitled "The Dozy Dozen".

It was published in the London Evening Standard in January last year.

Publishers Associated Newspapers withdrew any suggestion that the three MPs were inactive or ineffectual.

## Ramraiders' car gets stuck in window

# BUNGLING BANDITS

BUNGLING ramraiders fled empty-handed after their raid on a TV shop ended in chaos.

CRASH! Their getaway car became stuck fast in the shop window.

BANG! They dropped two TV sets as they tried to get away on foot.

WALLOP! They ran onto high-voltage railways lines to avoid being caught by the police — and trains were delayed when the power had to be switched off.

### By Caroline Storah, ECHO Crime Reporter

The three-man gang staged their botched raid at a Colorvision store, in Walton Vale, Liverpool, early today.

The car, a stolen Vauxhall Cavalier, was reversed at high speed and crashed into the shop window around 5am.

*But it became embedded in the shopfront, and the raiders were unable to move it for their getaway.*

They then dropped the two television sets at the scene, before fleeing on foot onto the railway as police moved in.

British Transport Police shut off the power on the 650-volt Liverpool-Ormskirk line for 40 minutes — from 5.40am to 6.20am — while a search was carried out close to Rice Lane Station.

A spokesman for Merseyside Police, said: "It appears they drove the car in too hard, and it became stuck fast.

"When it came to escaping they couldn't get it out of the window, so they had to abandon it.

"They were seen running onto the tracks, and the power had to be shut down for a thorough search."

The owner of the stolen Cavalier was unaware that his car had been at the centre of the drama until police informed him.

Nobody has been arrested. Anyone with information is asked to contact the CID at Walton Lane on:

051 777 3381.

## Widow hears crash that killed her son

A MERSEYSIDE mum rushed to the scene of a road accident outside her home, to find her only son lying critically injured.

Nine year old David Charsley died from his injuries a few hours later.

Today his distraught relatives were trying to come to terms with the second tragedy to strike the family.

For David's father died from cancer three years ago.

The road accident happened as David returned to his home in Border Road, Heswall, after school yesterday.

### By Vic Gibson

Moments after stepping off his school bus, he was struck by a van.

*His mother, Jenny, heard the accident and rushed from her home.*

Mrs Charsley, 44, who has a 14-year-old daughter, Vicky, was today being comforted by family and friends.

David, a pupil at the private Mostyn House School, in Parkgate, south Wirral suffered

● Turn to Page Two

□ Reely great . . . Jim settles down to watch the hit movie today

## Jim's Parking space

NOW HERE'S a reel treat!

Cinema boss Jim Walker has finally put his feet up — to watch the hit movie Jurassic Park.

The boss of Cannon Cinema, in Lime Street, Liverpool, has played the film close on THREE HUNDRED times for Merseyside fans.

*But he's been too busy to watch it himself.*

And it is just the sort of movie he loves to see.

So Jim decided it was time to give himself a treat.

He arranged to have a MORNING showing of the hit movie — all to himself.

Screenplay by Ann Todd
Picture: Tracey O'Neill

And his staff gave Jim the VIP treatment for a change.

Jim says: "It made a nice change to sit down myself, with my popcorn and fizzy drink, to enjoy a film.

"Usually, the only chance I get to see a film is at a tiny cinema on holiday in Cornwall — where I stand in the queue with everyone else to get in!"

And Jim's expert verdict on Jurassic Park?

*"Wonderful entertainment!"*

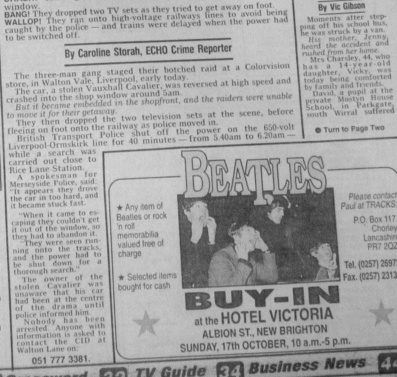
**INSIDE** Weather **2** Letters **26** Crossword **32** TV Guide **34** Business News **44**

*The last black and white Echo, Friday October 15, 1993*

# Liverpool ECHO

**OUTLOOK:** Sunny spells, rain later

35,270

SATURDAY, OCTOBER 16, 1993

26p

## My life after soccer
### One-time Anfield boy wonder fights back — Page 15

---

## Brand NEW Banger

BANGERS were really on the menu for this Merseyside family's Big Breakfast this morning.

John Campbell was in charge of the eggs.

Wife Jan took care of the bacon.

*Picture by Eddie Barford*

And nine-year-old son Johnathan took care of the pot of tea.

But the tastiest treat of all was being served up outside the front door of their home in Anfield.

□ Read their sizzling story — on Page 3.

---

### Police launch biggest-ever war on vice

# RED LIGHT BLITZ

POLICE are to launch their biggest ever crackdown on prostitution in Liverpool's red light district.

Officers will flood the streets of the city's notorious Anglican cathedral area, in a high-profile bid to show their commitment to cleaning up the problem.

From next Sunday until October, 31, **Operation Sara** — which stands for Safe And Reassured Area — will swing into action.

Up to 40 officers on foot, motorbikes and in cars, will patrol the streets of shame to highlight recent clampdowns on kerb-crawlers and vice girls.

The move comes in response to residents' fears that, despite a recent drop in offences, their streets remain unsafe for women and children.

Inspector Alex McGowan, who is in charge of the operation, said today that much of the police work in the area is undercover, and so goes unnoticed by locals.

*He said: "This exercise is to say: 'You may not always be aware of all our activities, but we are here'.*

#### ECHO Exclusive by David Walmsley

"We are dealing with the problem 24 hours a day — 365 days a year."

And he added: "We recognise that there IS a problem, and that residents do feel fearful and threatened in their community.

"We are determined to do everything in our power to prevent prostitution — and kerb crawling in particular — from affecting them in their daily lives."

The operation will be the biggest of its kind ever mounted by the Merseyside force.

*Insp McGowan says: "Police officers will be deployed in the area to such a level that it will be impossible for prostitutes to carry out their normal activities."*

But at a cost of £14,000, the plan could be seen as little more than an expensive public relations exercise.

But Insp McGowan counters: "This is not an operation in isolation.

"It supports our daily commitment to the area,

● Turn to Page Three

---

## Man is fined for watching pal's TV

A BABYSITTER was fined, after being caught watching television at the home of a FRIEND.

Mark Jones answered the door to TV licensing watchdogs — and ended up in court, where he was fined for using a TV without a licence.

*And officials confirm that anyone occupying premises where there is an unlicensed television is liable to be prosecuted.*

Mr Jones, 22, of Abbeystead Avenue, Bootle, says: "I was too honest for my own good, and gave them my own name and address.

### EXCLUSIVE by Barry Turnbull

"Even when I got a summons to go to court, I thought it would be no more than a formality to sort it out.

"But I was fined £10.

*"I am refusing to pay because of the principle."*

A spokesman for the TV licensing authority says: "Although individuals can be prosecuted in this way, we never knowingly prosecute a babysitter.

"I can only assume this person did not make the position clear."

● An official at Bootle Magistates Court said Mr Jones will be called back if he refuses to pay the fine.

---

*The first colour Echo, Saturday October 16, 1993*

# The National that never was

THE 1993 Grand National, on April 3, ended in confusion.
The popular Aintree horse race, which was being watched on television by around 300 million viewers worldwide, went dramatically wrong when the majority of competitors set off, not realising that it had been a false start.
Animal Rights protesters caused problems at the first fence which meant that the race needed to be started again but due to a breakdown in communications, officials could not notify 30 out of the 39 jockeys and their horses about their mistake, once they had started running.
It became known as 'the National that never was'.

*April 5, 1993*

# orts pecial

## SPONSORED BY Carlsberg

### Probably the best sports pull-out around

## on – but the only result is total confusion

● Starter Keith Brown is ushered away from a hos-e crowd into the weighing room.

● We want our money back ... punters line up to reclaim their stake money.

# ITEWASH

## Starting to find the right answers

THE promised full inquiry by racing's rulers into Saturday's Grand National fiasco will probe alternative methods of starting races.

The Jockey Club's investigation got underway at the London Portman Square headquarters today — and one idea will be the introduction of starting stalls for National Hunt races, a method used successfully in Australia.

A decade ago, the Jockey Club carried out false-start trials at Newbury with various new ideas, including flashing lights and a klaxon.

But both were written off because they scared the horses.

Former jockey Bob Davies, who won the 1978 National on Lucius and is now part of the Aintree team, said: "The communication system they have is very, very old —as old as the race itself."

Course marketing manager Nigel Payne said: "What happened has highlighted that there is a very big need to review the situation and to avoid an incident like this happening again."

Echo picture team at Aintree:
John Davidson
Frank Loughlin
Martin Birchall

### LUSIVE by Hargraves

destroyed in a matter of seconds ?

"A heck of a lot," says John Upson. "I am not pretending that our whole year was geared to Zeta's Lad winning the National — after all

he had won his five previous races — but we had certainly been concentrating on the National since Christmas.

"It is hard for an outsider to appreciate just how committed everyone becomes to ensuring that everything is right on the day.

"We might have been proved wrong, but we genuinely believed Zeta's Lad was going to win, because his form was right, the ground was right and his preparation was right.

"You cannot talk about coming back and trying again another year.

*April 5, 1993*

ORLD.

shero

---

The 1997 Grand National was abandoned after an IRA bomb scare which saw thousands of Merseyside racegoers stranded.

The big race was called off after two coded warnings were sent to Fazakerley Hospital and to Marsh Lane police station in Bootle.

Hundreds of people spent the night on the floor in churches, sports centres and schools across the region after what was the biggest mass evacuation in modern sporting history.

The Princess Royal was among those escorted from the course.

## LIVERPOOL ECHO

The best-selling newspaper on Merseyside

**SUNDAY SPECIAL**
Terror at the Grand National
*2am edition*

SPECIAL    APRIL 5, 1997    28p

### INSIDE: Pictures and reports from Aintree's day of despair

# STRANDED!

Ordeal of fans in bomb outrage

By Caroline Sforah, Peter Harvey and Debbie Johnson

TENS of thousands of racegoers were stranded on Merseyside today after IRA terrorists sabotaged the Grand National.

Huge numbers of people spent the night on floors in churches, sport centres and schools across Merseyside as the world of sport and politics

Emergency hotline:
0151-494 2421
Full details: Page 17

● Sad end to a sad day ... visiting Aintree race fans bed down for the night in Everton Park sports centre

*April 15, 1997*

# The day the Twin Towers came down

THE world stood still on September 11, 2001, holding its breath as one of the worst acts of terrorism in the history of mankind unfolded.

Most people will remember where they were on the day two planes crashed into the towers of New York's World Trade Centre, killing nearly 3,000 and altering the Manhattan skyline forever.

The first strike came at around 9am New York time, when hijacked United Airlines Flight 11 plunged into the side of one 110-storey tower.

Eighteen minutes later, a second plane, United Airlines flight 175, crashed into the other tower.

As smoke billowed from the building, witnesses on the street below saw trapped workers throwing themselves from windows moments before the towers collapsed.

On the day of the attacks, President George W Bush said: "The United States will hunt down and punish those responsible for these cowardly acts. The resolve of our great nation is being tested. But make no mistake: We will show the world that we will pass this test."

## Bush: We'll hunt down the people behind this

DISASTER: One of the planes that crashed into the World Trade Center was a 767

PRESIDENT George Bush was in Sarasota, Florida, reading to a classroom full of children when his chief of staff, Andrew Card, whispered the news in his ear.

The president briefly turned sombre before he resumed reading.

He then flew back to Washington for an emergency meeting of the National Security Council.

He ordered all resources go to help the victims and "hunt down and find those folks who committed this act."

He said: "Terrorism against this nation will not stand. We have had a national tragedy."

Prime Minister Tony Blair sent his deepest condolences to everyone involved.

He added: "These are the most terrible, shocking events.

Department HQ in Washington.

He said: "It was a huge fireball, a huge, orange fireball."

The White House was immediately evacuated amid fears of more terrorism.

CNN correspondent John King said the evacuation of the White House was orderly to begin with.

He added: "In the last 10 minutes, the last few hundred people were ordered by the Secret Service to run. They were running through the gate."

Shortly afterwards there were reports of an explosion, this time an Capitol Hill - the seat of US government - and claims that a fourth plane had been hijacked and was heading for Washington.

General Richard Myers, vice chairman of the Joint Chiefs of Staff, said of the attacks:

The astonishing terrorist strikes in the United States quickly reached a global audience, with many around the world watching live coverage of an aircraft hitting the World Trade Centre.

Audiences were transfixed by the awful images from New York, where one World Trade Centre tower collapsed.

Russian President Vladimir Putin expressed his condolences to the American people over the terrorist attacks, calling the "terrible tragedies," the Kremlin press service said.

"I'm afraid we can only imagine the terror," said Prime Minister Tony Blair, who cancelled a scheduled speech at a trade union conference.

"I know that you would want to

*The Echo brought images and reports from New York as the tragedy of the Twin Towers unfolded on September 11*

## Terrorist attack on America

# September 11 2001.. remember the date

## The infamous day that is destined to open a new and frightening chapter in the world's history

STREETS OF FEAR: Rescue personnel in Liberty Street after the first explosion at the New York World Trade Centre. Soon after, the horror continued with a second crash

OUTRAGE IN THE SKY: Smoke and fire surround the upper floors of the World Trade Centre this afternoon after the second plane crashed into the New York building

**LIVERPOOL**
# ECHO
www.icliverpool.co.uk

37,828  SPECIAL  TUESDAY SEPTEMBER 11 2001

**4.30pm EDITION**
Full story - Page 4

32p

# JETS ATTACK SKYSCRAPERS

- **Hijacked airliners hit New York twin towers**
- **Jet crashes at Pittsburgh**
- **Blast rocks Pentagon**
- **Thousands feared dead in terror attacks**

We will hunt ...ers - Page 4 • Twin towers collapse - Page 5 • World witnesses day of horror - Pages 6/7

Page 2  www.icliverpool.co.uk  Liverpool ECHO  Tuesday, September 11, 2001  Terrorist attack

# World's worst terror attack

Terrorists attack World Trade Centre

Plane two seconds before impact

"Terrorism against our nation we will not stand"
**President George W Bush**

# Royal visit to mark Golden Jubilee

## ECHO comment

### It's time to party

THE Golden Jubilee celebrations got under way in style at the start of this extended Bank Holiday weekend, with Merseyside playing its full part.

Today, they were due to move into top gear, with scores of street parties across the region, a day of entertainment at Liverpool's St George's plateau and several spectacular firework displays this evening.

However you have been marking this historic occasion we hope you all will be able to look back on the celebrations with fond memories.

The build-up to the Jubilee jamboree was lukewarm and there were fears it would be a damp squib,

The deaths so close together of Princess Margaret and the Queen Mother also cast an inevitable shadow.

However, as the reaction to the death of the Queen Mother so clearly demonstrated, there is still much warmth and affection for those at the top of this enduring institution.

Of course, Britain is very different now from when the Queen acceded to the throne 50 years ago and a great deal has changed even since the Silver Jubilee in 1977.

The mystique and blind allegiance that once cloaked the monarchy have gone forever. The spotlight now shines much more intensely on the Royal Family and they are no longer regarded with unquestioning deference by their subjects.

They themselves have had to change too, particularly after the death of Princess Diana five years ago. But the Queen remains the rock that underpins them all. To reign for 50 years in the way she has done is a remarkable achievement.

As we party today, there can be only one toast: "Her Majesty".

*Above: The Queen waves to the crowds on her way to St Paul's Cathedral*

*Below: It's the fireworks at the Jubilee concert making Prince William block his ears, not Sir Cliff's performance!*

## "Not even the weather has stopped people celebrating the Jubilee"

### Liverpool Lord Mayor Jack Spriggs

LIVERPOOL

**ECHO**

FINAL    TUESDAY JUNE 4 2002

8,058

## BACK WHERE HE BELONGS

Heskey set to partner Owen at heart of England's strike force - Back Page

**Bus fall girl is fighting for life**

ANDREA: Severe head injuries

A TEENAGE girl was fighting for her life today after falling from a slow-moving bus.

Andrea Sanders smashed her head on the ground after getting off the single decker vehicle on Saturday night.

She suffered severe head injuries in the fall outside Wirral's Leasowe railway station.

Andrea, 13, was taken to Arrowe Park hospital and transferred to the Walton Neurological Centre where doctors say her condition is critical.

Her mother Dawn Sanders and father Billy were at her bedside today.

Mrs Sanders, of Moreton, Wirral, told how it was touch and go whether Andrea would survive.

She wanted to know why the vehicle doors were opened before the driver had stopped.

Merseyside police have launched an investigation.

A spokeswoman for the Birkenhead-based firm A1A Travel said: "Our thoughts are with the girl and her family."

# MACCA'S BIG KNIGHT OUT

## Queen joins Sir Paul on stage

**By EMMA GUNBY** ECHO Reporter

SIR Paul McCartney stole the show as he ...

THREE CHEERS: The Queen joins Sir Paul and Cliff Richard on stage last night

*Above: Queen Elizabeth and the Duke of Edinburgh at Liverpool Town Hall*

*Left: Liverpool performers Paul McCartney and Atomic Kitten joined the Queen on stage for her Jubilee pop concert in London*

*Below: A street party held in Jubilee Drive, Liverpool*

# Liverpool: Capital of Culture 2008

*Right: Some images tell a thousand words, like this one on the front page of the Echo as the Capital of Culture announcement was made*

CELEBRATIONS were in order on June 4, as Liverpool fought off tough competition from 11 other cities to win the title of 2008 European Capital of Culture.

After becoming the first city to enter a bid for the award, Liverpool spent four years campaigning to convince a panel of judges that it had more potential than its competitors, which included Birmingham, Bristol, Cardiff, Oxford and favourites Newcastle and Gateshead.

The city was praised for its art, heritage, sport and "raw enthusiasm".

Supporters in the packed Empire Theatre cheered when it was announced that Liverpool had won the accolade.

The title would attract millions of pounds of investment to the city as well as bring thousands of tourists to the region.

Preparations immediately began for the party in 2008, when the world will focus on Liverpool.

*Below: The celebrations continued throughout the city*     *Right: The Echo's Capital of Culture special*

# LIVERPOOL ECHO

CAPITAL OF CULTURE 2008

*It will be Liverpool*
HERE WE GO!

A cultured performance: Gerrard looks to Europe
– Back page

38,370     CITY     WEDNESDAY JUNE 4 2003     32p

# WE DID IT!

## Liverpool: European Capital of Culture 2008

● CITY CELEBRATES: P2/3    ● REACTION: P4/5/8    ● COMMENT: P6/7

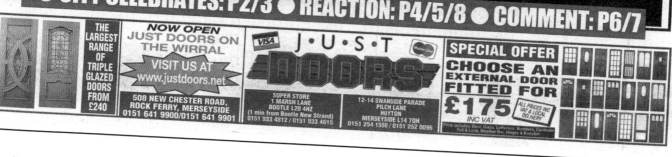

# 2057–2107
## ECHOES OF THE FUTURE

Where will Liverpool be in another 100 years?
It's a fascinating question and one that has had us back
in our Echo time machine, this time travelling forwards.

What will the Liverpool Echo front-page leads be
in 50 and 100 years from now?

We approached Echo Design Editor Gary Bainbridge with a simple challenge:
"Let your imagination run wild!"

Our man at the heart of today's page one covers didn't need asking twice.

His two contributions, one for 2057 and the other for 2107,
are both guaranteed to get you thinking.

In the first, Gary sees Liverpool's historic waterfront packed full
of skyscrapers, although some things never change. The Three Graces
continue to dominate their World Heritage Site home and the Liver Birds
are still very much in place on the city's most recognisable landmark.

However, you will find something very different dominating the Mersey
between the Pier Head and Birkenhead.

Gary's second vision, looking a full century on from 2007, will really stir
the imagination. Let it be! The cloned Beatles have been reformed and are
taking the world by storm for a second time. But what happens next?

One thing is for certain. Liverpool will continue to evolve
and change but the Echo will remain at the heart of city life.

Today's headlines will be tomorrow's history pages and the
"Echoes of Liverpool" will continue to unfold.

# Opening of the Mersey Bridge

AFTER the great year of culture in 2008, Liverpool continued to grow in stature. Along with its great rival Manchester, the city made the north west an economic powerhouse, and in 2025, the region established its own government as part of the federal structure of the United States of Britain, second only in financial and political clout to Greater London. Liverpool itself spread to encompass St Helens, Wigan and Warrington, a sprawling metropolis.

## LIVERPOOL ECHO

**SPECIAL EDITION**

Last-ever printed ECHO

70,940   MAIN   **TUESDAY, AUGUST 28, 2057**   £37.50

### NOW THAT'S WHAT WE CALL A BIRTHDAY PRESENT

Picture: EMILY ALLISS

BRIDGE OF SIZE: The Great Mersey Bridge, which officially opened today, dominates the Liverpool skyline

# RIVER BRIDGE OPENS

**850th anniversary party begins at the new look Pier Head**

By CATHERINE MATTHEW

KING Philip today declared the Great Mersey Bridge open.

The opening ceremony marked the beginning of the celebrations of Liverpool's 850th birthday.

Tonight, thousands will watch the

● Turn to Page 2

### LIVERPOOL CELEBRATES ITS BIG DAY - PAGES 2,3,4&5

Culturally, the city too grew in importance. An opera house, built on the banks of the Mersey in 2034, quickly established itself alongside the likes of La Scala and the Sydney Opera House. And it was to Sydney that Liverpool looked to solve one of its transport problems. As Liverpool had grown, it became a magnet to workers in the rest of the region. Despite the existence of two bridges at Runcorn-Widnes and two Mersey tunnels, the volume of traffic entering the city from Cheshire at rush-hour was intolerable. A grand plan to construct a Great Mersey Bridge, from Birkenhead to Liverpool, and based on the Sydney Harbour Bridge, was drawn up in 2040. The bridge would have six lanes of traffic, with two tramlines running alongside, connecting Birkenhead with the Liverpool tram system, as well as a walkway.

## The Big Gig

*Liverpool Arena and Convention Centre at Kings Dock*

THE year 2057 was an important one for Liverpool. The city celebrated its 850th birthday and the opening of the Great Mersey Bridge. It was also the 100th anniversary of the first meeting of John Lennon and Paul McCartney. To commemorate these three events, stars of the past and present came together for The Big Gig at Liverpool Arena. Dame Elizabeth MacClarnon of the Noughties "pop" group Atomic Kitten, and the surviving members of The Zutons, joined master waveform manipulators Robin Spratley's Monkey Troublers and 30s tone poet Beatrice McCartney, daughter of Sir Paul, on stage for the city's party.

## The Mersey Flood Barrier

*The barrier on the Mersey*

IT became clear that global warming would affect Liverpool badly. Although world governments had finally acted decisively to prevent climate change, some damage had already been done. Water levels had risen throughout the world, permanently flooding much of the coastline of south-east Britain. The sanddunes of Southport and Formby had also been eroded. To prevent flooding of Liverpool city centre, civil engineers constructed a £2bn flood barrier, based on the Thames barrier in London. The work began in 2019 and was completed in 2027. It was officially opened by King Philip I (the former Prince William) and Queen Catherine on April 12, 2029.

## Liverpool at 850

LIVERPOOL has expanded since its 800th birthday.

In the year 2057, the city has grown to incorporate several outlying towns.

The process of regeneration, which was spearheaded in the city centre with the Liverpool One development back in 2008, has spread throughout the city bringing prosperity to areas like Walton and Kensington.

Traffic congestion in the city centre has been reduced from its 2020 high, thanks to the introduction of a prompt and environmentally friendly tram system, extended to all areas of the city.

And the contribution of the Beatles to the city has been recognised with a 50ft statue of the band in Beatles Square (formerly known as Williamson Square).

# Diana 'made up' with new bridge

*Right: A vision of the future from tomorrow's Echo*

● From Page One

Big Gig birthday concert at Liverpool Arena.

Thousands more will be able to watch the concert at the ECHO's permanent holo-screen at Beatles Square, as well as at specially erected screens in Lennon Park, Stanley Park and Croxteth Park.

The King opened the new bridge at 11am today, accompanied by Queen Catherine and their younger daughter, Princess Diana, who studied art history at Liverpool Tesco University. Princess Diana said: "As an adopted Scouser, I would like to say I'm made up with the new bridge."

The Royal family then watched the Royal Liverpool Philharmonic Orchestra in conc

# The Beatles split up... for a second time

HUMAN cloning became possible in 2058, with ethical laws in place to restrict the practice.

But over the following decades, the laws became more and more relaxed. It was only a matter of time before entertainment impresario Ronaldo Macready decided the cloning technology could be exploited for profit.

Macready initially managed to procure some of Phil Collins' DNA and grew a clone of the Genesis singer. But this new Collins had an unimpressive impact on the charts. Undeterred, Macready tracked down DNA belonging to the four Beatles –

John Lennon, Paul McCartney, George Harrison and Ringo Starr. Fresh exciting Beatles songs were written by a reborn Lennon and McCartney partnership, the new Harrison was as influential to the current crop of rock guitarists as his predecessor... and the Ringo clone played the drums.

In short, the reborn Beatles rocked the world.

But it could not last. Macready's great rival, Gordon Clegg, was so envious of the impresario's success that he cloned Yoko Ono, who caused a rift between the Fabricated Four and split the Beatles for a second time.

## Love Me Two

*The first attempt at cloning the Beatles*

*The successful clones*

## Fly me to the moon

*A rocket prepares for launch at the airport*

LIVERPOOL John Lennon Airport grew throughout the 21st century, rivalling Heathrow and Manchester. This meant it was well placed to benefit from the advent of space tourism.

In the early days, space tourists had to be rich, and they were merely taken into orbit around the earth. But the invention of the nuclear fusion propulsion engine made more distant trips possible. The speed of craft using the engines made a visit to the moon as cheap and common as the

long-haul flight to Australia would have been in the late 20th century. In 2068, the first colony was established on the moon, and in 2084 the first hotels were built. In 2089, Liverpool John Lennon Airport started construction of its spacecraft pad, which was complete in 2091. It was only the second pad in Europe (the first was at Antoine de Caunes Airport in Paris). Nowadays, 48 million passengers pass through Liverpool John Lennon Airport every year, with 280,000 passengers flying to the moon alone.

## Liverpool at 900

LIVERPOOL has expanded since its 800th birthday. In the year 2057, the city has grown to incorporate several outlying towns. The process of regeneration, which was spearheaded in the city centre with the Liverpool One development in 2008, has spread through the city bringing prosperity to areas like Walton and Kensington. Traffic congestion in the city centre has been reduced from its 2020 high, thanks to the introduction of a prompt and environmentally friendly tram system, extended to all areas of the city. And the contribution of the Beatles to the city has been recognised with a 50ft statue of the band in Beatles Square (formerly known as Williamson Square).

# LIVERPOOL ECHO

**95,940 MAIN**  **SUNDAY, AUGUST 28, 2107**  £538.75

## Your ECHO

THIS special 900th birthday issue of the ECHO has been 'printed' on wood pulp using 'ink' to simulate how ECHO users would receive their news 100 years ago.

For advice on how to use this product, including help with 'turning' pages, contact your local customer services advisor on HeadNet.

WE HEARD THE NEWS TODAY, OH BOY: Paul II, George II, Ringo II and John II wound up the new Beatles after a row over the influence of postmodern artist Yoko Ono II

# ONO! NOT AGAIN!

## Yoko clone blamed for Fabricated Four split on birthday

**By CATHERINE MATTHEW**

THE reformed Beatles will NOT be playing at Liverpool's 900th birthday celebrations – because the band has split up.

The cloned Fab Four were due to appear at the concert at Liverpool Opera House this evening, but a spokesman today said the group had gone their separate ways.

● Turn to Page 2